Smart Home

2019

Cathy Young

Look Inside

• **Are you wondering what you can do with IoT?** IoT (the Internet of Things) is a term for digital devices connected to cloud services. We will look at the governing bodies behind IoT, the companies implementing IoT platforms today, and we discuss what IoT means to you right now. Chapter 2 introduces smart home devices, apps, and cloud services.

• **Engage your senses: sight, sound, and touch.** Amazon Flow, Samsung's Bixby Vision, and Google Lens use images from cameras as input. Virtual assistants like Alexa, Siri, and Hey Google respond to voice commands. The Apple Taptic Engine vibrates smartphones or taps your wrist to get your attention.

• **What do autonomous cars, robots, and Walmart have in common?** Use your voice to add items to your shopping list, and a personal shopper bags your groceries. Next, schedule a delivery or drive through Walmart. With connected smart home cameras and locks, you can talk to delivery drivers and watch them place the package inside your home. In the near future, autonomous vehicles will drive to your home, and robots will deliver packages to your door or drones will make airdrops. Chapter 2 has details on all these topics.

• **What role do virtual assistants play?** Learn how smart home devices and apps integrate with

Amazon Alexa, Google Assistant, Siri, Samsung Bixby, or Microsoft Cortana in Chapters 10 and 11. Use Siri Shortcuts and Caviar to order your favorite take-out, as shown in Chapter 11. Simply say, "Siri, order Wednesday dinner," and the Caviar app does the rest.

- **The field of Medicine and Healthcare is changing dramatically.** Smart monitoring devices will focus on prevention and early diagnosis, and healthcare will be centered around your well-being. Today, Accessibility Features are a fundamental aspect of many smart devices. Haptics plays a role in rehabilitation and virtual reality surgical simulators. Tiny microelectromechanical systems known as "Smart Dust" will instantly diagnose illness. Chapters 2 and 5 look at this exciting technology.

- **Cut the cord.** Explore Over-the-Top (OTT) solutions to "cut the cord" and expand your TV, video, gaming, and music libraries. Chapter 9 explores sharing photos, media, and more. Chapter 6 showcases VoIP options to replace a landline phone.

- **Meal planning has never been easier.** Browse recipes, use your virtual assistant to add ingredients to your shopping list, and pick up groceries at the Walmart drive-thru. This sounds like some futuristic dream; but Walmart, Google, Food Network, and Recipes by Myxx make all this possible today. I'll show you how in Chapter 2.

- **Set up a shared grocery list and add items with your digital assistant.** Everyone in your family can tap their wrist to view and check off items on your family's grocery list. The example in Chapter 12 covers setting up iOS family sharing and a shared iOS reminder list. Steps for creating IFTTT integrations that link iOS reminders and digital assistants are also included.

● **Explore cloud services and connected platforms in Chapter 5.** We'll look at the power of iMessages, Apple Pay, and account and password management platforms. We'll also explore iCloud, Dropbox, and Google Drive cloud services for storing and sharing data. The power of connected apps is showcased in an in-depth analysis of Apple's Activity View and App Tray.

● **Connected apps** share data in many ways. Learn how to connect all kinds of apps with your virtual assistants and simple ways to create connections between your apps. Examples in Chapter 12 showcase sharing data with reminder lists, e-mail, and more.

● **Are you wondering about the role of mobile operating systems?** If it's not an Apple device running iOS, chances are the mobile operating system is some flavor of Google's Android mobile operating system. Examples include Amazon Fire TV, Chromecast, and Amazon's Echo Show. Whether you like the iOS or Android mobile operating system, or a combination of both, the future looks promising.

● **Have you thought about automating lighting?** Enjoy mood lighting with smart colored bulbs that react to sensors, the weather, events, or schedules. Chapter 6 gets you started.

● **Would you like to use your voice to play music?** Simply tell your digital assistant to turn on your amplifier, switch inputs to your surround sound system, control volume, change stations, play a song or artist, or select a playlist. Follow along with a step-by-step example in Chapter 2, to see how it's done.

- **Learn verbal commands for Alexa, Google, and Siri.** Chapter 11 demonstrates task-based phrases you'll use again and again.

Table of Contents

1. Introduction

Like death and taxes, you simply cannot avoid IoT! It is everywhere! To use a ten-dollar word, it is simply ubiquitous. Love it or hate it; the choice is yours. Either way, get comfortable with it and understand it. I think you'll come to love it once you embrace how it works – and how you can make it work for YOU.

We think in terms of "Smart Homes," but with the advent of cybernetics that includes digital assistants, cloud services and personal medical devices (to name a few) our Internet of Things is unique. My Internet of Things includes a wide variety of emerging technologies. Examples include voice-controlled virtual assistants, robots, smart thermostats and blinds, and unifying platforms like

Chapter 1

SmartThings and IFTTT ("if this, then that"). In my home, I incorporated a combination of these things, selecting what I felt was the best product for each task – some overlap.

The technology is futuristic and, frankly, cool; but it required me to change the way I interacted with the world around me. Once my smart home was set up the way I wanted, I had to be mindful that it was there to help me - albeit not necessarily on my terms. I had to learn how to interact with my virtual assistants. That journey is still unfolding, and I expect both my smart home and IoT to keep expanding and improving as we add more things.

This book started simply as the notes I kept during my recent personal experience with selecting and setting up smart home devices for a new house. The scope of this book is broad because the technology isn't just one smart home device; it's all around us in our day to day lives. For that reason, I've included a lot of information on smart applications, mobile operating systems, cloud services, and how they overlap and share data.

While researching the project, my husband and I read a plethora of reviews from folks like us (real people, that is). Some reviews were admittedly more insightful than others, but we gained valuable insights into what to avoid, what questions to ask, and we found some great ideas. If you are a DIY type or just want a general idea of what is going on with smart homes, this book will show you a bit of what is possible. By the end of this book, indeed, I hope that you will be comfortable in the Internet of Things (or "IoT") world of connected devices, virtual assistants, skills, connected apps, or IFTTT applets.

Chapter 3 outlines the basics of the technology behind IoT, and then Chapter 4 discusses ideas for setting up a smart home.

Chapter 5 moves beyond smart home devices and covers apps, cloud services, and sharing data. Smart home solutions are discussed in Chapters 6-9. Chapters 10 and 11 deal with virtual assistants like Siri, Alexa, or Google Assistant. Smart apps are discussed in Chapter 12.

As you go through the chapters, you will learn the terminology and what really matters when buying equipment. In case you're like me and like to skip around as topics interest you, the Table of Contents is organized so you can quickly find what you're looking for. Now let's get started and show you how to:

- Select good equipment and plan for future growth.

- Set up and connect everything.

- Integrate apps and systems.

- Maintain your smart home.

- Select good equipment and plan for future growth.

- Set up and connect everything.

- Integrate apps and systems.

- Maintain your smart home.

Chapter 1

2. What Can IoT Do?

Your Internet of Things will include smart home automation with connected devices, skills, and cloud services. This automation involves more than the devices in your home since smart home devices interact with the IoT world beyond your home. This chapter is focused on smart home technology. Later in Chapter 5, we'll look at sharing data between connected devices or apps.

Combining smart devices and apps has the most potential to add value to your smart automation lineup. The ability to combine multiple connected things is starting to appear in virtual assistant's routines, as well as mobile apps like the IFTTT app, Apple's Shortcuts app, or Samsung's Bixby Quick Commands. With IFTTT, anyone can combine multiple devices and apps in whatever way they like. Take a look at Chapter 13, "IFTTT Applets Worth a Look" to see what others are doing with IFTTT. Chapter 11 also has suggestions for virtual assistant routines.

On another front, Amazon "Blueprints" let you create and publish your own Alexa skills. Chapter 11 has details about Blueprints. Since the initial release of Blueprints in 2018, Amazon has steadily added templates, such as:

- Houseguest

- Chore Chart

- Whose Turn

- Hallmark Holiday Greetings

- How Many Days (until my vacation!)

While I don't think I am a particularly creative person, I am curious. When researching a topic, it's not usual for me to end up going down countless rabbit holes. These virtual expeditions have shown me many of the creative ways others are using IoT - ways of which I would never have thought on my own. I've highlighted a few of my favorite ideas below. Please keep reading if you want to learn details and explore more ideas.

- TV & Video

- Food Delivery & Groceries

- Fall Detection

- Home Deliveries & Visitors

- Automotive

- Traffic Commute

- Travel

2.1 Alert Doors & Cabinets Open

As a tool to discourage our cats from opening and climbing in our kitchen cabinets, we use a Samsung sensor to detect when a door is open, and a motion sensor to detect movement. The alerts trigger an Aeotec Siren. The cats do not like the siren. My husband HATES the siren.

2.2 Appliances

GE, Jenn-Air, Samsung, and June are a few manufacturers of smart appliances available today. The ability to remotely preheat an oven, restart a dryer, or schedule the wash for off-peak times is impressive. Occasionally, available features are dependent on the mobile operating system - Android vs. iOS, for instance. If the only features that work on my smartphone are a diagnostic report informing me that the lint trap needs to be cleaned, the extra expense of a smart dryer isn't high on my priorities.

The majority of smart appliances will save energy and provide diagnostic information when things go wrong. Scheduling the dishwasher to run when the demand for hot water is low is useful, but the real savings come when your utility company gives you a break for electricity usage during non-peak hours. Integration with a smart system like NEST means the appliance learns when you're usually away and remembers times when hot water demand is low.

2.3 Arrive Home

When you arrive home, have your smart home turn off your security system, adjust the thermostat, open the shades, turn on lights and music, and stop surveillance camera recording.

2.4 Automotive

There are a number of advances in the automotive industry. Virtual assistants and automobile apps are now commonplace. As you'll see in a bit, I no longer have to worry about maintenance on my car because My Subaru e-mails me when it needs attention.

Our automobiles will soon use vehicle-to-vehicle communication, reducing crashes in the US by 600,000 a year. Smart cities will have autonomous vehicles like Nuro, to meet the demand for same-hour delivery. Once a package makes it to your house, a robot delivers it to your front door. This sounds like science fiction, but the Digit robot designed by Ford and Agility Robotics does just that.

With Apple CarPlay, Siri voice commands are available in your car. Ford, BMW, and Hyundai have Alexa skills that send alerts for maintenance issues or fuel levels. The convenience of remotely starting your car or unlocking doors, in fact, is showcased in a funny Hyundai commercial. An astronaut on the Space Station uses the Hyundai mobile app to unlock her husband's car door remotely.

In 2018 Alexa was integrated into BMW infotainment systems. Alexa will also be available on select Toyota and Lexus vehicles. Volkswagen has announced similar plans. Check out the Garmin Speak gadget if you want these features in your car today.

- Read messages.

- Add items to your to-do list or calendar.

- Control smart home devices.

The Automatic, Zubie, and Hum adapters plug into a car's standard OBD-II port to analyze the engine. These adapters record location and mileage. Through integrations, these adapters export statistics for use in expense reporting and diagnostics. Fortunately for me, My Subaru app sends me a monthly health report for my Crosstrek. On another front, Edmunds has an innovative Alexa skill that includes information about recalls, market value, and car shopping features.

2.5 Calendars

A virtual assistant makes adding events to your calendar a snap. There are other ways to take advantage of calendar information. An IFTTT applet, for instance, can flash your lights when a Google calendar event is approaching. Smart apps can also send notifications to remind you of events.

2.6 Calling or Messaging

Virtual assistants easily send text messages. Siri will answer and make calls on iPhones, Macs, or iPads. With CarPlay, Siri is also available while driving. The Google Assistant and Cortana also support calling and messaging, as shown in Chapter 9. Alexa sends messages and will make Alexa-to-Alexa calls. Alexa can also make mobile calls, or landline calls, in the US, Canada, or Mexico. To use these features, first configure calling and messaging on your smartphone in the Alexa app, as shown in Chapter 11.

In addition to virtual assistants, smart apps will place calls or send messages in response to events. Chapter 7 on Security systems outlines several systems that will call or message you when alerts are triggered. One example would be a message alerting you that the security system was disarmed, indicating your children are home from school. IFTTT applets are customized to your specifications and connect devices and apps. You can configure your IFTTT applets to send messages or place calls when certain events happen, as outlined in Chapter 13.

2.7 Close Garage Door for Severe Weather

At our old home, wind-driven rain would pool in one corner of the garage if the door was left open during a storm. Even if you don't automatically close the garage door when a storm approaches, a friendly reminder that the door is open could be helpful.

2.8 Shades & Temperature Changes

Temperatures on windows can change drastically when the sun is shining directly on them. One solution to this problem is temperature sensors and smart shades working together to adjust the shade position automatically as needed. The Samsung multipurpose sensor monitors temperature as well as motion, and the SmartThings hub can trigger shades to close when there is a temperature change.

2.9 Combine Motion, Lights, & Sound

There are mobile apps that integrate smart lights and music, and the apps trigger lights to move to the beat.

Alternatively, sensors detect an event and cause a device to react with sound and lights. Sample applications of this technology include alerts of intruders, fire, or water leaks.

2.10 Cooking

A personal virtual assistant can really help out in the kitchen. Here are several cooking-related questions you can ask your personal virtual assistant.

- How many tablespoons in a ¼ cup?

- What is a substitute for cornstarch?

- Set a timer for 30 minutes and flash the lights when done. (Ah, I remember the days when my only cooking timer was the smoke alarm!)

- Remind me to take the bread out of the oven.

- Add flour to my shopping list.

A smart temperature probe is also handy for the oven or grill. With IFTTT integration, simply program the lights to flash (or some other alert) when food is done cooking according to a predetermined temperature.

There are many ways a virtual assistant can help in the kitchen, as shown below.

- Add ingredients to shopping lists.

- Set timers.

- Convert measurements.

- Find substitutions for ingredients.
- Flash the lights when food is done cooking in the oven or on the grill.

Recipes

Good Housekeeping, Food Network, and AllRecipes have skills for reading recipes. There are several services for recipes that integrate with virtual assistants and smart displays. Good Housekeeping, Food Network, and AllRecipes both have skills for reading recipes.

Over the years, I have used various programs to organize recipes. The apps never seem to last long, and now I use a word processor. Ultimately, I'd love a personal virtual assistant that manages my recipes and reads them out loud while I'm cooking.

My perfect cooking scenario involves browsing recipes to find one I like. I click a button to add a recipe to my menu, and the ingredients to my grocery shopping list. Next, I want to swing by the drive-thru at my grocery store to pick up my groceries. Once I'm back home, I want my smart screen to display my menu, and then I'll decide what I'm in the mood for tonight. While cooking, my recipe is displayed on my smart screen, and my virtual assistant gives me verbal cues. For this dream to be my reality, it also works with Emeril's recipe website, as well as my own family recipes.

Fortunately for me, the company "Recipes by Myxx" has been working on a solution that matches my dream. Myxx has partnered with Albertsons, Walmart, Kroger, Safeway, and other grocery stores. While I can't enter my own recipes in the Myxx app, I can e-mail Myxx my recipes and Myxx will add them to their site!

Look for other sites like Food Networks that also have options to add ingredients to the Walmart shopping cart.

Check out these cooking apps and sites.

- AllRecipes

- Recipes by Myxx

- Food Network

- Good Housekeeping

- Recipedia

Smart Screens and Virtual Assistants

Good HouseKeeping has a visually based skill that allows Alexa to display recipes on the Amazon Echo Show or Echo Spot. Google has partnered with cooking partners like AllRecipes, Food Network, Chowhound, and others. After you search for a recipe on one of these sites, there is an option to "Send to Google Home," and display the recipe on the Google Smart Screen.

1. Open the Google app on your smartphone or tablet. Search for a recipe.

2. Tap "Send to Google Home."

3. Say, "Hey Google, start cooking."

4. Say, "Hey Google, read step one."

Chapter 2

Food Networks

Not only does Food Networks have some Emeril recipes, but there are also options to add ingredients to the Walmart shopping cart. Food Networks is also a partner of Google so that you can "Send to Google Home" and view the recipe on your smart screen while Google reads the steps out loud.

AllRecipes

AllRecipes.com also has a mobile app, as well as the web interface. When viewing a recipe online, there is a button to "Add all ingredients to your shopping list." AllRecipes goes a step further with an option to add your own recipes, as shown below.

1.   Log in to AllRecipes.com or start the AllRecipes app on your smartphone or tablet.

2.   Click on the favorites menu.

3.   Click on "Personal Recipes" and add the details.

4.   Open the Dinner Spinner App! to take your shopping list with you to the grocery store.

When entering recipes, spell out words like "teaspoon" or "green pepper" so that your virtual assistant's verbal instructions will be more natural.

If you need to make changes, use the Edit shortcut near the bottom of the ingredients list when viewing your recipes online.

"Alexa, open AllRecipes."

"Alexa, search favorites."

"Alexa, start cooking."

2.11 Document Collaboration

Sharing documents with friends or colleagues is easy with cloud services. Collaborating on the same word processing document is simple to set up in the Apple Pages app. Chapter 12 also shows you how to share spreadsheets and more with Apple apps. Cloud Services like Amazon Drive, Google Docs, Dropbox, and iCloud make it easy to share files. Chapter 5 has more information on these Cloud Services.

2.12 Drop in on the Nursery

Hear what's going on in the nursery on Echo devices with Alexa's "drop-in" feature. If your Echo has a video screen, you can also see the baby sleeping.

2.13 Find My Phone

A few years ago, I tried an Android phone, and the first thing I realized was I had to buy an app to locate my phone if I misplaced it. With the iPhone the "Find my iPhone" Apple app locates my iPad, Mac, Apple Watch, or iPhone. Chapter 12 has details on the Find My iPhone app.

Another option to locate smartphones is the "Life Bot" Alexa skill that calls your phone.

"Alexa, find my phone."

2.14 Fire Alarm

When a fire alarm is triggered, a smart home automatically turns on lights inside, flashes outside lights for first responders, plays loud audio, opens the garage door, turns on sprinklers, and notifies emergency services and contacts.

2.15 Food Delivery & Groceries

Until autonomous deliveries are a reality, grocery delivery, or drive-thru pick-up, are a popular service. Amazon, Shipt, Walmart, Google Express, Target, Instacart, Postmates, and other services either deliver to your home, car or a specified location. You decide on cost versus convenience as some services add membership fees, the cost of items is up to 15% higher, and you may have to tip the driver. Amazon Prime members have a "Prime Now" service included in their membership, and Walmart shopping is the same price as buying inside the store (with no tipping!)

Restaurant Deliveries

Uber Eats, Grubhub, Postmates, Caviar, and Door Dash deliver restaurant meals to your door. The "Amazon Restaurants" service provides food delivery in supported areas. The Caviar app integrates with Siri Shortcuts, so you can create a Siri shortcut for your "usual" order. A shortcut allows you to say "Siri, its pizza time," and the Caviar app does the rest. Learn more about Siri Shortcuts in Chapters 11 and 12.

Don't Wait in Line - Order Ahead

The convenience of drive-thru pick up and ordering ahead is at the top of my list of time-saving tricks. You can order online from Starbucks, Panera, Walmart, Target, or Amazon's Whole Foods, and pick-up in a designated location or locker at the store, without having to stand in line.

In 2019, Walmart Voice Order rolled out with support for Google Assistant. Walmart has invested billions in its online ordering systems, complete with drive-thru pick-up lines.

"OK, Google, talk to Walmart."

You'll also notice options to "Add to your Walmart cart," when browsing recipes on sites like Food Network.

Food Kits

Amazon Food Kits are available in some cities and integrate with Amazon's Echo Show. The advantage of a smart screen is a virtual assistant provides verbal clues as you read instructions on the display. Other popular Food Kit providers are Hello Fresh and Blue Apron.

Prepared Meals

On the other side of the coin, if you don't want to mix and prepare a meal, Icon Meals come prepared. This type of solution may be ideal for hospitals, nursery homes, or universities. Zune also offers "Baking-on-the-way" meals.

2.16 Geofencing

Location-based services, or geofencing, use GPS location services to gather relevant data on weather, pollen counts, or delivery routes. This data is also used to control smart things like lights, thermostats, and sprinklers. Platforms that combine smart devices and data can send messages and e-mails, or interact with your virtual assistant. Cities are also using beacons to gather location analytics for mobile apps that enrich tourism, sporting events, and traffic commutes. Apple devices running iOS 13 or later ask for your consent, to allow Bluetooth-enabled beacons, or tracking devices, to use your location information.

This is an illustration of this technology: You step off the plane and receive an e-mail with a map of your location, because you set up an IFTTT applet to send an e-mail with a map when you entered the area of Maui, Hawaii. This illustration uses geofencing and your smartphone - the tip of the iceberg as you'll see in the following chapters.

2.17 Haptics and Touch

Haptics is the science of applying tactile sensation (touch) and control when interacting with computer applications. Haptics encompasses both kinesthesia and cutaneous sensations. The kinesthesia sense involves location, motion, and force. Cutaneous sensations involve temperature, vibration, and texture. Chances are you're familiar with the role of Haptics in VR (virtual reality) games; but, are you aware that surgical simulators are also using Haptics to train the next generation of surgeons?

In 2012 Disney introduced a touch-sensitive technology called "Touche." Touche uses multiple frequencies to differentiate between one finger or a firm hand grasp. When closing a door, a firm grasp would lock the door, while a gentle touch could allow you to step outside and retrieve a package.

2.18 Health

Some exciting things are happening in the health industry today. We'll look in-depth at the topics below in Chapters 5 and 12. In the meantime, this section will discuss a bit of what is possible today.

- Wearable Smart Devices

- Accessibility

- Fall Detection

- Heart Rate Monitoring

- Exercise & Health Apps

- Virtual Assistants (in hospitals and care facilities)

- Mindfulness & Sleep Apps

When mobility is an issue, a Virtual Assistant that responds to verbal commands to control lights, TV, phone calls, messaging, and more is a great help. Amazon is working on HIPAA-compliant healthcare skills for Alexa with select developers and has a trial at Cedars-Sinai Hospital to place Alexa smart speakers in patients' rooms.

Wearable smart devices track heart rate, exercise, sleep, and more. For example, the Dexcom sensor continuously monitors glucose and integrates with the Apple Watch.

In the future, you can visit any doctor using VR. Doctors would implant "Smart Dust" and instantly diagnose your problem through a computer screen. Smart Dust is a system of tiny microelectromechanical systems, including sensors, robots, and other devices. These systems detect chemicals, magnetism, vibration, temperature, and light.

Haptics is also a useful accessibility feature for deaf or hard of hearing users that is available today. Drivers will appreciate the Map app that gently vibrates your Apple Watch to indicate an upcoming turn. Medical applications of Haptics in the future include rehabilitation.

We'll look at the Apple HealthKit platform and Accessibility features in Chapter 5. HealthKit includes apps, devices, and partnerships with hospitals and labs. Fall detection, emergency SOS, and heart rate & ECG monitoring are part of the Apple Watch health lineup. In November 2018, Apple won the prestigious Eleanor Roosevelt Humanitarian Award from the Center for Hearing and Communication for its accessibility features.

Fall Detection

The "Ask My Buddy" Alexa skill is designed for the elderly, or anyone who lives alone and wants a simple way to get help. Another similar solution is found in the Apple Watch, which automatically calls emergency services when it detects a fall.

Medical ID and SOS information are displayed on your Apple Watch screen when the side button is pressed for three seconds. Apple Watch Series 4 uses an accelerometer and gyroscope to detect a significant, hard fall. When your watch detects a hard fall, it taps you on the wrist, sounds an alarm, and displays an alert. You can choose to contact emergency services or dismiss the alert. Tap, "I fell, but I'm OK," or scroll down and tap, "I did not fall." Chapter 12 has details on configuring the Apple Health App and more.

Figure 2.1   The Hard Fall Alert

View Medical ID or Call Emergency Services

When anyone holds the side button on your Apple watch for three seconds, your Apple Watch will call Emergency Services. The Apple Watch counts down with an alarm, and a slider prompts if you want to end the call. Also, this option automatically detects if you take a hard fall. If you don't respond, it will tap your wrist, sound an alarm, and then call emergency services.

1.   On your Apple Watch press and hold the side button until the screen opens.

2.   Tap Medical ID, or Emergency SOS.

Follow the steps in the next sections to enable and set up emergency services and health information.

Enable Emergency SOS

1. Open the Apple Watch app on your iPhone.

2. Tap "My Watch," located in the left corner of the tab bar at the bottom of the screen.

3. Scroll down to "Emergency SOS."

4. Touch the "Emergency SOS" slider. Continue holding the slider as you move it to enabled. The slider is green when enabled and white when disabled.

Configure Medical ID in the Health App

1. On your iPhone, open the "Health" app.

2. Tap "Medical ID" located in the right corner of the tab bar at the bottom of the screen.

3. Enter your information.

Configure Emergency SOS

1. On your iPhone, open the Apple Watch App.

2. Tap "Emergency SOS."

3. Enter your information.

2.19 Holiday Greeting Cards

Hallmark teamed up with Alexa to send greeting cards to Alexa-enabled devices for the 2018 holiday season. On the Alexa Skill "Blueprints" website and select the "Hallmark Holiday Greetings" blueprint template. The "Hallmark Holiday Greetings" blueprint walks you through the process of recording a message and uploading a custom background image. You share your skill with others so they can receive the card through their Alexa-enabled devices. Alexa Blueprints are discussed in Chapter 11.

2.20 Home Deliveries & Visitors

With a smart home camera and smart lock, you no longer have to sit at home all day waiting on a delivery. You can remotely view and talk to visitors, workers, or delivery people, and unlock doors. In the near future, autonomous vehicles will drive to your home, and robots will deliver packages to your door or drones will make airdrops

With a UPS Smart Choice account, you can sign a delivery release and provide a garage code for the UPS delivery driver. UPS will send text alerts to your smartphone.

UPS Smart Choice also has a skill for Amazon Alexa so you can check on scheduled deliveries.

The US Postal service has an app to track mail. The USPS "Informed Delivery" app shows images of mail and includes a list of packages scheduled for delivery. The app will also send e-mail and text alerts.

Another interesting delivery option is provided by the virtual assistant, Microsoft Cortana. Cortana can track packages from specific retailers like Amazon, Target, Walmart, Apple, eBay, or the Microsoft Store by scanning your e-mails. If you search for a FedEx, USPS, or UPS tracking ID, Cortana will start tracking it.

For information on Amazon delivery options, see the section "Alexa Purchasing" in Chapter 11.

2.21 Houseguest

The first Alexa "Blueprint" skill I set up was "Houseguest." I included our smart home phrases, trash days, and TV instructions. Honestly, I thought it was cute, but wasn't sure how useful it would be. My daughter texted me the first night she was house sitting, asking me to turn off the Hue bedroom lights. I forgot to include that command. There is no light switch for the HUE lights behind our headboard, and the lights automatically come on each evening. I appreciate that Amazon designed and implemented a solution for this situation before I realized I needed it.

2.22 Leave Home (or Sleep)

It is a bit tricky to define when you have left home. There are automotive sensors, arrival sensors, and location services on smartphones. The challenge is deciding what defines "away." What if one person leaves and someone else is home that day? One option is the SmartThings or Apple Home apps, that track mobile phones for everyone in the family. The apps automatically run tasks when everyone in the family has left the house. Here are several things your smart home can do when you are away, or about to leave your home.

1. Close the shades.

2. Adjust the thermostat.

3. Turn off the lights.

4. Lock the doors.

5. Close the garage door.

6. Turn off the TV.

7. Turn off all speakers.

8. Call your cell phone with the weather from Weather Underground and IFTTT.

9. Turn on the security system.

10. Report traffic for your commute.

2.23 Music

There are many music-related skills. The Apple Music app is covered in Chapter 12. In addition to the providers found in the Music, Video & Books Alexa skill topic mentioned in Chapter 11, check out these skills.

- Chart music

- Song Quiz

- Sound system skills like Yamaha MusicCast

Because I love listening to my favorite music while cooking, I thought I'd share an exact example of how I listen to music with Alexa. Although I can use a Logitech Harmony activity for this, I prefer Alexa. The advantage with a virtual assistant is I can play a particular song, switch channels or playlists, and add new songs to a playlist.

Not all smart speakers support Bluetooth external speakers. The original Amazon Echo and Google Home didn't connect to Bluetooth speakers.

Turn on Receiver

"Alexa, use MusicCast to turn on Family Room Yamaha."

Change to Bluetooth Input

"Alexa, ask MusicCast to switch input to Bluetooth in the Family Room."

Play Music

"Alexa, ask MusicCast to play pop music."

Create a Playlist

"Alexa, create a playlist called Pop Music."

Add a Song to a Playlist

"Alexa, add this song to Pop Music."

2.24 Photos & Videos

A few years ago, a digital picture frame was all the rage. Today's smart TVs and smart screens display photo slideshows by default. The background of my Echo Show is set to my favorite Amazon photo album. My husband is an amateur photographer, and I like to display his vacation photos on our 4k Sony TV, which uses my Google photo album.

Chapter 9, "Home Entertainment" has information and examples of unique ways to make the most of your photo albums. Chapter 12 outlines the Apple Photo app and how to share photos with friends.

- Display photos on your smart TV

- Stream media with Apple TV or Chromecast

- Setup slideshows on Echo Show

- Share photos with friends

2.25 Printing

Call me old fashioned, but I like a printed copy of some things. On those occasions, I can say, "Alexa, print my shopping list." Since we already use the HP Print Bot with Facebook messenger, and we also print via e-mail to 2019SmartHome@hpeprint.com, we wondered if HP has an Alexa skill, and it does! Granted, it only prints Alexa lists as of this writing - meaning that we can't have Alexa print one of the recipes that we mentioned in the previous section. The steps to set up an HP printer with Alexa are shown below.

1. After unpacking your HP printer on the menu, go to **settings** and Apps to select the HP Connect icon. The printer will print out a Web Services Summary with your **Printer Code**.

2. Download and install the HP Connected app on your mobile device. When prompted, enter your **Printer Code**.

3. Launch your Alexa app and search for the HP Alexa skill. Follow the prompts to log in and link accounts.

HP printers that support HP ePrint can print from smartphones, tablets, or computers.

1. Install the HP ePrint app on your mobile device.

2. Select Remote Printing. Log in to your ePrint account and enable HP ePrint.

3. Enter your printer's e-mail address – for example, 2018SmartHome@hpeprint.com.

4. Send a message and/or e-mail to other devices and computers to download the smartphone app and use the printer.

2.26 Freezer Temperature Change

My kids are grown, so I don't have to worry that they left the refrigerator door open. When on vacation, however, I would appreciate an alert that there was a temperature change or that the freezer lost power.

2.27 Reminder to Buy a Birthday Gift

For once, I won't forget to buy a gift because it's easy to ask my virtual assistant to set a reminder for me. Another interesting use for reminders is the Grocery app that uses reminder lists to store your shopping list. With a combination of iOS "Family Sharing" and an IFTTT applet that automatically links my Grocery shopping list with my iOS reminder lists, I can easily add items to my grocery list with Alexa, Google Assistant, or Siri. Chapter 12 has the details on setting up reminders, IFTTT, and family sharing.

2.28 Schedule Appliances

Smart appliances use a schedule and integration with other systems to identify non-peak times of electrical use or to start cycles. Some utility companies, in fact, have conservation programs for electricity use during non-peak times.

2.29 ScoreKeeper

Do you play Scrabble, darts, or card games? Check out the Alexa Scorekeeper skill that keeps score for you.

2.30 Shopping List

One of the handiest things a virtual assistant can do is add items to a shopping list. With a smartphone or tablet, you can easily print the list, e-mail a copy, or access the list from your smartphone or smartwatch.

2.31 Smart Cities

Smart Cities are emerging - the LA City skill for Alexa is available today. In 2019 Georgia citizens have a new Alexa skill to access Georgia.gov. A company called Imaginuity is helping municipalities across the US engage their citizens. Cities like Raleigh, NC, and Marietta, GA have skills. Try asking, "Hey Google, when is my trash day?"

2.32 Sports

There are IFTTT channels like ESPN that can automatically add your team's games to your calendar. If you're wondering when the next game is or what the final score was, Alexa can answer your questions.

2.33 Surveillance

Smart cameras and motion sensors provide home surveillance. Another option is to set up your spare smartphone as a surveillance camera with IFTTT and the smartphone app "Manything." This is one way to catch your resident cookie thief or the dog getting into the trash. Imagine the look on their face when Alexa's voice says, "I see you; put that cookie back," when no one else is in the room!

2.34 TidePooler

Surfers will appreciate the TidePooler Alexa skill that looks up tide information for various cities.

2.35 Timer

Virtual assistants are perfect for setting times for cooking or reminders. Take timers a step further with IFTTT applets to flash the lights when the Alexa timer reaches zero.

2.36 Traffic Commute

Ask your virtual assistant for traffic information for your daily commute, or trips to the airport.

2.37 Travel

Travel can be grueling, so I'll try anything that makes it less of a hassle. There are travel apps where you enter a destination, and the apps use geofencing to send you a map of your location when you enter an area. Chapter 12 includes more detail on travel apps.

2.38 Turn on Christmas Lights

Set outdoor lights to be controlled by a WeMo smart electrical outlet programmed to turn on and off at certain times. Philips Hue also has several outdoor lights. An interior smart wall outlet is handy for Christmas tree lights.

2.39 TV & Video

Over-the-Top, OTT, streaming media devices allow you to stream subscription music or video networks and services to your TV. Popular streaming media devices include Apple TV, Google Chromecast, Roku, and Amazon Fire TV. Other OTT providers are OnRewind, Tedial, Dozn, Sportradar, Deltatre, and Maestro. Both Disney and Apple have plans to launch their own OTT network. Today's smart TVs also include support for a variety of streaming service apps.

Over-the-Top streaming media services like Hulu, Prime Video, or Netflix charge monthly fees. Some solutions like "slingtv" or Amazon's "Fire TV" support local channels with antennas. Amazon's Fire TV adds support for video streaming from websites. Antennas are one way to avoid monthly fees and are discussed in Chapter 9.

TV providers with a skill give you even more control of your TV. With Logitech Harmony's Alexa skill, for example, you can turn on the TV, change to a specific channel, or adjust volume with your voice. Google Home has a skill for Netflix and Chromecast. Look for skills from Amazon Fire TV, smart TV manufacturers like Sony, LG, or Vizio, or service providers like Netflix, DirectTv, Verizon, or Dish.

With the DirecTV skill, say "Alexa, tune to HGTV."

"Hey Google, turn on Friends on Netflix with Chromecast."

2.40 Vacuums

Although pricey, a smart vacuum is a gem. If we have a choice between a regular vacuum and a robotic vacuum, the decision is quite simple. Our only complaint with our Neato vacuum is that we have to empty the cat hair almost every day. On the positive side, however, this simply reminds us how well the machine is working. Perhaps it will eventually clean the litter box as well!

Figure 2.2   This is George, Jr., Our Second Robot Vacuum

Although Neato offers more expensive robotic vacuums that integrate with their mobile app, we have the model that works best for pet hair. We can still set up a cleaning schedule, but we can't use Alexa to move the vacuum around the room like the iRobot model.

Our vacuum advocates for itself. It asks us to empty its bin or says, "put me down." After a few of those interactions, we named our robot, "George." It reminds us of the Jetsons when we ask, "Did George clean already?"

A few of the popular robot vacuum manufacturers are shown below.

- iRobot Roomba

- Neato Botvac

- Samsung POWERbot

- Dyson

2.41 Visual Advice & Shopping

Fans of the Big Fang Theory TV show may recall the episode, "The Bus Pants Utilization." Penny had an idea for an app and asked Sheldon to help her create it. She said, "When you see someone wearing shoes you like, you just snap a picture of them, and the app goes on the Internet and finds out where you can buy them." Sheldon, of course, dismissed the idea saying, "The simplemindedness of your idea is exceeded only by its crass consumerism and banality."

Sheldon's objections notwithstanding, Penny's idea has become a reality (to some extent, anyway.) Today, the Amazon Echo Look and Galaxy smartphones both use cameras to provide visual-based skills. The Echo Look is designed as a closet assistant for fashion advice. Galaxy phones with the virtual assistant Bixby have Bixby Vision that allows you to shop for products right when you see them.

The Google image search engine "Google Lens," Amazon's "Flow," and some mobile apps available today, can search for plants or animals based on photographic images. With the Vuzix augmented reality glasses you can ask Alexa, what is it I'm looking at?" Sometime in the near future, taking a picture and asking a virtual assistant, "What is this?" will be commonplace.

2.42 Wake

Why not take advantage of all your smart devices to kick start your morning routine? Some ideas for reminders and controlling your home are shown below.

- Take medicine.

- Turn on lights and music.

- Adjust thermostat.

- Start heating water for showers.

- Make coffee.

- Read appointments.

- Reminder to allow extra time on your commute if you need to stop for gas.

- Set a timer for 5 minutes before departure time, and flash the lights as a reminder to kids that it's almost time to leave.

2.43 Weather

The IFTTT weather applets are powered by Weather Underground and include some interesting recipes.

- Send weather reports.

- Send e-mails when the UV Index is high.

- Send notifications of high pollen counts.

- Change the color of lights when snow or rain is forecast.

2.44 Window Coverings

Although motorized shades aren't unusual, they are certainly useful. I love to be able to say "Alexa, start 'goodnight';" and, through her IFTTT link, she closes the shades, turns off the lights, adjusts my thermostat, and turns off the TV.

Learn more about the free IFTTT web service Maker in the section Combine Several Actions in Chapter 13.

Your smart shades ideally will have integration with your virtual assistant, IFTTT, or your central control platform of choice. A few manufacturers make motorized shades, and that list seems to be growing daily.

- Bali Shades

- Hunter Douglas

- Pella

- Lutron

- Somfy

Hunter Douglas Shades

Our favorite smart thing is our PowerView shade. We have 3 rooms with motorized shades, one PowerView hub, and two repeaters. Each blind has a battery wand that uses 12 AA batteries which require replacement once a year. PowerView recommends Energizer Alkaline AA batteries.

Setup PowerView

Once the equipment is installed, the technician will configure the shades in the Hunter Douglas PowerView mobile app.

1. On your mobile device, download the PowerView app and create a login.

2. Add each device.

3. Create rooms and add shades to the rooms.

4. Create scenes.

Keeping detailed notes will help you avoid becoming needlessly frustrated when trying to remember settings after replacing batteries, updating software, or reconfiguring the shades. At a minimum, document:

- The model of the shades and hub.

- How long the batteries will last and how to replace them.

- How to do a factory reset.

- Your account login and password.

Why are there Duplicate PowerView Scenes?

Duplicate scenes confuse Alexa. This can happen when you have more than one hub in your PowerView account. Avoid this problem when you replace a hub by deleting the old hub from your account. If you suspect there are duplicate scenes, go to the skill section in the Alexa app and click on the scenes tab.

To remove duplicate scenes, remove the duplicate hub in your PowerView account and then rediscover scenes in the Alexa app. Log in to your PowerView mobile app and click on Account in the top right corner. We want to keep the active hub. The old hub should be shown as "remote." Select the remote hub and click on the information symbol next to the hub name. Select the option "Hub Info" and click on "deregister."

Learn more about Duplicate Alexa Scenes in Chapter 11.

Backup Your PowerView Configuration

You may, at some point, have to replace your PowerView hub, at which time a backup of shades and scenes will come in handy. To back up your hub, select the information symbol next to your hub name in the Powerview app. Then select Hub Info. Finally, choose Hub Backups to turn on automatic backup.

Reset to Factory Settings

When shades are unresponsive, a factory reset might resolve the issue. To restore shades to factory settings, take the batteries out of the wand and hold the manual control button on the headrail for a few seconds.

2.45 IoT News

To keep our imaginations piqued, our family subscribes to newsletters like the Amazon weekly e-mail, "What's New with Alexa?" New products are showcased at the annual CES convention that provides a fascinating view of new trends and emerging technology. Another resource, CNET, publishes a current list of all Alexa or "Hey, Google" commands. iMore has interesting articles on how to use apps and virtual assistants.

2.46 What's Next

For the purposes of this book, smart home devices are grouped into a few major categories in Chapters 6-9.

- Lighting, Electrical, HVAC and Plumbing

- Security

- Outdoor: Garage, Lawn and Garden

- Home Entertainment

- Smart Speakers and Virtual assistants

Next, I will showcase some of the more unusual smart devices that are a bit harder to classify.

- Window Coverings

- Smart Vacuums

- Cooking

- Printing

3. The Basics

In this Chapter we discuss

Since first learning such a thing existed, I wanted a smart home. Now that we have a smart home, every day reveals a new feature to be explored. Consequently, our smart home grows progressively smarter, because we keep trying out ideas other people post on social media and experimenting with new skills. We love that others are as excited about this technology as we are. I'm glad they take the time to share their ideas.

The fact that you picked up this book suggests that you might have asked the question, "How do I build a smart home?" The answer can be as simple as a whole-home solution like Insteon or SmartThings. These platforms include sensors, switches, and a control unit, and everything pretty much works right out of the box. These control units usually connect to the Internet, so you have remote access, and may also add integrations to other systems. With a whole-home solution, all you have to decide is where to put the unit and provide a Wi-Fi or Ethernet connection for Internet access.

Technical issues such as interoperability, control, and communication are relevant if you want to combine various systems, selecting the best system for each task. We also think that allowing for growth is important, and that means standardization if it's available. Addressing these issues now will make it easier to add new smart things to your home in the future. This chapter covers these technical details.

If you choose a single platform strategy such as SmartThings, you probably don't need to delve into these details right now, and you can move forward to the section on platforms. If you're curious about what goes on under the hood or need to know more in the future, we've provided the basics for you to review.

We'll also explore what is the "Internet of Things" in this Chapter. In Chapters 5 and 12, we'll look beyond devices to the role apps play in your Internet of Things.

3.1 A Solid Foundation

As quasi-normal, everyday working-class homeowners, our main objectives for our smart home were, indeed, the most practical. We wanted to select devices with proven reliability and that, accordingly, would be around for a while. Moreover, we wanted devices that had free integration, since some manufacturers charge a monthly fee to be connected. We also planned for future expansion with additional equipment and devices. In this regard, I learned the importance of planning for easy access to existing equipment. Why you may ask, is this important? I have spent too much time peering into dark closets trying to read electrical panels and other such items. The lesson: carefully consider where you'll put your devices. You may need to access them again someday.

3.2 The Internet of Things

Since this Chapter deals with basics, let's get the nerdiest aspect out of the way first by addressing standardization. Given the plethora of smart devices already on the market, we wondered if any universally accepted standard existed that applied to them. Spoiler alert: As of this writing, there really isn't.

British technology pioneer Kevin Aston coined the term "The Internet of Things" (or IoT), and Amazon, Microsoft, AT&T, and other corporations do have IoT platforms. Nevertheless, we find no one protocol or system that would represent a "gold standard." IoT, therefore, refers more to a concept of connected devices, than to any standardized reality. What this means to you and me, is that the present state of smart devices is sort of a digital wild wild west, and there is no sheriff in town. To form an analogy, if the state of electricity and electrical devices was similar to the smart things industry, a microwave oven that works in our house may not work when plugged into the outlets in your home. The potential for chaos is clear.

CAGS refers to the web of connected things across Cyberspace, Aquaspace, Geospace, and Space. I think the term itself illustrates the vast changes occuring in the foundation of the Internet.

A group known as the Internet Engineering Task Force (IETF) is working to develop standard protocols and systems, and the IETF IoT Directorate working groups are facing the same challenges today as did the groups in the '70s and '80s pioneering the Internet standards we use today. We mention this here simply to promote awareness of the bigger picture, and to say that you will likely encounter some frustrations. Don't let those frustrations discourage you.

3.3 Controlling Your Devices

For the purposes of this book, we will approach smart devices in three tiers - the third being the most burgeoning of them. Tier 1 has been around for a while and includes devices in which the "intelligence" is entirely self-contained. An example is the keypad outside your garage door. Our robot vacuum is another example. It is a smart appliance that operates on a schedule that we program. It has no interface or integration with any other systems - although some now exist that do. Tier 1 devices, therefore, serve very specific purposes and function independently of any other device. Each will have its own manual.

Tier two takes us more into the realm of what anyone over 40 may still regard as "cool." The hallmark of this level is its reliance upon mobile apps - hence the allure to Millennials and others addicted to their smartphones.

Mobile apps, of course, run on smartphones, tablets, or "wearables" like the Apple Watch - and the list grows every year.

The third tier takes us into a developing and exciting world, in which devices are integrated with other smart things using software or virtual assistants. The potential in this arena is staggering. Say, for example, you want to be able to talk to Alexa hands-free to control something (your TV, music, or blinds). Or perhaps a family member is locked out of the house, and you need to unlock the door remotely. Integration becomes vital in these situations.

Tier three is also where smart devices are configured to react to other smart things. The NEST thermostat, for one, can cool or heat according to established patterns that it figures out by itself. Moreover, the thermostat can adjust the temperature to compensate for oven heat or trigger hot water based on your normal morning schedule.

Another example is Rain Bird's irrigation sprinkler systems. The irrigation systems read weather reports from the Internet and automatically adjust settings accordingly. So the system will not water your lawn during a monsoon, and it will increase watering during a drought.

3.4 Communication and Connectivity

How a device communicates on a network is important. Communication influences where you establish your devices. And it absolutely influences the compatibility of one device with another. That is what this section is all about. Some of it is nerdy, so be patient.

The International Standards Organization (ISO) introduced the network OSI Reference Model in 1978. OSI stands for Open Systems Interconnection. This 7-layer model is sort of a Bible for Internet nerds. The lowest layer or Layer 1, is the Physical Layer - the network cards, cables, etc. Layer 2 is the Data Link layer, and this is where the MAC address of the network card comes into play. MAC stands for "media access control," and is a unique identifier associated with every network card. Think of it as a gadget's social security number. Smart devices that can communicate over Layer 7, the Application Layer, provide the greatest interoperability. Google's Weave platform operates at the Applicaiton Layer. (We spared you the pain of going into all seven layers. You're welcome!)

Devices connect to a network using a protocol for communication. Bluetooth, Ethernet, and Wi-Fi protocols are probably familiar, and for smart home automation, there are several well-known protocols. We'll talk a little about these protocols and why they are fundamental to your project's success in the next few pages.

Protocols and Networks

Today, mobile devices typically connect to home networks over Wi-Fi, Bluetooth, or possibly Ethernet protocols. These networks can also include routers, repeaters, and switches. An ISP premises router connects a home network to the Internet.

Home automation hubs and their mobile apps leverage these networks. Sensors, locks, thermostats, cameras, and other smart devices, generally also use home automation protocols like ZigBee, or Bluetooth to communicate with their respective control units. For example, a sensor or camera connects to the SmartThings hub using the ZigBee protocol. Next, we are going to get the discussion of protocols out of the way, and then we'll discuss the different kinds of control units.

There are popular Wi-Fi protocols today that operate at 2.4Ghz and 5Ghz. The Wi-Fi Alliance announced a new 802.11ah (HaLow) protocol in 2016. This solution for the Internet of Things is optimized for home automation applications and uses the 900Mhz band.

Bluetooth

Bluetooth is a global standard celebrating 20 years of success. Bluetooth utilizes the 2.4 GHz or 5.0 GHz radio frequency. This wireless protocol is ideal for short distances and supports point-to-point, broadcast, or mesh network topologies. A router or switch is not required. For example, a smartphone connects to headphones.

With predictions of 50 billion devices connected to the Internet by 2020, the age of IoT is around the corner. 30% of these devices will use Bluetooth.

Low Energy Bluetooth has speeds around3 Mbps, and classic Bluetooth speeds up to 2.1 Mbps. When selecting hearing aids and other devices, take into account that Bluetooth speed impacts direct streaming.

An excellent example of home automation solutions that use Bluetooth is provided by the company "Unikey." Its platform forms the foundation of Kevo locks. Unikey utilizes a security protocol to encrypt all Bluetooth traffic with military-grade encryption.

Pairing Bluetooth devices is covered in the next Chapter.

Other Network Protocols

Other common network protocols like Z-wave (or Zywave), x-10, Insteon, or ZigBee are designed specifically for home automation. Google's NEST Weave platform has a Weave Message Layer, BTP Layer, an Advertising Format Layer. Google also has an Open Weave version available to all developers. Smart devices use the same network as the control unit, and then the devices can communicate with each other.

- Z-wave

- x-10

- Insteon

- NEST Weave

- ZigBee

- RedLink

- Powerview

- EnOcean

The EnOcean wireless technology operates at 902 MHz in the US and Canada and has 868 Mhz products in Europe and China. This green solution includes self-powered IoT devices that use energy harvesting technology to retrieve energy from the environment in the form of temperature changes, kinetic energy, or light changes.

Why Do I Care about Protocols?

If you're rolling your eyes and wondering about the point of all this detail, I encourage you to hang in there a little longer. The cost of home automation increases with every protocol, or network, you add. When you buy additional components for a network, your wallet takes a hit.

Let's look at my home for an example. I wanted remote access to our Honeywell thermostat. After a little research, I discovered that Honeywell has its own RedLINK wireless protocol - the first in the HVAC industry. While a RedLINK Internet Gateway that pairs with the thermostat is available, the technology requires the purchase of a separate Honeywell Equipment Interface Module that manages the RedLINK wireless connections.

Another example is my Hunter Douglas Powerview shades. The shades use a proprietary wireless Powerview protocol to communicate between shades, repeaters, and a Powerview hub. If only we could buy one hub and have it work with everything, but that day is not here yet!

Honeywell, Hunter Douglas, and Kevo are closed systems. Closed systems communicate with each other over a proprietary network, using their own protocol. The control units do expand this communication to the Internet. There are several advantages to these systems in that they are designed for a particular purpose (i.e., HVAC), and the manufacturer can easily make modifications without having to garner a global consensus.

Whether or not these protocols are more secure is a debate that is beyond the scope of this book.

Unfortunately, a manufacturer may employ a proprietary implementation of a well-known protocol. That manufacturer, then, may only support their own version of Z-wave, for example, in which case it will not work with Z-wave devices from other manufacturers. We recommend you specifically ask if a device works with other manufacturer's Z-wave devices before making your purchase decision.

We spoke earlier about the absence of standardization. The multiple protocols and control units discussed here illustrate the free-for-all that exists today. In our own home, we have Bluetooth, Wi-Fi, Ethernet, PowerView, RedLINK, and ZigBee networks, to name a few. Don't despair - we'll take this one step at a time so that you become comfortable with one or two systems before you try to juggle multiple systems and protocols.

Bridges, Gateways and Hubs

Let me take a moment to explain the difference between bridges, gateways, and hubs. These are control units that govern a manufacturer's smart things, and they manage communications.

A **bridge** acts as a repeater to amplify signals and helps with communications between devices at the lower network layers. A bridge keeps track of device MAC addresses so that it delivers messages efficiently. A message is a packet, or chunk, of data. The bridge also isolates "conversations" and, in so doing, increases available bandwidth. Bridges aren't fancy or very smart, but they get the job done.

A **gateway** translates protocols and provides connectivity to foreign servers (that is, servers outside of one's own network). Translation takes time as messages have to be repackaged and then forwarded through the gateway.

A **hub** might add RJ-45 Ethernet ports and may store configuration data. IoT hubs connect to cloud services and utilize device data.

A Sample Conversation

Let's take what we've learned and put it all together using a real-world example. Devices begin communication at Layers 1-3 using Bluetooth, Wi-Fi, Ethernet, or another protocol. For example, our smartphones communicate with our Kevo lock over encrypted Bluetooth radio frequencies.

Next, device manufacturers add a control unit. Our Kevo lock communicates with our Kevo Plus Gateway. As shown in the diagram below, at step 2, the gateway connects to our home network with an Ethernet connection. Once connected to the Internet, the gateway communicates with Kevo Smart Lock Servers in the cloud. Now we have remote access to our locks and can unlock our doors when away from home.

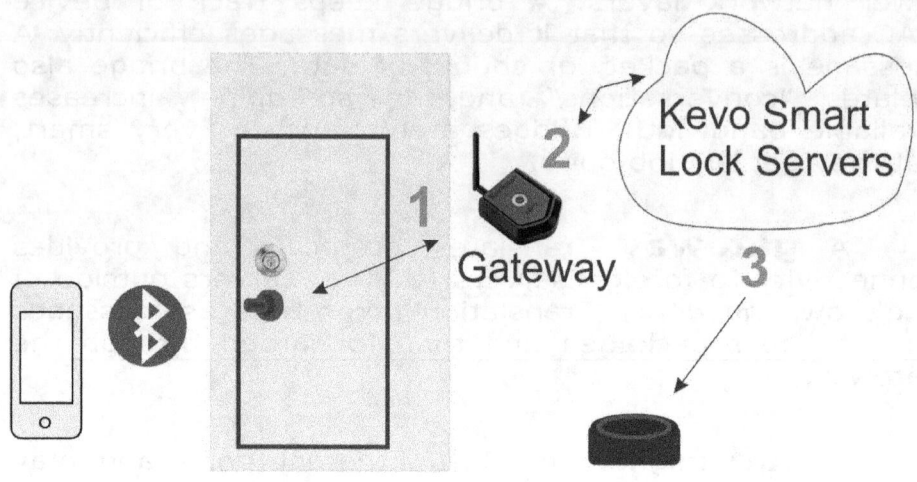

Figure 3.1   Kevo Communication

The last step in the conversation is application integration between the gateway and virtual assistants, IFTTT, or the Samsung ARTIK Cloud. This integration may leverage a microchip from the Samsung ARTIK Internet of Things (IoT) platform, or software that communicates with Amazon Alexa, Google Home, Apple HomeKit, or the IFTTT platform.

Manufacturers also add custom integrations within their mobile apps. For instance, Logitech's Harmony Remote Control app also works with Philips Hue lights. A manufacturer could also use the Amazon API from the Smart Home Skill Set to connect their device to Amazon Alexa. In the previous diagram, Step 3 shows the integration of the Kevo Servers with Alexa.

A Network Strategy

After researching all the choices, I decided my strategy would be control units (hubs, gateways, or bridges) with Wi-Fi (wireless fidelity) or wired Ethernet for connection to the Internet. Sensors, locks, and other smart devices communicate over Bluetooth, ZigBee, Z-wave, or some other protocol to their respective control unit. Although this approach offers considerable flexibility, we do have quite an array of control units.

When deciding which device is right for you, I suggest you create a chart of the supported protocols and integrations. The Chapter, "Setting Up Your Smart Home," has a sample chart, in the section "Checklist."

3.5 Platforms

SmartThings, Insteon, IFTTT, Qubino, and Yonomi are a few of the platforms to combine multiple devices, events, and actions. When integrated with virtual assistants, you can control your smart home with your voice.

For things like irrigation or vacuums, you rarely make changes after the initial setup, so integration isn't that important. However, devices you want to control on a day-to-day basis should probably integrate with SmartThings, Alexa, HomeKit, Siri, or a similar platform.

Yonomi One is "software as a service" (SaaS), with a mobile app to integrate devices and apps. IFTTT is an acronym for **If This happens, Then do That**, and is a free web-based platform. With IFTTT, you can easily create applets (pieces of code) to control your home automation devices.

Learn how to combine smart home commands in Chapter 13, "IFTTT."

Samsung smart technology is found in digital cockpit vehicle displays, TVs, washers, dryers, vacuums, ranges, and refrigerators. The Samsung SmartThings platform includes smart home devices for security, lighting, and more. Underlying this technology is the Samsung Connect Cloud, which is Samsung's unified IoT platform. The Samsung ARTIK IoT Platform provides hardware-backed security and public key infrastructure to protect information. To make all of this technology easier to use, Samsung plans to roll out its voice-controlled virtual assistant "Bixby" to all their connected devices by 2020.

Learn more about SmartThings in Chapter 7, "Home Security."

Qubino takes the approach of transforming existing things into smart devices that communicate over a Z-wave network. A Qubino relay can control lights, fans, ovens, washing machines, irons, power sockets, garage doors, electric radiators, or water heaters, and also measures power consumption.

3.6 Mobile Operating Systems

Generally, your smartphone, tablet, smart screen, or smartwatch will run one of these mobile operating systems.

- iOS

- Android

The Apple iOS mobile operating system apps and devices are tightly integrated and focused on ease of use. Apple apps are available from the Apple store. Google's Android mobile operating system is an open system and is free for manufacturers to use on their devices. Apps are available in "Google Play." Both Google and Apple have a cloud service for sharing files: iCloud or Google Drive.

Android

While Apple's iOS is proprietary and only available on Apple devices, Google's various Android operating systems are used by many manufacturers in an array of devices.

- Smartphones

- Tablets

- Smart TVs

- Smart Screens (Echo Show, Portal from Facebook, Lenovo Smart Display)

- Amazon Fire TV

When Google releases a new version of their Android mobile operating system each year in August, they use a naming convention modeled after desserts. Android v9 is "Pie," and Android v8 is "Oreo."

A few years ago, I tried an Android phone and tablet. At the time, I was surprised I had to download, and pay for, a third-party app to do what I thought were basic tasks. For example, I missed the simplicity of searching for a business in the Maps app and then clicking a button to save the business as a new contact. These days I also forward contacts to friends in Messages or e-mail apps, because it's an easy way to share address or phone information.

While I absolutely love Google Maps, the Google search engine, and the Google Calendar app, I couldn't adjust to life with an Android phone. Android is a powerful and elegant operating system, it's just not for me. I like the simplicity of Apple iOS because I don't have to research what is possible or search for apps.

iOS 12

The Apple iOS 12 operating system encompasses the logistics of how an iPhone or iPad works. In many ways, the functionality of an iPhone or iPad is similar when they are both running the same iOS version, regardless of the device model. iOS 12 includes these features:

- USB-C

- Group FaceTime (up to 32 participants)

- Camera effects (filter and stickers)

- Screen time (limits, allowances)

- Grouped notifications

- A new Shortcuts App

- Siri Shortcuts

- The Measure App

- Do Not Disturb (based on location, time, actions)

- Apple Pencil Support

The iOS supports your interaction with your iPad - tapping, swiping, and controls. This engineering is elegant and simple to use, provides Wi-Fi and Bluetooth connectivity, and app updates from the Apple Store.

There are several app Changes in iOS 12. The "Files" app now integrates with iCloud Drive, Dropbox, and other providers. There is a redesigned interface for the Stocks app with iOS 12. The new "Shortcut" app expands the Siri virtual assistant shortcuts, as shown in Chapter 12.

3.7 Location Services & Geofencing

In Chapter 2, we looked at location-based services or Geofencing. Smartphones, smart TVs, and virtual assistants all use GPS information to determine your precise location. This data is also used to control smart things like lights, thermostats, and sprinklers. For example, your smart TV uses your location to determine the program guide for local shows.

Apple Location Services

Apple's "location services" are used for apps like Messaging, Do Not Disturb, Maps, Find My Friends App, and Intelligent Siri. Apps and settings like Nightshift or Home use location services to determine sunrise and sunset.

1. Open the Settings app on your iPad and tap "Privacy." Swipe and tap "Location Services."

2. In the list of apps, configure location services for each app. The options are "Never," "Always," or "While Using the App."

Alexa Location and Time Zone

Location and time zone settings are used by Alexa for navigation, traffic, skills like Uber, weather reports, scheduling activities, and Geofencing skills.

Figure 3.2   Set Your Location

1.   Go to the menu and select **Settings**.

2.   Select your device.

3.   Under the General section, select **Device location** and **Device time zone**.

3.8 Accessibility

In Chapter 2, we looked at IoT and virtual assistants in the context of medical and health issues. For those who have suffered a broken leg or other disability, smart devices can drastically improve your quality of life. Whether it is listening to music, turning lights on or off, cleaning the floor, or sending a message, a smart home is an assistant worth having. Accessibility is another area where this new technology is changing people's lives, and I wanted to mention a few practical applications here.

Initially, I used accessibility features on my smartphone for convenience. A flashing light when my iPhone rings is a handy way to find my iPhone in the dark. Next, I ran across the setting for larger text, so I can read my screen without glasses. The new MFi (Made for iPhone) hearing aid integration means I can listen to my iPhone playlist or calls without disturbing those around me. Eventually, I decided to do a little research on accessibility and see what else would make my life easier.

The work Apple has done for accessibility is outstanding. In fact, in November 2018, Apple won the prestigious Eleanor Roosevelt Humanitarian Award from the Center for Hearing and Communication for its accessibility features. The iPad, iOS, and Apple Apps work together to provide accessibility in three areas.

- Vision

- Hearing

- Physical and Motor Skills in the Workout App

In the next sections, we will discuss accessibility settings, app integrations, wheelchair settings, and workouts.

Haptics and Touch

In Chapter 2, we discussed Haptics and Touch. Haptics is the science of applying tactile sensation (touch) and control when interacting with computer applications. Apple introduced the Taptic Engine with the iPhone 6s. Chances are, you've found your muted iPhone at one time or another by following the vibrations. Haptics is also a useful accessibility feature for deaf or hard of hearing users, and drivers will appreciate the Map app that gently vibrates your Apple Watch to indicate an upcoming turn.

Read Out Loud

The first time my Kindle app started reading my book out loud, I was so startled I knocked over my glass of water. I was quietly reading as I ate lunch at my desk, and frankly didn't want my coworkers to hear what I was reading. Even though I hadn't bought an Audible subscription, Amazon decided to give me a free demonstration. I already knew the Apple Books app displays a microphone button at the top of the screen in books that support voice narration. Children's books are a prime example of read-aloud options. In the Apple Books app, words are highlighted as you read along.

Another option is to turn on "Speech." Open the Settings app and in the left sidebar tap "General." In the right pane tap "Accessibility," and then tap "Speech." Control which voice is used with the "Voices" setting. Highlight the words as Siri is reading. Toggle "Highlight Content" to highlight words as they are spoken. When you have a book open in the Books app, swipe down with two fingers from the top of the screen to hear the contents of the screen.

Read Screen Contents Out loud

Apple devices have an accessibility feature called "Speak Screen." The voice isn't as nice as a professional narrator, but it will read my book to me as I'm driving and that's pretty cool. This feature works in the Books app or any app running on the iPad. In apps like Safari, you can say, "Hey Siri, turn on Speak Screen."

1. Open the "Settings" app.

2. Tap My iPad, go to "General."

3. Tap Accessibility.

4. Tap "Speech" and toggle "Speak Screen" on.

Swipe down from the top of the screen with two fingers to hear the content of the screen.

Accessibility Shortcut

The "Accessibility Shortcut" uses the iPad Home Button to turn on "Zoom," "VoiceOver," or other accessibility options with a triple-click. You can choose one of these options for your accessibility shortcut.

- Assistive Touch
- Classic Invert Colors
- Color Filters
- Reduce White Point
- Smart Invert Colors
- Switch Control
- VoiceOver
- Zoom

1. Open the "Settings" app on your iPad.

2. Tap My iPad, go to "General."

3. Tap Accessibility, scroll all the way down to the bottom and tap "Accessibility Shortcut."

4. Choose "Classic Invert Colors" or another option.

Customize App Notifications

Some apps allow you to customize notification options, as shown below.

- Allow Notifications
- Banner
- Notifications Off

To set app notification options, follow these steps.

- On your iPad, open the "Settings" app.
- Tap "Notifications."
- Tap an app and select the option.

Vision

Apple has several settings on the "Accessibility" screen to accommodate vision. Visual enhancements include these "General" settings.

- Bold Text
- Reduce Motion

- Reduce Transparency
- VoiceOver
- Zoom
- On/Off Labels
- Grayscale

VoiceOver

VoiceOver is a built-in screen reader on Apple devices. As you move your finger over the display, each item is announced. The VoiceOver feature has 37 supported languages and works with all native apps including mail, calendar, maps, or messages.

During the initial setup process, press the Home Button three times to activate "VoiceOver." There is also a setting to toggle the Accessibility Shortcut on, as mentioned earlier.

Siri excels at toggling VoiceOver on or off. Press the Home Button twice to wake up Siri and say, "Turn on VoiceOver." Siri responds with "VoiceOver on." If you prefer, you can turn on VoiceOver in "Settings."

1. Press the Home Button to open the Home Screen.

2. Tap Settings, and then tap General.

3. Swipe to select "Accessibility."

4. Tap "VoiceOver" to toggle on or off.

Tap twice to open an app, switch an option, or perform any action that would normally be done with a single tap. To go back to the last screen swipe a "Z" on the screen. While using VoiceOver, there is a "Screen Curtain" setting to turn off the iPad display for privacy. Quickly tap the screen three times to activate the screen curtain.

Set the Reading Rate

The reading rate for VoiceOver on your iPad is controlled by "Accessibility" settings.

1. Press the Home Button on your iPad to open the Home Screen.

2. Tap "Settings," and then tap "General."

3. Swipe to select "Accessibility."

4. Drag the slider bar to adjust the reading rate.

Zoom

The Zoom magnification setting on an Apple iPad is fifteen times the native size. Pinch the screen with two fingers, to control the zoom level.

On/Off Labels

Apple Accessibility options include the "On/Off Labels" setting. This setting displays additional label information when toggled on.

Grayscale

The "Grayscale" settings on an iPad assist users where color might impair visibility. Grayscale is a system-wide setting.

Hearing

If you're deaf or hard of hearing in one ear, you may miss some stereo audio or alerts. The "Mono Audio" setting plays both audio channels in both ears. You can also adjust the balance for greater volume in either ear. Tap the "Mono Audio" switch on the "Accessibility" screen in the Hearing section to toggle the setting on or off. There is a slider to adjust the volume for the left or right side.

1. Press the Home Button to open the Home Screen.

2. Tap "Settings," and then tap "General."

3. Swipe to select "Accessibility."

4. Tap the "Mono Audio" switch to toggle the switch on or off.

5. Drag the slider bar to adjust the volume for the left or right side.

Bluetooth Accessories

If you are using hearing aids, look for hearing aids that are "Made for iPad" or MFi. Some models, like Phonak Audéo Marvel hearing aids, support direct Bluetooth streaming to both ears. Chapter 8 discusses how to add Bluetooth accessories.

Hearing Aids

Your iPad connects to hearing aids over Bluetooth. Hearing Aids that support Classic Bluetooth with speeds up to 2.1 Mbps are better for direct audio streaming. Low Energy Bluetooth is3 Mbps, and Classic Bluetooth is up to 2.1 Mbps. For innovative hearing aid designs, check out the annual CES Innovation Awards for accessibility products.

Another option instead of traditional Bluetooth is to connect hearing aids with the MFi (Made for iPhone) setting. By default, "Control on Lock Screen" will be on as outlined in the next section. Leave this setting on to control your hearing aid from the Lock Screen (using the Accessibility Shortcut) and from Control Center. The following is a list of MFi options.

- Play Ringtones
- Audio Routing
- Control Nearby Devices
- Audio Handoff
- Control on Lock Screen

With MFi Audio Routing you select the default device for audio playback. MFi Audio Handoff allows you to continue listening with your hearing aid when you switch between your iOS devices.

The "Control Nearby Devices" applies to iOS devices. Your iOS device will adjust hearing aid settings when devices are on the same Wi-Fi network and connected to your iCloud account.

1. Open your hearing aid's battery doors, or power rechargeable hearing aids off.

2. On your iPad, tap Settings > General > Accessibility > Hearing > MFi Hearing Devices.

3. Close your hearing aid's battery doors, or turn on your rechargeable hearing aid. Your iOS device will search for your hearing aid.

4. Under Devices, tap the name of your hearing aid.

5. Tap Pair when you see the pairing request on the screen. If you have two hearing aids, you will get two requests. The pairing process can take up to a minute.

Control your MFi Hearing Aid

Control the volume of your Phonak Audéo Marvel hearing aid with your iPad. Use the Volume Buttons to adjust the volume.

Use your iOS device to see your hearing aid's battery life, turn on Live Listen, and more. To configure your hearing aid, use "Settings" or the Accessibility Shortcut. Tap your hearing aid name for these options.

- View battery life.

- Unpair your hearing aid.

- Adjust volume levels for either or both hearing aids.

- "Live Listen" options (Basic, Restaurant, Outdoor, Party.)

Messaging & Video Calls

Text messaging, FaceTime, and video conferencing on smart screens are a great alternative to close-captioned phone calls.

Subtitles

The "Audio & Subtitles" control is available when watching videos in the Apple TV app. Tap the screen to see the playback controls. On the right side, tap the "Audio & Subtitles" control. You can also turn subtitles on in the Settings app. In the left sidebar tap "General" and in the right pane tap "Accessibility." Swipe to scroll down to the "Media" section and tap "Subtitles & Captioning."

3.9 What's Next?

Chapter 4 will cover the logistics of setting up your smart home, ensuring a good foundation so you can continue to add new technology when it becomes available.

4. Setting up Your Smart Home

In this chapter we discuss

Where to Put Smart Home Equipment

Stands for Mobile Devices

Network Switch

Quality LAN Cables

Naming Devices and Scenes

Setting Up Devices

Accounts and Passwords

What to Buy

Checklist of Features

What's Next

My goals for a smart home are for everything to work as expected, to be simple to maintain, and to be readily expandable in the future. To do that, I needed a reliable, solid infrastructure that includes a network switch for all the smart hubs, quality cabling, and a fast ISP connection to the Internet. With a little planning at this stage, I'll help you avoid some pain points down the road.

When we get to the part about a central location for your smart things, we hope you will understand why the discussion of protocols in Chapter 1 was necessary. It should illuminate why we make some of the choices that follow. The salient points from Chapter 1 are recapitulated here - just in case you skipped through Chapter 1 (which, frankly, would just be a shame)!

4.1 Where to Put Smart Home Equipment

Placing your smart home equipment (smart hubs, gateways, bridges, network switches, and repeaters) in a central location is a good idea for several reasons. Firstly, the devices must connect to a network and maintain a strong signal for successful communication. Secondly, you need to wire the location with additional power outlets and a cable to your ISP router. Finally, you need easy access to your equipment - for set up, viewing status lights, and adding new devices. A few of our suggestions are:

- Select a central location with easy access.

- Provide a port to your ISP Internet router.

- Choose a network switch with multiple ports.

- Add extra electrical outlets for all those powered devices.

The close proximity of devices and control units is essential for devices that require line of sight signals. One example is the Wii sensor bar that uses IR (infrared) wireless signals. Also, keep in mind that Bluetooth radio frequencies are meant for short distances. If your Wi-Fi router does not have a good signal throughout your house, you can add a Wi-Fi extender, also known as a repeater, to ensure a strong signal.

In the past, we had a wiring hub in a closet and had to add an electrical outlet for video equipment and routers. We were worried, however, that the temperature would become too high in the closet with the door closed. Our solution was to install a wiring hub, along with the main AT&T network premises router, in our laundry room. Our smart home hubs and network switch, however, are centrally located in our family room, in a large entertainment center.

4.2 Stands for Mobile Devices

Since a mobile phone or tablet is integral to a smart home, you will want to know where yours is at all times. Having a dedicated stand for this purpose will provide a home base for your device. It will also prove to be convenient when cooking or streaming music.

There are lots of designs available to choose from, ranging from styles that include an iPad holder to a vertical charging stand. Most third-party docks leverage existing charging cables. Two stands I considered were (1) the HiRise 2 Deluxe with three height levels and a charger, and (2) the adjustable Lamicall stand with rubber cushions. You will find a wealth of stands from which to select. Pay attention to features such as:

- Adjustable Height
- Rotation
- Charging
- Solid and Sturdy Base

4.3 Network Switch

You probably already have a premises router from your ISP. Hopefully, it supports both 2.4GHz and 5GHz Wi-Fi radio frequencies and Ethernet. 2.4GHz is an older technology and can reach farther than 5GHz. It is important to note that some devices like the Harmony Hub are only compatible with 2.4GHz frequencies. The router provided by our ISP uses Wi-Fi band steering so that the network name and password are the same for both 2.4GHz and 5GHz Wi-Fi radio frequencies. This is convenient because we only need to know one network name and password combination. To ensure a strong Wi-Fi signal throughout our home, we also have a Wi-Fi repeater recommended by AT&T specifically for their router.

In addition to the router provided by our ISP (AT&T), we have a NetGear switch for Ethernet wired LAN connections to our Smart TV, DVD, Yamaha Amplifier, Wii, PlayStation, Apple TV, Wi-Fi extender and numerous home automation hubs. When we moved into our new home, we realized within 3 days that an 8-port switch didn't have enough ports. We decided to go with a 24-port switch so we would not have to think about it again for a long time.

Configuring a router behind a router can be tricky - assuming your ISP even allows it - so we chose to add a network switch for our smart devices over another router. A router with Wi-Fi can also introduce conflicts on the Wi-Fi network, so we decided having a separate Wi-Fi repeater for that purpose would be less troublesome.

The model switch we selected has auto up-link. With auto up-link, all you have to do is plug the switch into the ISP router LAN jack, and setup is done. The NetGear switch we selected, with which we are satisfied, has all of these features:

- Auto-switching between 100 and 1000 MBps ports

- Auto up-link

- 24 ports

- Gigabit Ethernet (1000 MBps)

4.4 Quality LAN Cables

To allow for the future of Gigabit Ethernet, we chose Cat 7 cables that would support Gigabit speeds or 1000 MBps. Although Gigabit Ethernet is not very common today, we don't want to have to replace cables in the future when it becomes commonplace.

A quality LAN cable ensures reliability and performance, so we splurged on Ortronics cables in various colors and lengths. Ortronics is actually a part of the Legrand family and has been around a long time.

When troubleshooting, the last thing you want to worry about is a bad cable. It is not uncommon for poorly constructed (aka cheap) cables to go bad after a few months. Practically any time a device suddenly stops working and I didn't change anything, a bad cable proves to be the culprit.

4.5 Naming Devices and Scenes

Unless you work in the IT field, you probably haven't paid much attention to network names. For the purposes of this discussion, "name" refers to either the device or scene name configured in the mobile app or the network name. Often the name is the same in both places. Basically, every device on your Wi-Fi or Ethernet network has an IP address and network name. For most smart things you configure names in a mobile app, and you're good to go.

Examples of setting network names for different types of devices can be found in the "Home Entertainment" chapter.

When you have more than one device for the same task, for example casting or playing music, it's a good idea to update the device name or scene name to ensure there are no duplicates anywhere in your smart home. In the case of an Echo dot, in the mobile app, you can set the network name, and Alexa uses that name going forward for all tasks.

Unique names that include location or purpose avoid confusion. Names that use hard consonants are also more likely to be understood by your virtual assistant. We've also noticed our virtual assistants are sometimes literal. For example, "bedroom light" is not the same as the plural "bedroom lights."

- Family Room Yamaha

- Family Room Lock

- Family Room Lights

- Family Room Blinds

- Family Room Outlet

- Upstairs Thermostat

- Downstairs Thermostat

In our family room alone, we have these smart devices: speakers, a thermostat, lights, blinds, an outlet, and our smart vacuum George. It's easy to see how we might get confused about names if we name all these devices "family room."

Names vs. IP Addresses

As mentioned earlier, every device on your Wi-Fi or Ethernet network has an IP address and network name. Personally, I like to know what all the devices are that are connected to my home network so that I can identify intruders. With a little detective work, you can match devices to IP addresses. If you're curious about the process or run into an issue, there is an in-depth section in the Day to Day chapter, in the section on troubleshooting network names and IP addresses.

4.6 Setting Up Devices

Obviously setting up each device will be a unique experience, but I have found it generally involves some combination of the following steps.

1. Unpack the device and write down codes from the packaging if required.

2. Connect the device to power.

3. Download and install an app on your mobile device or computer.

4. Launch the app and create an account.

5. Connect the device to a Wi-Fi or Ethernet network.

6. Configure the device in the mobile app and create scenes, schedules, etc.

7. Install skills for your virtual assistants.

8. Create IFTTT applets.

When I took a new hub out of the packaging, I got distracted for a few days before I tried to set it up. There was a "device code" on the packaging needed for setup, and I had to dig in the recycle bin to find the box. The lesson: hold on to packaging until everything is working as expected, and make a note of codes.

Connecting to a WPS Network

During the initial setup, some devices use a WPS (wireless protected setup) network. If your router supports WPS, to connect the router and new device to the WPS network you typically press a button on the router or Wi-Fi repeater to activate WPS and another button on the new device.

Instead of using WPS at the router, another option is for the new device to create a temporary Wi-Fi WPS network. You switch your smartphone (or PC) from your home network to the new device's WPS network, and complete the setup instructions.

Note the WPS Wi-Fi network is only available during the setup process. After setup is complete, the new device will use your regular home Wi-Fi network.

Bluetooth: Pair Devices

Because you'll probably be pairing Bluetooth devices a lot, I wanted to mention the process briefly. These days it's not uncommon to use a Bluetooth keyboard with a smart TV or to connect your smartphone and amplifier to play music. My Internet of Things world includes these Bluetooth devices.

- TVs

- Music Amplifiers

- Harmony Remote

- Smartphones and Tablets

- Smart Speakers

- Keyboards

The steps below walk you through pairing a Bluetooth accessory with an iPad and illustrate the basic pairing process.

1. Turn on pairing mode on your Bluetooth accessory.

2. Press the Home Button on your iPad to open the Home Screen.

3. Tap the gear button to open "Settings." If you don't see the gear, swipe and move your finger until you locate the gear button.

4. Scroll and select "Bluetooth."

5. Tap to select the Bluetooth accessory.

Once connected, you can switch between Bluetooth devices in the Control Panel on the iPad. Tap the Bluetooth control to disconnect paired Bluetooth devices. To turn off Bluetooth completely, use the Settings app on the iPad.

Smart TVs

Once you pair a Bluetooth device with a smart TV, you can use the "input" option to select the Bluetooth device. On TV's the option to pair a Bluetooth device might be found under:

Settings, Network & Accessories, Bluetooth Settings.

Chapter 9 has an example of pairing the Logitech Harmony Remote with your smart TV.

Smart Speakers and Amplifiers

Not all smart speakers support Bluetooth external speakers. The original Amazon Echo and Google Home didn't connect to Bluetooth speakers.

"Alexa, ask MusicCast to switch input to Bluetooth in the Family Room."

Hearing Aids

If you are using hearing aids, look for those that are "Made for iPhone." Some models, like Phonak Audéo Marvel hearing aids, support direct Bluetooth streaming to both ears.

1. Open your hearing aid's battery doors.

2. On your iOS device, tap Settings > General > Accessibility > Hearing > MFi Hearing Devices.

3. Close the battery doors of your hearing aid. Your iOS device will search for your hearing aid.

4. Under "Devices," tap the name of your hearing aid.

5. Tap Pair when you see the pairing request on the screen. If you have two hearing aids, you will get two requests. The pairing process could take up to a minute.

Once paired, the MFi Hearing Device screen has several options. By default "Control on Lock Screen" will be on. Leave it on to control your hearing aid from the Lock screen (using the Accessibility Shortcut,) or from Control Center. Chapter 10 has additional information on controlling MFi hearing aids.

Use the volume buttons to adjust the volume on your Phonak Audéo Marvel hearing aids.

Device Details

This is where I want to shout, "Save yourself heartache; write down everything!" Instead, I'll just say I referred to my notes constantly and was glad I had them. During the initial setup, these details ensure the process goes smoothly. Later, you will refer to your notes when reprogramming or troubleshooting a device. If you sell your home someday, the buyer will want details about your smart home.

A housesitter will also need to know the phrases you set up. My daughter texted me the first night she was house sitting, asking me to turn off the Hue bedroom lightstrip. I forgot to include that command in my Alexa "Houseguest" skill covered in Chapter 11 in the topic Blueprints. There is no wall switch for the HUE lights behind our headboard, and the lights automatically come on each evening. I learned a lesson from that experience. I need to record all my smart home commands somewhere for visitors too, not just if I sell my house.

1. What devices are smart?

2. Is there a generic "home e-mail address" used to set up devices? Do you have account names, login information, and passwords?

3. Is there a list of device IP addresses?

4. What are the model numbers?

5. Do you know how to do a master reset to reprogram a device?

Default System Settings

To bridge the gap between what is possible today in an app and your ideal smart home environment, use default system settings. When you turn on a device like a TV or your sound system, you probably prefer a particular color light or intensity, and volume of sound. It's a little annoying to change the sound back to the level you prefer, but if you have the remote control in hand already, it's not a big deal.

Now change to the same situation in a smart home where there is no remote, and you use your voice to control everything. Default settings take on a new meaning. Imagine you're cooking dinner and you have a Harmony activity called "dinner" that has these actions.

1. Turn on the TV and change to a music channel.

2. Turn on the surround sound system.

3. Blink lights in other rooms.

4. Send a text message that dinner is ready.

5. Turn on the dining room lights.

6. Close the blinds.

Our cable TV DVR box cannot start on an initial channel we select, but a Harmony activity can. Also, as of this moment, we have been unable to find an initial color or intensity setting for lights in the HUE app, but we can control those settings with IFTTT applets. There is an option in our Yamaha amplifier on the setup screen under sound settings to set an initial volume of 50Db. Your preferences and devices will vary, but we wanted to point this out because it's a nice customization.

Schedules

Let's take a moment to mention device schedules. Schedules are used to tell a device when to automatically turn on or off, adjust the temperature or change light intensity. Look for smart devices that support schedules with daily, weekly, and recurring options. Some apps support a solar calendar that uses "sunrise" or "sunset." We prefer to set a specific time.

4.7 Accounts and Passwords

There will be many accounts to juggle for each smart home manufacturer, and we would suggest you consider using a separate login ID and password for each account. To increase security, a unique ID and password for every account are ideal. Also, a separate e-mail account or ID for your home, instead of your personal e-mail, makes it easier to transfer to a new homeowner if you sell your house. An account manager app, as outlined in Chapter 5, would be helpful in this situation.

If you use your virtual assistant to order from Amazon, read text messages or check deliveries, you probably want to use your personal e-mail for those things. However, when it comes to smart electrical, lighting, or thermostat devices, using a separate "home" e-mail makes the most sense. Whatever you decide, we recommend you keep a record of IDs and passwords for future reference.

4.8 What to Buy

This section is geared toward advice on how you can decide what to buy and where to get it. Although we mention specific brands with which we have experience, the decision of what to buy is entirely up to you. We have included a checklist of features we have found important at the end of this chapter. Hopefully, with that in hand, you have enough information to go shopping.

When deciding where to buy things, we have learned that it's not just about price. As careful as we were in our research, not everything we purchased worked as expected. The customer service aspect, therefore, became a critical factor in deciding where to buy this new technology. We found Amazon, the big-name stores or manufacturers like Legrand and Samsung make it easy to return items.

Until you're sure everything works properly, keep the receipt and original packaging to speed up returns.

This is the checklist we used when selecting and setting up our smart devices. It also comes in handy if you have to "reconfigure" a device or if you sell your house. Even a shortlist of all your smart Wi-Fi devices is a huge help in case you have to replace your ISP router. You have my condolences in that scenario if you have to re-type the Wi-Fi password 20 times.

The devices you want to control on a day-to-day basis should probably work with Alexa, HomeKit, or a similar system. For things like irrigation or vacuuming, you will probably set it up and never interact with it again, so integration doesn't matter. The checklist section "Does it work with" is for comparing whether the device works independently controlled by its own mobile app or has integration features.

4.9 Checklist of Features

Basics	
Brand/Model	
IP Address	
Host Name	Family Room TV
Account Name	2018SmartHome@att. net
Account Password	
Device Code	
Bridge/Hub	
WPS (wireless protected setup) network	
Connect Button on Bridge for Pairing	

Connectivity	
Wi-Fi (2.4GHz or 5GHz)	
Ethernet LAN (Wired)	Ethernet
Bluetooth	
Other	

Does it work with a Virtual assistant?		
	Device	Skills
Amazon Alexa		
Google Home		
Microsoft Cortana		
Apple HomeKit		
Other		

Does it Support...?	
IFTTT	Yes
NEST	
Other	
Scenes	
Device Groups	
Automations	
Widgets (Apple Watch)	

Does it Have a Scheduler?	
Recurring Events	
Daylight Savings Time	
Sunrise/Sunset	Yes

Questions	
Does it work when the network is down?	
Is it reliable? Does it have good reviews?	
Is there a monthly fee?	No
Is there a door key, fob or remote?	
Can you open blinds without power?	

4.10 What's Next?

Although much of what we talk about in this book pertains to smart home technology, the Internet of Things incorporates so much more. Indeed, any business or agency we deal with can be part of the IoT. In the next chapter, we'll look at the technology that extends beyond your home.

5. Sharing Connections, Data, & More

In this chapter we discuss

Sharing Wi-Fi and Cellular

Two-Factor Authentication

Accounts and Passwords

Health and Activity

Handoff Apps & Continuity

Share Files or Photos with Cloud Services

Background App Refresh

Side-by-Side Apps

Integrating Apps & Sharing Data

Apple Activity View and App Tray

Credit Card Information & Purchasing

Audio

There are complex systems behind your Internet of Things. In Chapter 2, we talked about the basics of how devices communicate. Moving beyond smart home devices, this chapter outlines other technologies and architectures that expand your Internet of Things with connections between devices, cloud services, and apps. While this chapter is on the broad-reaching platforms, Chapter 12 discusses individual apps with real-world examples.

- Sending audio signals, photos, or video signals from a smartphone to devices like speakers or smart TVs.

- Cloud services like Dropbox, Amazon Drive, or Apple iCloud, that store or exchange files.

- Apps and devices are utilizing Geofencing or location services.

- Accounts & Passwords

- Credit Card Accounts

- Health & Activity Sharing

- Ways to exchange and share data between apps. We'll explore using e-mail, reminder lists, macros, and shortcut apps.

Managing your information in one place, and sharing it with other apps or devices is possible in a variety of ways.

- Share Wi-Fi and Cellular

- Share Accounts and Passwords

- Share Credit Card Information

- Health and Activity Data

- Challenge Friends with Activity Workouts

- Listen to Audio Across Devices

- View Photos and Video Across Devices

- Share Data with Family or Friends (photos, files) with cloud services

- Integrate Multiple Apps

Sending audio signals, photos, or video signals from a smartphone to devices like speakers or smart TVs is an example of connected devices. Apps and devices utilizing Geofencing or location services are other examples. Another simple example is two different apps exchanging data through e-mail.

Maintaining the privacy and security of your accounts can be a challenge, and I outline account management apps and two-factor authentication later in this Chapter. We'll also look at Apple's Wallet and Apple Pay platforms.

In the Health topic, we'll look at platforms that integrate health and workout information in one place, utilizing input sources from an app or device data. For example, there are workout apps like Strava or Paddle Logger, as well as apps with clinical data like LabCorp. Device data examples are a heart rate monitor, the Apple Watch, or the Dexcom sensor for continuous glucose monitoring.

5.1 Sharing Wi-Fi and Cellular

During the initial setup of your Apple device, you probably connected to your home Wi-Fi network. Unless you choose to "Forget this Network," the network name and password are automatically stored once you've connected at least once to a Wi-Fi network. Occasionally you might want to connect to a different Wi-Fi network, and the steps to manage Wi-Fi connections follow.

1. On your iPhone or iPad, open the "Settings" app and tap "Wi-Fi" in the left sidebar. A green slider next to "Wi-Fi" at the top of the right panel indicates Wi-Fi is on. The line below that has a checkmark next to the Wi-Fi network you're currently connected to.

2. In the section "Choose a Network," a list of Wi-Fi networks in range of your iPad is displayed. Tap to select a network, and enter the network password when prompted.

3. At the bottom of the right panel, tap "Ask to Join Networks," if you want to be prompted any time your iPad is looking for a Wi-Fi network.

Personal Hot Spot

Personal hot spots are a way to tether another device to a smart device, and "share" the Cellular or Wi-Fi connection. For example, when you assign a name to your iPad, it is used as a network name for AirPlay, iCloud, or for your personal hotspot. Cellular iPad models have an option to create a personal hotspot to share your Wi-Fi with other devices. Check with your cellular carrier to see if your plan includes personal hotspots.

5.2 Two-Factor Authentication

To protect account security, 2FA or two-factor authentication is becoming common. Instead of using only your normal account password, a second category is involved.

- Something you have. A smartphone, credit card, etc.

- Something you know. A PIN, password, answers to secret questions.

- Something you are. Your fingerprint, for example.

One way to provide two-factor authentication is a text message or e-mail with a verification code displayed on one of your other Apple devices. You then enter the authentication code on your new device.

Some apps add an additional level of passwords along with two-factor authentication. In that case, you generate a specific password for that app. For example, I don't share my Google password with Apple Calendar.

Instead, at Google, I generate an "Apple app" password. I then enter that new special password and also enter my normal Apple password. You could think of this as a subordinate Google password that only works with my Apple app.

You enable two-factor authentication for your Apple ID in the Settings app. Tap your Apple ID on the top left of the Settings screen, and then tap "Password & Security" on the right side of the screen. Toggle Two-Factor Authentication on.

5.3 Accounts and Passwords

When you trust an account manager app like Dashlane to keep track of your accounts and passwords, all you have to remember is your Dashlane ID and password. Apple introduced its "Passwords & Accounts" manager in iOS 12. All your accounts and passwords are stored in one place - your iCloud Keychain. Your security information is available on any Apple device when you authenticate with Face ID, Touch ID, or your passcode. The Password & Accounts app generates strong passwords for you, identifies weak passwords, and will autofill account information when you visit a login web page.

5.4 Health and Activity

Medical devices integrate with smartphones and smart watches to gather your health data. Medical devices include blood pressure monitors, CGM or continuous glucose monitors, or biosensors that measure respiratory rate and temperature. For example, the Dexcom CGM sensor connects to a transmitter. The transmitter communicates with a smartphone app, and has a watch complication that displays data on your Apple Watch.

When it comes to Health, Exercise, and Activity apps, Apple has covered all the bases with its HealthKit and GymKit platforms, which we'll look at in this section. HealthKit includes apps, devices, and partnerships with hospitals and labs. Fall detection, emergency SOS, and heart rate & ECG monitoring are part of the Apple Watch health lineup.

The Apple Watch heart rate monitor and health and fitness apps work together to meet your health and fitness goals. Features like an electrical heart rate sensor, built-in electrodes, optical heart sensor, accelerometer, and gyroscope are ideal for health and fitness apps. The accelerometer can differentiate between a walk and a run and enables features like "Running Auto Pause," to identify when you're taking an exercise break.

- Activity App
- Workout App
- Breathe (Mindfulness) App
- Health App
- ECG App
- Heart Rate App

The Apple Activity app has three goals: move, stand, and exercise. Apple calculates your exercise and stand goals for you, but does allow you to change your move goal. The goals change weekly, adapting to your lifestyle. The goals are designed to be a challenge that is within your reach.

The Apple Workout app includes walking, running, cycling, hiking, swimming, and yoga workouts, to name a few. If you don't see the workout you want, the "other" category allows you to record a workout and then give it a custom name.

The Apple Health app displays the Activity, Workout, Mindfulness, and Heart rate records. When linked to other health apps, the Health app displays body measurements, health records, lab results, and vital statistics in one place. The Heart Rate app also shows insights into your heart rate, such as your Heart Rate Recovery results.

GymKit

Recently you may have noticed elliptical or treadmill equipment compatible with Apple's new GymKit platform. Tap your watch against the machine's NFC reader at any time during your workout. Your Apple Watch pairs with the machine, and the "Workout" app opens on your watch. Look for the green logo "Connects to Apple Watch."

For those who regularly use gym equipment, you're familiar with entering your age and weight to gauge your optimal heart rate and calculate calories burned. Until now, you had two options; enter information every time you work out, or create an account and log in. The GymKit interface automatically connects with a tap of your Apple Watch, and your workout data syncs with the Health Kit app automatically. Manufacturers supporting GymKit include:

- Life Fitness (Elevation, Integrity, Discover)

- TechnoGym

- Matrix Fitness

- StarTrac

- Stairmaster

- Schwinn

- Nautilus

Activity App

The Activity app ensures you are getting enough exercise every day, and will send you reminders to stand, move, or exercise. In addition to notifications and reminders, there are special challenges, and daily coaching designed to encourage you to meet your goals. My goal is to be active enough that I'm not embarrassed to turn on "Activity Sharing Notifications" with my nieces and nephews. Activity sharing works with friends who also have an Apple Watch.

Set Activity Settings

1.   Open the Apple Watch app on your iPhone.

2.   Tap "My Watch," located in the left corner of the tab bar at the bottom of the screen.

3.   Scroll down and tap "Activity."

4.   Tap the "Stand Reminders" switch to turn off. The switch is green when on.

Share Activity with a Friend

Activity Sharing is a great way to find out just how serious your friends, or husband, are about winning. In hindsight, working out with my husband wasn't one of my better ideas. For friends who also have an Apple Watch, you can share your activity. The information listed below is shared. Personal information is not shared.

- The day's activity rings which include exercise and stand minutes.

- The number of active calories you burn throughout the day.

- Workout information, including type and duration.

- Daily step counter.

Enable Sharing

You can share your activity with up to 40 friends. Use preset replies to lend encouragement, or choose a "smack talk" reply.

1.   On your iPhone, open the "Activity" app.

2.   In the tab bar along the bottom of your screen, tap "Sharing."

3.   Tap the "Add" icon in the top right corner of the screen. The icon looks like a red plus sign.

4.   Tap "Add" again to select a contact, or simply type the e-mail address.

When your friend accepts your request, the next time you open the Activity app, you can accept the request.

Accept a Sharing Request

Seriously, you may want to think twice before accepting an invitation from a friend (or spouse). If you want to go forward, this is how to accept the invitation.

1.   On your iPhone, open the Activity app.

2.   Tap the "Sharing" tab.

3.   Tap the account icon at the top of the screen.

4.   Tap Accept, or Ignore.

View Your Friend's Progress

1.   On your iPhone or Apple Watch, open the Activity app.

2.   Tap the "Sharing" tab.

3.   Tap the name of your friend to see their progress.

Enable Activity Sharing Notifications

1.   Open the Apple Watch app on your iPhone.

2.   Tap "My Watch," located in the left corner of the tab bar at the bottom of the screen.

3.   Scroll down and tap "Activity."

4.   Tap the "Activity Sharing Notifications" toggle to turn on. A green switch indicates the switch is on.

Move, Exercise, & Stand Rings

There are three rings in the Activity app: move, exercise, and stand. The idea is to close your rings every day. When the rings overlap, you've exceeded your goal. While "Wheelchair mode" is active, the "stand goal" in the Activity app changes to a "roll goal," and the "steps" counter changes to "pushes."

Move Ring

The move ring tracks steps or "pushes." Each week your Apple Watch displays a weekly summary and suggests a new weekly move goal based on your daily average for the week. Tap the plus or minus symbols, and then tap "Set Move Goal."

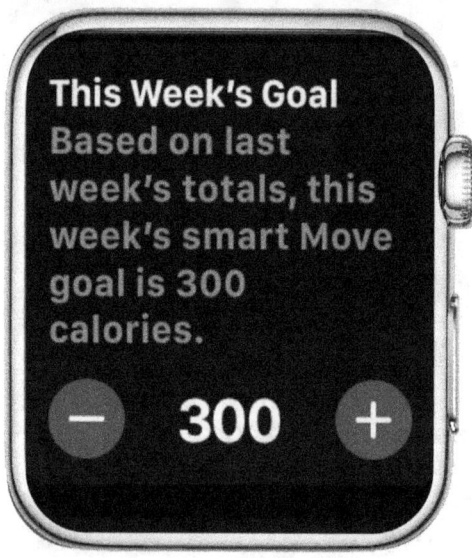

Figure 5.1   The Weekly Goal

Exercise Ring

Your vital statistics are used to calculate your personal exercise goal. Set vital statistics like age and sex in the Health app outlined in the next section.

Stand Ring

The Stand goal is one minute every hour, for twelve hours a day.

Change Goal

Follow these steps to change your Move Goal in the app.

1. On your Apple Watch, press the Side Button.

2. Scroll and tap the Activity app.

3. Firmly press the screen and tap "Change Move Goal."

4. Use the symbols or turn the Digital Crown to adjust your goal.

5. Tap "Update."

Challenge a Friend

For a little friendly competition, challenge a friend. During a 7-day competition, you both earn points by filling your Activity rings. You can earn up to 600 points a day. When you are sharing Activity with a friend, you can reply to a notification with a "challenge." In the Activity app, you can also issue a challenge at any time.

1. On your Apple Watch, open the "Activity" app.

2. Swipe left, tap a friend, then tap "Compete."

History, Weekly Summary & Details

On Monday morning, your watch displays a weekly summary, along with a new Move goal suggestion. When the weekly summary is displayed, tap the plus or minus symbols, and then tap "Set Move Goal."

Workout and Activity History

1.   On your iPhone, open the "Activity" app.

2.   In the bottom tap: History, Workouts, or Awards.

3.   Tap a day, and then swipe up to see details.

4.   Swipe to the bottom of the page to see steps, distance, and flights climbed.

Weekly Summary or Activity Details

1.   On your Apple Watch open the "Activity" app. Force touch the dial (press firmly and hold) to open the options.

2.   Select "Weekly Summary."

3.   Scroll up to see calories, steps, distance, and flights climbed.

Activity Reminders

1.   On your iPhone, select "Settings," and scroll to Notifications.

2.   Tap "Activity," and then tap "Allow Notifications."

The Health App

The Health app stores daily logs for the Activity app on your iPhone. iOS 12.1.1 introduced blood pressure monitoring, EKG monitoring, and irregular rhythm notifications. Apple's HealthKit technology includes partners like the National Cancer Institute, the National Heart Lung and Blood Institute, and Mayo Clinic. So, if you're browsing "Vitals" and wonder what normal body temperature is, you will notice a citation from Mayo Clinic. Right now, there is a beta program underway designed to store your health data in one place - the Health app, of course. The list of companies supporting this feature includes LabCorp, Quest, and many hospitals and medical practices.

Your Vital Statistics

Your vital statistics are used by app algorithms to ensure your health and activity data are accurate. I'd encourage you to enter this information in the Health app. These are important settings used by fitness, exercise, health apps, and other types of apps. For example, the Fitzpatrick Skin Type Scale measures how susceptible your skin is to the sun's rays. In combination with weather apps, this information is used to predict the effects of the daily UV index.

- Birth Date
- Sex
- Blood Type
- Fitzpatrick Skin Type
- Wheelchair

Edit Your Personal Informational

1. On your iPhone, open the "Health" app.

2. In the top right corner tap the "Account" icon that looks like a person.

3. In the top right corner of the screen, tap "Edit."

To see apps that are using your health data, tap the "Sources" button in the tab bar at the bottom of the screen.

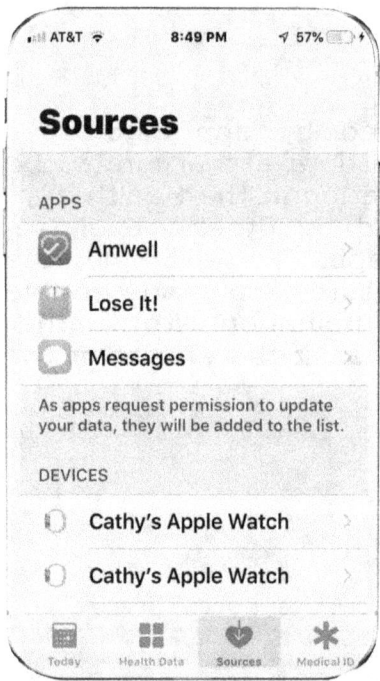

Figure 9.1   Sources for the Health App

Health Data Backups

In case you replace or upgrade your iPhone, note that if you use iCloud and your iPhone has iOS 11 and later, iCloud already has your Health and Activity data. Data is automatically kept up to date on devices where you've signed in with the same Apple ID.

The Health Data Screen

The Health Data screen has four categories: Activity, Mindfulness, Nutrition, and Sleep. Tap the Activity button to see your daily and weekly logs. The data sources are the apps you installed and linked to your Health app. For instance, my sleep app reports my sleep analysis in the "Sleep" category.

1.   On your iPhone, open the "Health" app.

2.   In the bottom tab bar tap "Health Data."

3.   In the top right corner of the screen, tap "Edit."

4.   Tap Activity, Mindfulness, Nutrition, or Sleep.

On the Health Data tab, you can add accounts like Quest, LabCorp, hospitals, and other supported medical providers. After account linking you can see LabCorp diagnostic reports on the "Results" screen, as shown below.

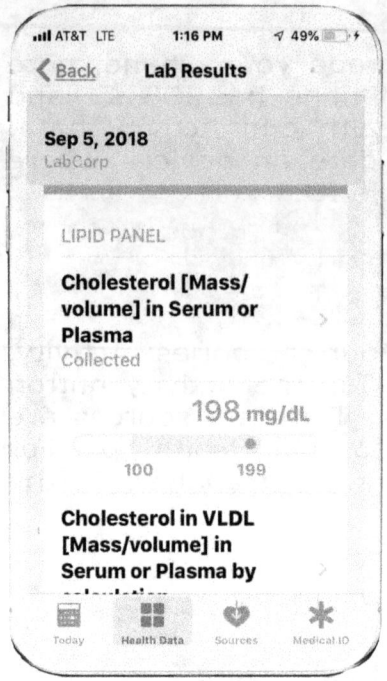

Figure 5.2   Health Data

View Heart Rate Data

The Health Data tab is also where you can view data from the "Heart Rate" app.

1.   On your iPhone, open the "Health" app.

2.   In the bottom tab bar tap "Health Data."

3.   Swipe up and tap "Heart."

4.   Tap the arrows at the top of the screen to move between days. Tap again to change the view to Hour, Day, Week, Month, or Year. Tap anywhere on

the graph to view the day, time, or minimum and maximum information.

Explore Recommended Apps

In each Activity category, Apple includes a section called "Recommended Apps." Simply tap on the app you are interested in, and it opens in the App Store.

Although the Apple Health app reminds you to set a consistent time to go to sleep, at this time, it doesn't monitor your sleep patterns. To track your sleep patterns, install a third-party app such as one shown below, or explore the recommended apps. Sleep affects diet, motivation, energy levels, muscle growth, and tissue repair. Proper sleep means you are more focused and have better blood sugar regulation. And most importantly, in my opinion, a fat-burning growth hormone is released while you sleep!

- Auto Sleep
- Sleep ++
- Sleepwatch
- Pillow

Export Health Data

Not only can you save your health data, but you can also export the data to XML files and e-mail or message to anyone. The new Apple ECG app has an option to "Export a PDF for Your Doctor." No more fudging our answers when your doctor asks how much you exercise a week!

As far as I know, there isn't a handy app to interpret the XML files at this time, but you can export them following these instructions.

1.   On your iPhone, open the "Health" app.

2.   In the top right corner tap the "Account" icon that looks like a person.

3.   In the top right corner of the screen, tap "Edit."

4.   Scroll down and tap "Export Health Data."

The ECG App

The new Apple ECG app arrived with watchOS 5.1.2 and iOS 12.1.1. Providing heart rate monitoring with an electrocardiogram (EKG), the app has FDA clearance in the U.S. for the ECG and atrial fibrillation detection features. The ECG app works by measuring your heart rate on your wrist while you touch the opposite hand to the Digital Crown, creating a circuit.

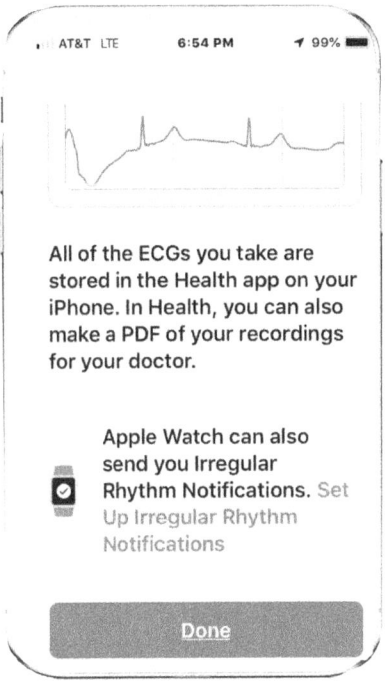

Figure 5.3   ECG App

When the latest software is installed, the ⌁ ECG icon appears on your watch. Follow these steps to check if you have the latest watchOS software on your iPhone.

1. Update your Apple Watch to the latest watchOS version.

2. On your iPhone, open the "Health" app. The app will prompt you to set up the ECG app.

3. Tap "Health Data," located in the tab bar at the bottom of the screen.

4.   Swipe up and tap "Heart."

5.   Swipe up and tap "Electrocardiogram."

Figure 5.4 · Take an ECG

Export a PDF for Your Doctor

Follow these steps to take an ECG, view the ECG Detail, and then export for your doctor.

1.   To take an ECG open the ECG app on your Apple Watch.

2.   Touch your finger to the Digital Crown for 30 seconds.

3.   On your iPhone, open the "Health" app.

4.   Tap "Health Data," located in the tab bar at the bottom of the screen.

5.   Swipe up and tap "Heart."

6.   Swipe up and tap Electrocardiogram (ECG).

7.   Tap a recording, and swipe up. Tap "Export a PDF
     for Your Doctor."

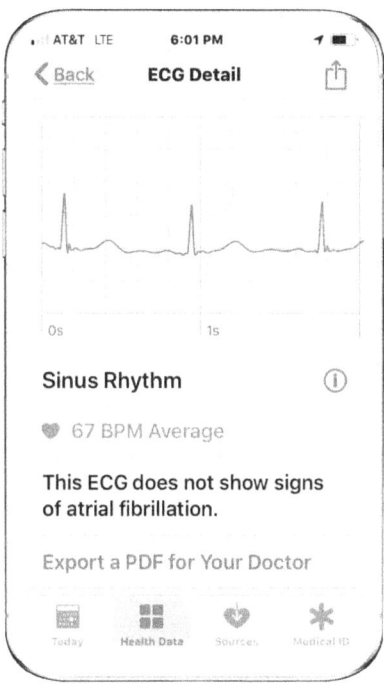

Figure 5.5   Export a PDF for Your Doctor

The Workout App

The Apple workout app is quite sophisticated and
encompasses several different components. First, we will
look at the mechanics of a workout: starting a workout,
viewing progress, pausing, and stopping.

Chapter 5

Recording a workout is effortless with the Apple Watch. The watch is engineered with an accelerometer and gyroscope to correctly identify your movements, and pause workouts when you stop moving. The app even asks if you want to end the workout when it detects a change in your movements.

To help the time pass, Apple provides entertainment in the form of podcasts, music, or Audible books. Lastly, for motivation, Apple hasn't overlooked the social aspect of workouts. watchOS 5 includes challenges and sharing your Activity data.

Running Auto Pause

Thanks to the Apple Watch accelerometer, your workout will automatically pause when you take an exercise break. Workouts automatically resume when you start moving again. Enable this feature in the Apple Watch App, as shown below.

1. On your iPhone, open the Apple Watch App.

2. Tap "My Watch," located in the left corner of the tab bar at the bottom of the screen.

3. Tap "Workout," then toggle "Running Auto Pause" on.

Metrics

Each workout has its own set of metrics, which you can reorder and customize to your personal preferences. Metrics vary by workout and may include the items listed below. So, for example, the hiking workout uses pace, heart rate, and elevation gain.

- Duration

- Active Calories
- Heart Rate
- Average Pace
- Current Pace
- Distance
- Current Cadence
- Average Cadence
- Total Calories
- Elevation Gain
- Rolling Mile

Cadence is your steps per minute. Elevation gain ensures you will get credit when hiking those tough hills. We recently biked up a mountain in Acadia National Park, and I like knowing I get credit for that since it almost killed me. While working out, you can view metrics when you raise your wrist and turn the Digital Crown.

1. On your iPhone, open the Apple Watch app.

2. Tap "My Watch," located at the left corner of the tab bar at the bottom of the screen.

3. Tap "Workout."

4. Make sure "Workout View" is set to "Multiple Metric."

5. In the "Workouts" section tap the workout you are interested in, for example, "Outdoor Walk."

6. The top of the list displays included metrics. To remove a metric tap "Edit" in the top left corner of the screen.

7. Drag the three horizontal bars to reorder the items. Swipe left to delete.

Scroll down to the "Do Not Include" section to add metrics.

Start a Workout

1. On Your Apple Watch, press the Side Button to open the Dock.

2. Swipe and tap "Workout."

3. Swipe to find your workout, and then tap to start the workout.

Tip: When running at night - for safety, try turning on the strobe flashlight. Swipe up on the Apple Watch face, tap the flashlight, and then swipe left.

Set a Goal

On your Apple Watch, select a workout as outlined above, and tap "more." The more icon looks like an ellipsis. This is also where you can set a pace alert. Goals include Calories, Distance, or Time. When you reach your goal, the workout automatically ends.

Figure 5.6   Workout Options

Add to Your Workout

To add another type of workout without ending your session, open the Workout app, swipe right, then tap the "Add" icon that looks like a green plus symbol.

Track Your Progress (View Metrics)

Raise your wrist and turn the Digital Crown to highlight a metric.

Listen to Music While You Workout

When working out with your Apple Watch, swipe left to play music.

Watch a Podcast or Tune in a Show

1. On our Apple Watch, open the "Podcasts" app.

2. Tap "Podcasts" in the top left corner of the screen. Tap on "iPhone" or "Library."

3. Tap Listen Now, Shows, Episodes, or Stations.

To play podcasts stored on your Apple Watch, in the Podcasts app, turn the Digital Crown to scroll and tap a podcast.

Pause Your Workout

On Your Apple Watch, press the Digital Crown and the side button at the same time. Press both buttons again to resume your workout.

End Your Workout

On Your Apple Watch, swipe right, then tap the red X.

Name Your 'Other' Workout

At the end of an "Other" workout, you can choose a name for the workout such as Barre, Core, Cross Training, Kickboxing, Dance, Badminton, Table Tennis, Tennis, Archery, AUS Football, Baseball, Basketball, Bowling, Boxing, Climbing, or Cricket. It's a long list so I'd encourage you to check it out yourself.

1.   On your Apple Watch, open the "Workout" app.

2.   Tap "Other."

3.   Complete your workout.

4.   Swipe right and tap "End."

5.   Tap "Name Workout," then tap Save.

Workout and Activity History

1.   On your iPhone, open the "Activity" app.

2.   In the bottom tap History, Workouts, or Awards.

Sample Workouts

The Apple Workout app includes these workouts: yoga, hiking, cycle, stair stepper, rower, run, walk, strength training, elliptical, or interval training. You can also expand your workouts, utilizing third-party apps. These are a few features related to workouts that may be of interest.

- Listen to podcasts or Audible books. Install the apps on your Apple Watch, as shown in Chapter 12.

- Set custom metrics for each workout. See the earlier section for specifics on Metrics. While working out, you can view metrics when you raise your wrist and turn the Digital Crown.

- At night turn on the strobe flashlight. Swipe up on the Apple Watch face, tap the flashlight, and then swipe left.

Running

Since I have specially fitted running shoes, I have no excuse not to run. But I don't. I find running really difficult. For those of you amazing people who have mastered the experience, there are a few ideas for your running workout.

- Listen to podcasts or Audible books. Install the apps on your Apple Watch, as shown in Chapter 12.

- Enable the metrics for average and current cadence, or average and current pace. While working out, you can view metrics when you raise your wrist and turn the Digital Crown. See the earlier section for specifics on Metrics.

- At night turn on the strobe flashlight. Swipe up on the Apple Watch face, tap the flashlight, and then swipe left.

- Enable "Running Auto Pause." On your iPhone, open the Apple Watch App. Tap "Workout," then toggle "Running Auto Pause" on.

- The option "Set Pace Alert" ensures you're not running too fast or too slow. When starting an Outdoor workout, tap the "More" icon (that looks like an ellipse). Then swipe up and tap "Set Pace Alert." There is an option for minutes per mile.

Swimming and Water Sports

The Workout App has an option for "Open Water Swim" or "Pool Swim" workouts. Third-party apps like Paddle Logger or "Waterspeed," are ideal for water sports. Real-time speed, direction, distance, heart, weather, and stats make this a popular app.

Please keep in mind Apple's guidance on water resistance and avoid scuba diving, water skiing, or high-velocity water while wearing your Apple Watch.

Turn on Water Lock

1. On your Apple Watch, swipe up from the bottom of the screen to open Control Center.

2. Tap the water lock icon. It looks like a drop of water.

When you're finished with your workout, turn the Digital Crown to unlock the screen and clear water from the speaker.

Yoga

There is a new Yoga Workout with Apple Watch Series 4. To avoid bumping your watch during a workout, you could change the watch orientation, or turn on water lock.

Workout Playlist

Whenever you start a workout, you can automatically play music from a workout playlist you configure in your iPhone Apple Watch app.

1.   On your iPhone, open the Apple Watch app.

2.   Swipe to scroll down and tap "Workout."

3.   Swipe up and tap "Workout playlist" to select a playlist for your workouts.

If you haven't already added music to your Apple Watch follow these steps.

1.   On your iPhone, open the Apple Watch app.

2.   Swipe to scroll down and tap "Music."

3.   Tap the playlist or album you want to add.

Additional Workout Apps

There are third-party workout apps geared toward specific activities like sailing, kayaking, or climbing. Social networking and entertainment apps add a little fun into your workout, and apps like Forest and Breathe promote mindfulness. Check out these and other apps in Chapter 12.

- Audible
- Gymatic
- Lifesum
- Music
- Paddle Logger
- Podcasts
- Pokémon
- Runtastic

- Seedling Scavenger Bingo
- Strava

Strava is a social network created specifically for athletes. You can configure devices like your Peloton bike with Strava. The next step to complete integration is to configure the Strava app with Apple Watch.

Entertainment apps like Music, Podcasts, and Audible help your workout pass by quickly. Amazon's "Whispersync" technology allows you to listen on one device like your Apple Watch, and then seamlessly continue reading on your Kindle. How awesome is it to go for a run and listen to the new number one bestseller? Honesty compels me to point out I didn't say when "I" go for a run since my exercise level is more along the lines of a brisk walk. I also want to add a shameless plug here for my books: "Smart Home, Digital Assistants, Home Automation and the Internet of Things," and as soon as Amazon accepts it this book will also be available on Audible.

Don't limit yourself to boring gym workouts. Why not do something fun for exercise? Although I don't even know what the Pokémon game is, when I read sessions can be logged as workouts and traveling certain distances for egg hatching counts as steps, I thought, "Why not?"

A few years back, National Geographic had a scavenger hunt in grocery stores. I find it amazing how many countries are represented at my local grocery store. Anyway, the App Store has scavenger hunt games like Seedling Scavenger Bingo. Seedling Scavenger Bingo works on an Apple Watch or smartphone so that most everyone can play. This app would have been simply awesome for sleepover parties when my daughter was younger, or for rainy afternoons when the kids are bored and driving you out of your mind. Oops, did I just say that? Let me try the politically correct version. I loved raising my daughter, but it came with challenges.

Nature and sports enthusiasts will appreciate these apps that are available today for your Apple Watch. Several of these apps also have complications for your watch face.

- AllTrails
- Big Year Birding ABA
- Gaia GPS
- Gardenia
- Golf Shot
- Komoot
- Scavenger
- New York City Museums
- Paddle Logger
- Santa Fe Botanical
- Trails

Similar to Apple's "Breathe" app, the "Forest-Stay Focused" app has a unique approach to being mindful. Forest is hard to describe so I'd encourage you to check it out. There's a reason it's the #1 app in 113 countries.

Explore Apps

Why not search the App Store today for your favorite hobby, or try searching for sailing, hiking, nature, botany, or birding? Another option is to explore "Recommended Apps" in the Health app. Simply tap on the app you are interested in, and it opens in the App Store.

1.   On your iPhone, open the "Health" app.

2.   In the bottom row, tap "Health Data."

3.   Tap Activity, Mindfulness, Nutrition, or Sleep.

4.   Scroll down to the "Recommended Apps."

5.   Tap the app.

5.5 Handoff Apps & Continuity

Handoff is the ability to switch an application from one Apple device to another and is part of Apple's Continuity platform. For example, if you're reading mail on your iPad, you can continue reading the same message on your Mac or iPad.

1.   Open the "Settings" app on your iPad.

2.   Swipe to scroll to "Settings" and tap "General."

3.   Scroll down and touch the "Enable Handoff" switch to toggle it on or off. The switch is green when on, and white when off.

Handoff From Apple iPhone to iPad

When the two Apple devices are in range, the active app appears on the other device. For example, when you have mail open on your iPad, on your iPhone, the "Mail" app appears as an "app banner," along the bottom of your iPhone screen.

Enable Handoff on your Mac

1. On your Mac: Choose the Apple menu, System Preferences, then click General.

2. Select "Allow Handoff between this Mac and your iCloud devices."

Enable Handoff on your iPad

1. Open the "Settings" app.

2. Swipe to scroll down to "Settings" and tap "General."

3. Scroll down and touch the "Handoff" switch to toggle it on or off. The switch is green when on, and white when off.

Requirements

Apple devices must be signed in with the same Apple ID, and Bluetooth and Wi-Fi must be active to use Continuity.

*   Bluetooth is enabled.

*   Wi-Fi is enabled.

*   Both devices are signed in with the same Apple ID.

*   Handoff is turned on.

Universal Clipboard

Apple's Universal Clipboard supports copying text, images, photos, or videos between Apple devices. You can also take screenshots of the iPad screen. Screenshots are saved in the Photos app, as outlined in Chapter 12. When you copy text on one device, the text is automatically added to the clipboard on the other device for a few seconds.

In the following example, I am copying selected text from my Notes app on my iPad, to the Pages app on my Mac. Handoff is enabled, and Bluetooth and Wi-Fi are active on both devices.

1. Open the Notes app on your iPad, and type some text. Double-tap to select some text.

2. Open the Pages app on your Mac. Right-click and tap "Paste." If you pause for a few seconds, the clipboard may be empty. In that case, repeat the steps and paste again.

Use the iPad Camera on Your Mac

1. Open the Pages app on your Mac. Right-click to open the menu and tap "Import from iPhone or iPad."

2. In the sub-menu for "Cathy Young's iPad," tap "Take Photo" or "Scan Documents."

5.6 Share Files with Cloud Services

Cloud services are at the forefront of smart homes and are discussed throughout this book. In fact, we highlight these specific cloud services in context with smart home devices and virtual assistants.

- Music and TV subscription services.

- Smartphone location-based services and apps.

- Add on virtual assistant "skills."

- Printing services.

- Cloud storage for video and camera streams.

One use of cloud services is to share photos with friends. Integration between cloud services and your Smart Screen or Smart TV turns these devices into digital photo frames. My Android Sony TV uses my Google Photos for a background slideshow app, and my Amazon Echo Show is set up to use Amazon Photos as my background slideshow.

Amazon Photos

My Amazon Echo Show is set up to use Amazon Photos as my background slideshow.

Apple iCloud

Analysts estimate as of February 2018; there are 850 million iCloud users. Apple's iCloud service shares files, passwords, and payment information across your devices. iCloud is also used to share photos and files with others, and to back up your iPhone or iPad. Setup iCloud in the "Settings" app to access your files and contacts from any Apple device. When "Text Messaging Forwarding" is active on your iPhone, your entire message history is stored in iCloud.

When iCloud drive is enabled, you'll have several folders available. Third-party apps like Drafts and Grocery add folders to iCloud. Apple Apps, like Pages and Numbers, also add folders. In addition, you can make your own folders. The next list is a few examples of folders.

- Documents
- Drafts
- Grocery
- Numbers
- Pages
- Shortcuts

To configure iCloud, in the Settings app on your iPad, in the left panel, select your Apple ID name. The right panel options will change. Now tap "iCloud," swipe up, and then tap "iCloud Drive." Tap each app name, if you want to store that app's data in iCloud Drive. Apple apps are shown at the top of the list, and third-party apps like Amazon Drive, Drafts, Grocery, or Procreate are grouped at the bottom of the list.

Note the "Password & Accounts" system stores accounts and passwords in your iCloud Keychain. Your security information is available on any Apple device when you authenticate with Face ID, Touch ID, or your passcode. iOS 12 will generate strong passwords for you, identify weak passwords, and autofill account information.

Your Apple ID

When you set up your iPad, you are prompted to create or log in with your Apple ID. Your Apple ID is your account with Apple and is based on the e-mail address you enter when you create your Apple ID.

Write down your Apple ID and password and keep it somewhere safe, you'll be using it again for many of the Apple apps and services like Messages, FaceTime, the App Store, Apple Wallet, iTunes, and iCloud to name a few. When creating a new Apple ID, keep in mind your Apple ID password will be unique to your Apple ID. It is not the same password you are already using for your e-mail. If you take advantage of the new "Passwords & Accounts" iOS 12 feature to autofill account information, you'll have your Apple ID handy with a touch of your finger on the Home button. Later in this Chapter, the topic "Passwords & Accounts" has additional information on password management.

Because I have family sharing enabled, when I buy apps or songs in the App Store or iTunes, my husband and daughter can also download the same content.

On your iPad Home Screen, tap the gear button to open the Settings app. When you tap an option in the left sidebar, the choices in the right panel are updated to display options specific to the item selected in the left sidebar.

In the following example, I selected my "Apple ID" in the left sidebar. When I select my name "Cathy Young" on the left, the items in the right panel change to display Password & Security, Payment & Shipping, iCloud, iTunes & App Store, Share My Location and Family Sharing. My Apple devices are also shown at the bottom of the right panel.

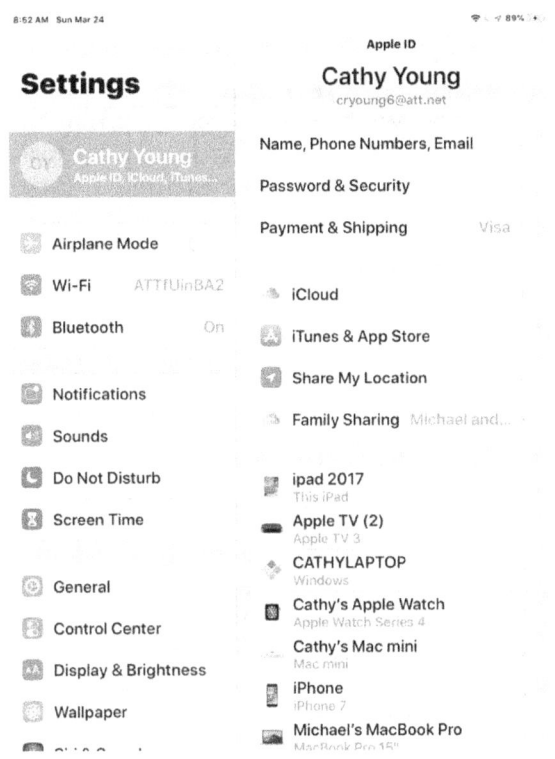

Figure 5.7 Apple ID in the Settings App

Name, Phone Numbers, E-mail

Siri will customize your experience by using your Apple ID information in "Name, Phone Numbers, E-mail." The Mail app will use the e-mail addresses you add to "Name, Phone Numbers, E-mail."

Family Sharing

With iCloud "Family Sharing," you can share your calendars, reminders, and more with up to six contacts. Family Sharing includes sharing purchases in the App Store, Apple Music, iCloud Storage, Location Sharing, and Screen Time. When you turn on family sharing a shared calendar is automatically created called "Family."

Third-party apps like the Grocery app also utilize shared reminder lists. The Grocery app outlined in Chapter 12 uses the iOS reminders lists to store your shopping list. With a combination of iOS "Family Sharing" and an IFTTT applet that automatically links my Alexa shopping list with my iOS reminder lists, I can easily add items to my grocery list with Alexa, Google Home, or Siri. Everyone in our family can access our family shopping list on their Apple device. I'm particularly fond of the Grocery app because while I may forget to bring my Smartphone to the grocery store, I will probably be wearing my Apple Watch with the Grocery app installed.

Enable Family Sharing

1.   Open the Settings app. Tap "your name" at the top of the left sidebar.

2.   In the right panel, tap "Set up Family Sharing." Follow the prompts to invite contacts to join your family.

Ask to Buy

Ask to Buy is automatically active for children under 13. When enabled for a family member, the family organizer receives a request to approve all purchases.

1.   Open the Settings app. Tap "your name" at the top of the left sidebar.

2.   In the right panel, enable "Ask to Buy" for the 13 and under child.

There are also choices to receive announcements, new releases, news, and special offers for Apple subscriptions and services.

iCloud Keychain

iCloud Keychain stores your passwords, credit card, Wi-Fi network configurations, and other accounts. An example of sharing Wi-Fi configurations is when your iPhone is nearby a family member's iPhone and you "share" a Wi-Fi password with their iPhone. Both devices must be logged in with the same Apple ID or family sharing account.

iCloud Keychain is set up in the Settings app, in the "Passwords & Accounts" section in the left sidebar.

iCloud Photo Stream

When enabled iCloud Photo Stream copies your photos iCloud. Images are available from any of your Apple devices.

1. Open "Settings."

2. Tap "your name" at the top of the left sidebar. In the right panel, tap "iCloud."

3. Tap "Photos" and make sure the option "iCloud Photos" is toggled on. Also, tap "Upload to My Photo Stream."

Turn on Find My iPad & iCloud Backup

By default, "Find My iPad" is turned on after the initial setup with your Apple ID.

1. Open "Settings."

2. Tap "your name" at the top of the left sidebar. In the right panel, tap "iCloud."

3. Ensure "Find My iPad" is turned on. This is also where you turn on "iCloud Backup."

iTunes & App Store

Configure automatic downloads for purchases in the "Automatic Downloads" settings. There is also an option to offload apps you aren't using.

Share My Location

The "Share My Location" option is used with family and friends in the Messages, Find My Friends, and "Home" apps. Usually, I leave the "From" setting as my "iPhone and Cellular Apple Watches," because when I leave the house, I'm more likely to have my iPhone than my iPad.

The other section on the screen is to Enable "Share My Location" with family. Tap names to enable location sharing for each individual.

Share a Reminder List

Family sharing is active on my iPad. My "Family" reminder list is shared with both my husband and daughter.

1. Open the Reminders app and tap the "Family" list. Any list would work, but in this example, I happen to have a "Family" list.

2. Tap "Edit" and then tap "sharing." Select a contact and click "Add" (the plus sign) to send an invitation to join the family.

Share Calendars

The bottom tab bar of the Calendar app has options for the Today view, Calendars, or Inbox. Tap Calendars to see all your calendars.

To add a new calendar tap "Add Calendar" in the bottom right corner of the pop-up menu. Tap the information symbol next to a calendar to see who the calendar is shared with, and set a color. Swipe to the bottom of the list to delete this calendar.

View Photos on Apple TV

When you enable iCloud and set up a shared folder, you can view photos from your phone or MacBook on your Apple TV.

1. On your iPad, connect to your home Wi-Fi network.

2. In the Photos app, select a photo.

3. Tap the share button ⬆️ to open the Activity View.

4. Tap **AirPlay** ⬛.

5. Select your Apple TV.

iCloud Photo Sharing is another option to view photos on your Apple TV, instead of AirPlay. Once configured the Apple TV will display iCloud Photos.

1. Open the Photos app and select the photo(s).

2. Tap the Share ⬆️ button.

3. Click on Shared Albums 🌸 .

4. Add comments for the photo(s).

5. Invite people to view the photo(s).

6. Select the shared ☁️ album for the photo(s).

To manage iCloud settings on your Windows computer, download and install the iCloud app for Windows.

1. Launch the iCloud app on your **Windows** computer.

2. Select Photos, and click on **Options**.

3. Scroll down to enable iCloud Photo Sharing.

4. Click **Apply.**

Dropbox

Dropbox has been around for a while and provides a central place for storing files. App developers write an interface to Dropbox, and Dropbox takes care of synchronizing your files across your smartphone, PC, Mac, or tablet.

Facebook

A few years ago, I couldn't imagine I'd use Facebook as a place to store photos. With the advent of the "portal" smart screen from Facebook, I realized I do have quite a few photos in my timeline.

Google Photos and Google Drive

My Android Sony TV uses my Google Photos for a background slideshow app. To download photos from your account to your device, please follow these steps:

1. On your iPhone or iPad, open the Google Photos app.

2. Select a photo or video.

3. Tap "More" and choose "Save to Device." If the photo is already on your device, this option won't appear.

Alternatively, you may download all photos or videos in a folder on Google Drive. Here's how:

1. In the Google Photos app, select the folder you want to download.

2. Tap "More," then tap "Select All." Finally, tap "Download."

Microsoft OneDrive

Microsoft launched OneDrive in 2007 as part of its suite of online Office applications. Windows 10 users can also sync there Windows 10 settings across devices.

5.7 Background App Refresh

With Apple apps, when you are not actively using an app after a short time, it changes to a suspended state and stops using system resources. When you turn on "Background App Refresh," suspended apps will check for updates or new content. For example, the Weather app can check if there's an advisory and send you a notification.

On your iPad, in the Settings app tap "General" in the left sidebar, in the left sidebar, and then tap "Background App Refresh" in the right panel. Toggle the setting on, and then swipe down to turn "Background App Refresh" on for particular apps.

5.8 Side-by-Side Apps

The iPad Split View and Slide Over multitasking features have been around for a few years. Simply drag an app from the Dock onto another app to run both apps in a split view. To enable this feature, open the Settings app, and in the "General" section tap "Multitasking & Dock."

Videos will continue to play in a "Picture-in-Picture" when you enable "Persistent Video Overlay." In addition to the options mentioned here, Safari can display two browsing windows side-by-side, as shown in Chapter 6.

Slide Over

In the following example, the Numbers app is in my Dock.

1. Open the Mail app.

2. Swipe up from the bottom of the screen to open the Dock.

3. Touch and hold the Numbers app and drag it onto the Mail app screen.

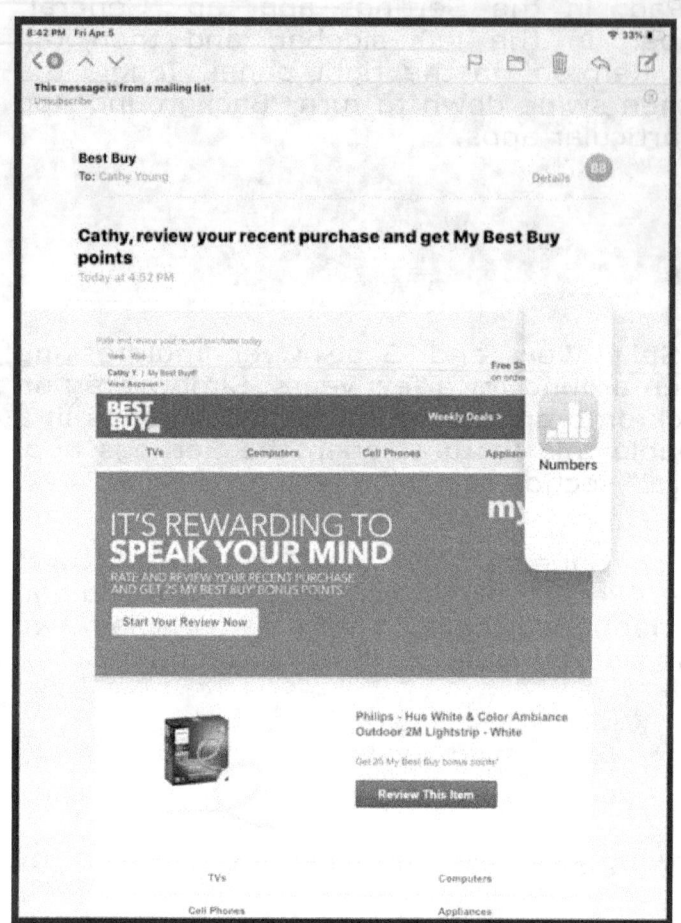

Figure 5.8   Dragging an App From the Dock

4. Drop the app onto the screen to create a Slide Over, as shown below.

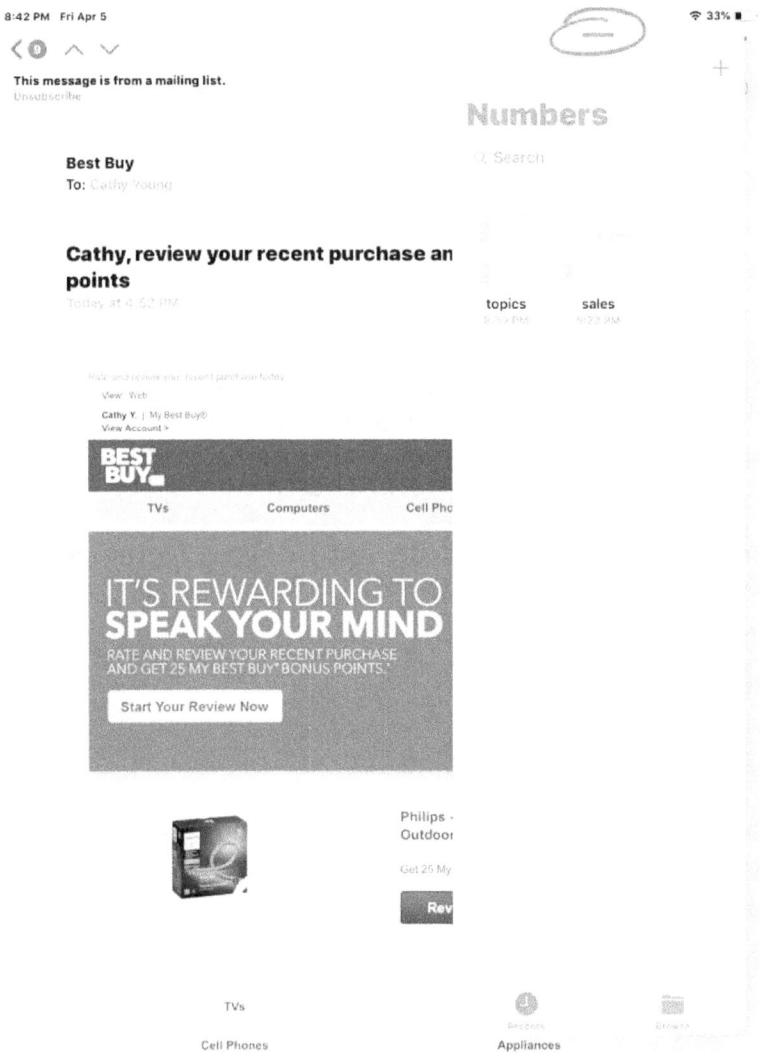

Figure 5.9   Slide Over App

Split View

The next example outlines the process for creating a Split View.

1.   Open the Mail app.

2.   Swipe up from the bottom of the screen to open the Dock.

3.   Touch and hold the Numbers app and drag it onto the Mail app screen.

4.   At the top of the Split View screen, touch the small bar and swipe up. The screen is now split, and the "App Divider" is displayed. The App Divider is a vertical bar with a handle in the middle.

5.   Touch the handle and drag left or right to resize the split-screen windows.

6.   To close the Split View, drag the App Divider to the right.

After you close an app that was in split-screen, you can still touch the right side of the screen and swipe to the left to reopen it.

Picture-in-Picture

When a video is playing, tap the control and the video changes to a "Picture-in-Picture" and moves to the bottom right corner of the screen. Tap the control in the Picture-in-Picture window to return to full-screen viewing. Not all videos are compatible with "Picture-in-Picture," and in that case, you won't see the controls.

5.9 Integrating Apps & Sharing Data

App designers have a variety of creative ways to share data with other apps. These integrations may use existing platforms like text messages or emails. Apps like "Grocery" leverage smartphone components like reminder lists.

- Reminder Lists

- SMS Messages (Short message service)

- MMS (Multi-media messages)

- Emails

Whenever possible, I've included examples throughout the book, although please keep in mind these are subject to change, since developers are continually changing their apps. You'll probably also notice most examples will be based on Apple's iOS apps, simply because I typically use Apple devices.

As a side note, in my experience, things don't always go according to plan. For example, I've linked my Google calendar account with another app with no problem, and the next time, I simply could not get it to work. Unfortunately, when apps with different developers have communication problems, you're usually on your own to figure out what went wrong.

AirDrop

On your iPad or iPhone, tap the AirDrop control to see AirDrop options. AirDrop shares your data, website passwords, and accounts, or Wi-Fi setup information with nearby devices over Bluetooth and Wi-Fi. Sign in to your iCloud account and ensure iCloud Keychain is set up. To transfer data between your iPad and another Apple device or Mac use Airdrop. In the next section, the Activity View example demonstrates using Airdrop with the Photos app.

AirDrop uses Wi-Fi. The connection can be between your iPad and Mac directly, without the need to connect to an existing Wi-Fi network.

Configure AirDrop in Settings under the "General" section under "AirDrop." The Apple keychain is set up in the Settings app. Tap your name in the top left sidebar and then tap "iCloud." Tap Keychain and turn on iCloud Keychain.

Share a Password over AirDrop

In the Settings app, tap "Passwords & Accounts." Tap "Website & App Passwords" to view and manage passwords, or share them over AirDrop. Select the account you want to share and then tap "Password." A menu opens with a choice to "Copy" or to use "AirDrop."

AirPlay

AirPlay is a technology to mirror music or videos from your mobile to your TV. AirPlay is often referred to as "casting."

AirPlay TVs

Look for TVs that support Apple AirPlay. Sometimes communication is via the local network (wired Ethernet or Wi-Fi) and other times it utilizes Bluetooth. My older Bowers and Wilkins speaker supports AirPlay through a direct LAN Ethernet connection. My Yamaha amplifier utilizes a direct Ethernet or Wi-Fi connection for AirPlay.

Cast from iPad

While playing music or videos in your music app, swipe up and click on the "AirPlay" button to send music, images, or video to a smart TV.

5.10 Apple Activity View and App Tray

On the Apple iPad or iPhone, the Action or Share button opens the Activity View. This control is often shown in the top right corner of an app. The Activity View displays relevant activities for the current task. So depending on the app and what you are doing, the choices in the Activity View will change.

There are three tab bar rows in Activity View, as shown below. The first row is "AirDrop." The second row has "Share Extensions," and the third row has "Action Extensions." To see the Activity View in action, open Photos and tap the "Share" button in the top right corner of the screen.

Figure 5.10   Share and Action Extensions

The second row below AirDrop has Share extensions such as those shown below. Third-party apps also have share extensions.

- Share with Messages

- Share with Mail

- Shared Albums

The third row has Action extensions which include Copy, Slideshow, Airplay, Add to Album, Use as Wallpaper, Save to Files, Assign to Contact, Print, and more.

Tip: When the Activity View is open, swipe left and right in the tab rows to view more buttons.

Reorder Extensions

Swipe left and tap any "App button" to drag it to the new location. You can also swipe left and tap the "More" button. Touch the three horizontal lines to reorder the items.

Add or Remove Extensions

To toggle extensions on or off swipe left and tap the more control that looks like three dots or an ellipsis. To turn an extension off, toggle the switch on or off. Tap "Done" to confirm changes.

5.11 Credit Card Information & Purchasing

There are many payment systems popping up today with integration to smart devices. Samsung Pay, Amazon, and Google Pay will store your credit card information. My favorites are Amazon Alexa Voice Purchasing and Apple Pay.

Alexa Purchasing

Enable voice purchasing and set the voice code in the Alexa app. Alexa even remembers past orders to simplify purchasing. A voice code provides an added layer of security. When this feature is enabled, Alexa won't place an order without the code. The first time Alexa responds to a command on a commercial, it can be funny, but after that, you probably want to stop that behavior. Purchasing settings are found under the "Alexa Account" section of the app.

1. Open the Alexa app on your smartphone or tablet. Go to the menu and select "Settings."

2. In the section "Alexa Account" select "Voice Purchasing" and add a code.

Amazon offers Prime members the "Prime Now" service to order groceries. The Amazon "Restaurants" service provides food delivery in supported areas. The Amazon Key service for deliveries even has an in-car delivery option.

Apple Pay

Apple Pay is easy because it works across my iPhone, iPad, Mac, and Apple Watch. Apple Pay is integrated with Apple Wallet and is configured in "Settings" on the iPad. Open the Settings app, and scroll down in the left pane to "Wallet & Apple Pay." In Apple Pay, when setting up your account, add your shipping information, e-mail, and phone. I probably went overboard with examples in this section. There are so many ways to use Apple Pay!

First, we'll look at what's in your wallet. Next, I explain how to use your iPad with Apple Pay and Siri in messages, or how to complete a transaction in Safari. Funds for Apple Pay come from credit cards or Apple Pay Cash stored in the Apple "Wallet" app.

There are several ways to use Apple Pay with your iPad, as outlined in the detailed examples that follow.

- Ask Siri to send cash in a message.

- Complete a Safari transaction with Apple Pay.

Ask Siri to Send Cash in a Message

Before sending funds in a message, set up Apple Pay Cash. Open the Settings app and tap "Wallet & Apple Pay." In the section "Payment Cards," tap "Apple Pay Cash."

Apple Pay is integrated with SiriKit. On your iPad, ask Siri to "Pay Michael one dollar," and Siri does the rest.

Apple Pay is available on your iPad if you've enabled "Apple Pay Cash" in your Apple Wallet app on your iPad. If you've added "cash" to your account, you can send cash to friends or family in a message.

1.   On your iPad, press the Home Button.

2.   Swipe and tap "Messages."

3.   Start a new conversation or continue an existing conversation.

4.   Tap the button for Apple Pay in the App drawer at the bottom of the screen.

5.   Select an amount to send using the plus or minus symbol.

6.   Tap "Pay."

Safari Apple Pay and iPad

On Apple devices, you can also use Apple Pay in Safari. Start the transaction in the Safari web browser, and when prompted, click on "Buy with Apple Pay."

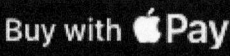

Figure 5.11   Confirm Apple Pay Transaction

Activate Credit Cards on Your iPad

Although you may have credit cards set up in Apple Pay, you must activate the card on your iPad. Enter the corresponding card security code in your "Settings" app to activate the card. Student IDs require the eAccounts and Duo Mobile apps.

Apple Pay & the Wallet App

Apple Pay is integrated with the Apple Wallet App. I probably went overboard with examples in this section, but it's not my fault you can use Apple Pay in so many ways!

First, we'll look at what's in your wallet. Next, I explain how to use your watch with Apple Pay and Siri in messages, at a store, or how to confirm a transaction in Safari on your Mac. There are five examples of adding third-party app cards and reservations (Fandango, Hilton, Marriott, Sephora, and Starbucks.) Next, we'll look at how to add any card, ticket, or pass that has a bar code to your wallet using the "Pass2U" app.

Funds for Apple Pay come from credit cards or Apple Pay Cash stored in the Apple "Wallet" app. The "Wallet" app houses this information:

- Hotel Reservations
- Credit Cards
- Membership Cards
- Airline Boarding Passes
- Movie Tickets
- Coupons
- Transit Cards

- Student IDs
- Tickets

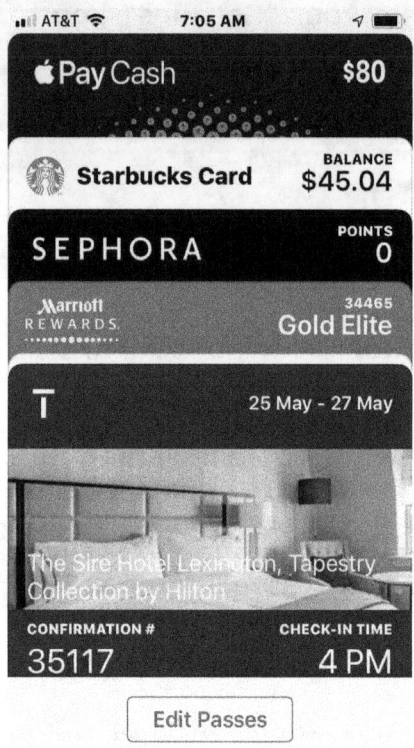

Figure 5.12   The Apple Wallet App

There are several ways to use Apple Pay with your Apple Watch, as outlined in the detailed examples that follow.

- Ask Siri to send cash in a message.

- Confirm a Safari transaction with your watch.

- Pay a store merchant using your watch.

For example, at Subway, you click the side button on your watch twice to pay the merchant.

Ask Siri to Send Cash in a Message

Apple Pay is integrated with SiriKit. On your Apple Watch ask Siri to "Pay Michael one dollar," and Siri does the rest.

Figure 5.13   Sending Cash in a Message with Apple Pay

Safari Apple Pay and Apple Watch

On Apple devices, you can also use Apple Pay in Safari. Start the transaction in the Safari web browser, and when prompted "confirm" the payment on your Apple Watch.

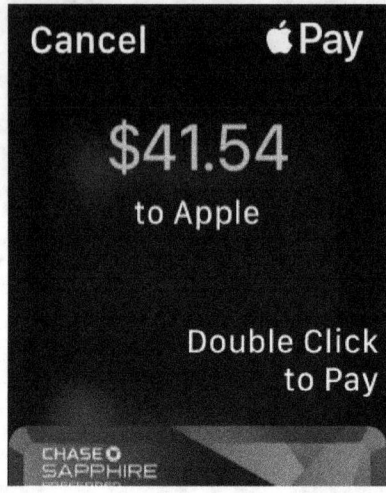

Figure 5.14   Confirm Safari Apple Pay Transaction

Pay a Merchant on Your Watch

To initiate an Apple Pay transaction, the merchant activates Apple Pay on their payment terminal. Next, you press the side button on your Apple Watch twice.

Tip: Apple   Pay   is   unavailable if you turn off passcode.

1. Open the Apple Watch app on your iPhone.

2. Tap "My Watch," located in the left corner of the tab bar along the bottom of the screen.

3. Scroll down to "Passcode."

Add Cards and Passes to Apple Wallet

Third-party apps that support the Apple Wallet PassKit framework include a button to "Add to Apple Wallet," as shown in Figure 6.4.

Figure 5.15   Add to Apple Wallet Logo

The instructions for adding third-party cards to the Wallet app vary depending on the particular third-party app, so I've provided a few examples below. The Marriott example includes adding both the Marriott Rewards card, as well as a particular hotel reservation.

- Fandango
- Hilton
- Marriott
- Sephora
- Starbucks

Once a third-party app is installed on your iPhone or Apple Watch, look for an option to add the card or pass to Apple Wallet. The following examples demonstrate the steps, although they vary slightly.

Starbucks: Launch the Starbucks app, select Manage, Details, and click "Add to Apple Wallet."

Hilton Honors: Launch the Hilton app, select Stays, Upcoming, and click "Add to Apple Wallet."

Marriott: Launch the Marriott app and select "My Account." Swipe up and tap "Add to Apple Wallet." To add a reservation, tap the menu icon to see your reservations. Tap the confirmation number, and then click "Add to Apple Wallet."

Sephora: Open the Sephora app and click on Beauty Insider. Click "Add to Apple Wallet."

Fandango: Open the Fandango app and go to "Account." Select "Purchases," swipe up and tap "Purchase Details." Click "Add to Apple Wallet."

Another option to add cards to your Wallet is to scan a QR code to add a card.

1.   Open the Wallet app on your iPhone.

2.   Tap "Edit Passes."

3.   Tap "Find Apps for Wallet" or "Scan code."

When scanning codes, the Apple Wallet app launches the camera and displays a square finder marquee to select a "QR code." The Apple PassKit framework supports 128

QR Codes. To add tickets or passes with a bar code, that does not have direct integration with Apple Wallet, use a third-party app like "Pass2U."

Add Bar Code Tickets with Pass2U

There are probably several third-party apps that create QR codes for your Apple Wallet, but I use "Pass2U." In the figure below, you can see a ticket for the Atlanta Symphony in my Apple Wallet. I scanned the bar code on the original ticket into the "Pass2U" app, added a logo photo, location, time, and seat.

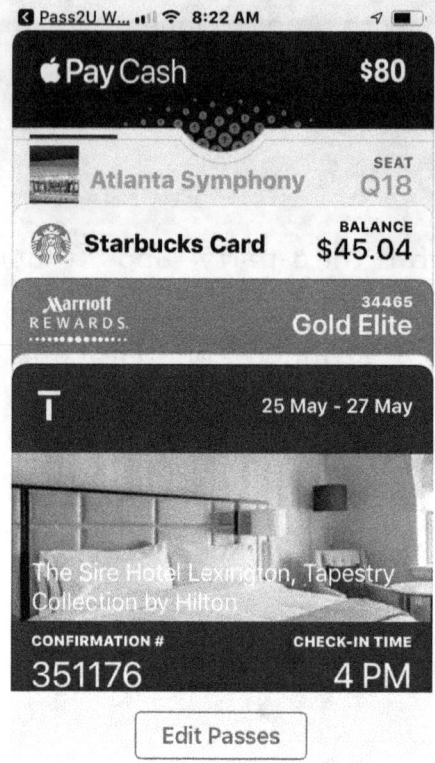

Figure 5.16   Symphony Ticket in Apple Wallet

After clicking "Add," the new ticket is shown in my Apple Wallet.

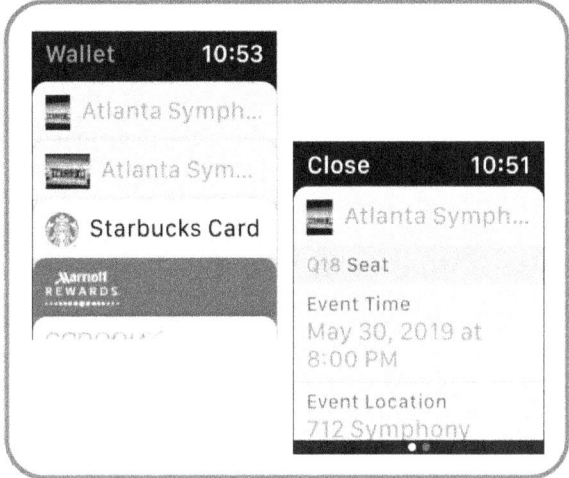

Figure 5.17   The Wallet App on Your Watch

Activate Credit Cards on Your Watch

Although you may have credit cards set up in Apple Pay, you must activate the card on your Apple Watch. Enter the corresponding card security code in your Apple Watch app on your iPhone to activate the card. Student IDs require the eAccounts and Duo Mobile apps.

Reorder Cards in the Wallet

To reorder cards touch the card in the Wallet app and drag it up or down to change the order. This is also how you set the default card.

Transit Cards

In Japan, the Tokyo transit Suica card works with Apple Pay. When Suica is set as your Express Transit Card, simply hold your watch close to the ticket gate scanner. There is no need to wake or unlock your watch. In Beijing and Shanghai, you can also use transit cards; just make sure your region is China in the "Settings" app. Change the "Language or Region" on your iPhone in "General" settings.

Status of the Apple Pay System

It is possible that the Apple Pay system is down for maintenance. You can check the Apple Pay system status at https://www.apple.com/support/systemstatus/.

5.12 Audio

To stream music or videos to your favorite speakers, AirPods, or headsets, use the Audio Output in the Control Center on your iPad. Audio Output is located in the top right quadrant of the Control Center.

1. Swipe down from the top right corner of the Home Screen on your iPad to open the "Control Center."

2. Tap the Audio Output button.

Tapping the audio output button will also switch the audio output between paired Bluetooth or Airplay devices.

1. Swipe up on the Apple Watch face to open the Control Center.

2. Tap the Audio Output icon.

Control Audio Volume

Tapping the audio output icon will also switch the audio output between paired Bluetooth devices.

Use the volume buttons on the top right area of your iPad to control volume.

Tap the audio  status icon on your watch face and turn the Digital Crown to adjust the volume. Control music, podcasts, or hearing aid volume. If you have Bluetooth speakers or a headset connected to your Apple Watch, this is a simple way to adjust the volume.

Figure 5.18   Change Volume

When playing music, firmly press the screen to view these options.

- Shuffle
- Repeat
- Source
- Output

Download Music to Your Apple Watch

To listen to music on the go when you don't have your iPhone with you, download albums or playlists to your Apple watch. If you subscribe to Apple Music, the "Favorites Mix" and "New Music Mix" are automatically added.

1. On your iPhone, open the Apple Watch app.

2. Tap "My Watch," located in the left corner of the tab bar at the bottom of the screen.

3. Swipe to scroll down and tap "Music."

4. Tap "Add Music" and then tap the playlist or album you want to add. This is also where you could delete a playlist.

5. To download music, connect your watch to Power and place it near your iPhone.

Check Available Space for Music

Music files can use up a lot of storage space. In case you're wondering how much space is used, on your iPhone open the Apple Watch app to see detailed information.

- The count of songs on your watch.

- The count of photos on your watch.

- The number of applications on your watch.

- The total capacity.

- The available capacity.

1. On your iPhone, open the Apple Watch app.

2. Tap "My Watch," located in the left corner of the tab bar at the bottom of the screen.

3. Swipe to scroll down and tap "General."

4. Tap "About" to see available capacity.

6. HVAC, Lighting, Electrical & Plumbing

Who doesn't want to save money? Utilities are a great place to start. Aside from saving money, lighting can also play a significant role in security. The phrase "leave the light on" takes on a whole new meaning when your abode welcomes you home by automatically adjusting lights and temperature.

Before buying smart home electrical, lighting, plumbing, or HVAC devices, I'd encourage you to find out if your local municipality has a rebate program. Even without a rebate, smart home options provide worthwhile opportunities for saving money on your utility bills.

Smart lighting is useful and fun. Colors can have different meanings. For example, a flashing red light indicates the door is open, a green light means the delivery driver is almost here, or a blue light means it's going to rain today. We use soothing tones in our study, and vary the color depending on the time of day or activity. When I'm in charge of lighting the Philips Hue lights behind our bedroom headboard are color-coordinated to our decor. My husband isn't a fan of the blue Hues and changes the color whenever I'm not looking.

6.1 HVAC

Heating and cooling systems were early adopters of home automation. A wide variety of features are readily available today.

- Receive e-mail alerts.

- A daily 24 x 7 schedule, and special vacation or holiday schedules.

- Integration with mobile apps and IFTTT.

- Wireless outdoor temperature and humidity sensors.

- Wireless entry or exit remotes.

Air Filters

The previous list is primarily related to thermostats and HVAC systems. There are also innovations in smart air filters. The Filtrete smart air filters are relatively inexpensive, and the sensor monitors when the filter is clogged. Since I never can remember when to check my air filter, I really appreciate the reminder from the app that my air filter is dirty. The mobile app also keeps track of the filter size and type to make reordering simple.

Nest

The Nest Learning Thermostat was one of the first smart thermostats to market and has since been acquired by Google. The Nest Weave platform includes a network and application protocol at the Application layer, as discussed in Chapter 3.

The Nest Thermostat is a beautiful piece of engineering. When you turn down the temperature at night or when you are away, Nest learns what you like. The Nest technology "Home Away/Assist" automatically switches to Eco Temperatures when no one is at home. The Nest Time-to-Temperature is similar to Honeywell's Adaptive Intelligent Recovery and estimates how long it will take to reach your desired temperature.

Figure 6.1   Nest 3rd Generation Learning Thermostat

The Nest Protect sensor works with the Nest Learning Thermostat and will turn off your furnace when the Nest Protect senses carbon monoxide. The Nest Thermostat will tell a connected dryer or dishwasher when energy demand is low.

Additional Nest security system products are discussed in Chapter 7.

If you have new air conditioning equipment, before replacing a thermostat, make sure you don't inadvertently void the warranty. The HVAC company may require that work be performed by a licensed installer.

Ecobee

The Ecobee Thermostat is compatible with many smart products, as shown below. Ecobee makes room sensors to prioritize temperature based on occupancy. They also make light switches. The Ecobee 4 Thermostat has Alexa and Google Assistant built-in.

- Apple HomeKit

- Google Assistant

- Amazon Alexa

- Apple Watch

- Sonos

Honeywell

The VisionPRO series with RedLINK from Honeywell controls humidity and ventilation, and the Adaptive Intelligent Recovery system learns how long it takes to reach the temperature you want.

- Wireless outdoor/indoor temperature sensors.

- Wireless outdoor/indoor humidity sensors.

- Leak detection sensors.

- Wireless entry/exit remote.

RedLINK includes an Internet gateway with integration to IFTTT and virtual assistant skills.

"Alexa, decrease MyHome to 76."

Installing the Gateway at the Thermostat

The gateway must be installed by a registered technician or else the warranty on the HVAC system will be voided. The installation itself, however, is a simple process. Nevertheless, we highly recommend shelling out the $200 or so for the installation - but be righteously indignant about it! A warranty is a terrible thing to waste.

If your HVAC warranty has expired or you simply don't care, feel free to follow the instructions below to install the gateway - but understand that it's at your own peril.

1. At the thermostat, select Menu, **Installer Options** and enter the Date Code (found on the back on the thermostat).

2. Scroll down to Wireless Manager and select **Add Device**.

3. Plug the Honeywell internet gateway into a wall outlet and connect the LAN Ethernet cable.

4. Press the connect button on the gateway.

5. The thermostat confirms the connection was successful. Press **Done** to exit the menu.

Pair the Honeywell Gateway

The next step is to create your Total Connect Comfort account and pair the gateway.

1. Log in and create an account on Honeywell's Total Connect site.

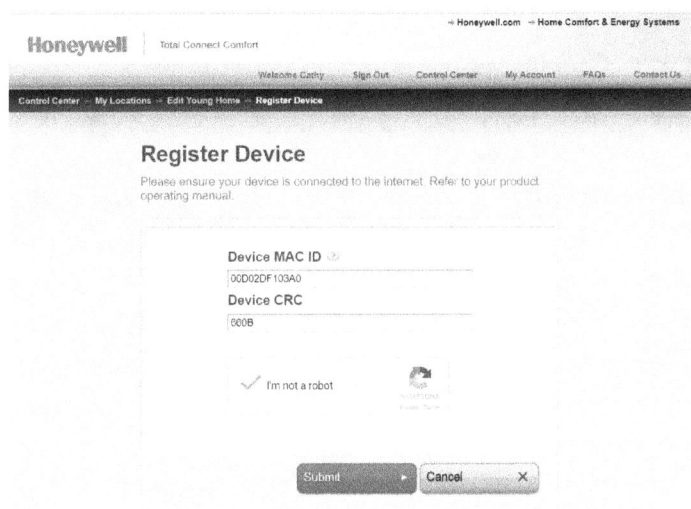

Figure 6.2   Register with Honeywell

2. Click on Add Device to register your new gateway. Enter the information from the bottom of the hub.

3. Follow the prompts to complete pairing the gateway. After a few moments, you will receive a message that the registration was successful.

Figure 6.3   Gateway Registration Successful

The last step is to install the Honeywell app on your mobile device.

1. Download the "Honeywell Total Connect Comfort" app on your mobile device and log in.

2. Initially, the app asks if you want to allow voice control. Select yes or no.

3. On the left side, you can select Heat, Cool, Off or Em Heat. The **Menu** button shows you your current schedule. I think it is much easier to set up a schedule in the app, then at the thermostat unit.

4. To change the thermostat name, go to Thermostat(s) in Your Home. Select the thermostat and click on the **Menu** icon.

5. Type the new thermostat name. You can also set notification alerts on this page.

6. After making changes click on the **Submit** button.

The Honeywell gateway also integrates with Amazon Alexa.

1. Open the Alexa app and click on **Skills**.

2. Search for the "Honeywell Total Connect Comfort" skill and follow the prompts to link Alexa. Once linked, the Alexa app will switch to the Smart Home screen.

3. Click Discover to locate the Honeywell gateway.

If you change the name of your thermostat after linking to Alexa, find the device in the Alexa app under Smart Home and forget the device. Then click on "Discover" to find the device again.

6.2 Lighting and Electrical

Our initial goal for smart home electrical equipment was simply to have our lights turn on or off with home automation. We found a wide range of actuators, as well as an impressive array of features. Our smart home automation goals quickly expanded to include dimming lights, changing colors, and linking the devices to other systems. Our research revealed there are several approaches to connected lighting and electrical actuators. By "actuators," incidentally, we mean the following:

- Smart Light Switches

- Smart Electrical Outlets

- Smart Bulbs

- Smart Light Bulb Sockets

6.3 What Can Smart Lighting Do?

Smart lighting involves smart electrical outlets, smart bulbs, or smart sockets. Smart bulbs allow you to move lights and their array of 16 million colors around the house. This can be useful if you want to use changing color to indicate a delivery or a change in air quality. Electrical outlets are handy if you know you'll always plug the Christmas tree in the same location.

A photograph of colored LED light strips behind crown molding in a tray ceiling inspired us to try that in our office. The color options of the Philips Hue LED light strips open up a whole new world of possibilities, such as:

- Turning on lights in response to a sensor (motion, fire, etc.).

- Changing the color of lights when a delivery is due.

- Setting the lights to red when an alarm occurs.

While building our new home, we asked our builder to add an electrical outlet in the corner of the tray ceiling so we could plug in an LED light strip.

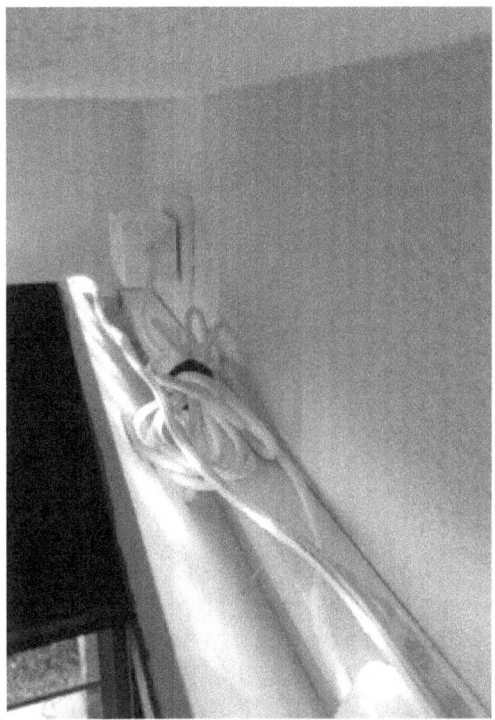

Figure 6.4   Power Outlet at Ceiling With LED Light Strip Behind Crown Molding

With a power outlet in the tray ceiling behind the crown molding, all we had to do was plug the LED light strip in and lay it in the crown molding tray. The entire installation took less than 5 minutes.

Figure 6.5 Tray Ceiling with Philips Hue Lightstrips

In response to an air quality report, or when the pizza delivery driver is close to our home, the lights will automatically change color. Visitors are impressed when Alexa closes the blinds, but they think the lights changing color is the coolest thing our smart home does.

Please keep in mind visitors won't know how to control lights that don't have a wall switch. You'll have to provide instructions for virtual assistant commands or the smart app. I learned that lesson when my daughter texted me the first night she was house sitting, asking me to turn off the Hue bedroom lightstrip. The lights automatically come on each evening. One solution to this dilemma is the "Houseguest" skill from Alexa Blueprints covered in Chapter 11.

Dimmable Lights

The cost of dimmable light switches and bulbs, when compared to regular bulbs, is minimal. We definitely encourage you to consider this option. The perfect light intensity is great for task lighting to avoid eye strain. Moreover, we find it relaxing and comfortable. Lutron changed the industry in the 1950s with the invention of an affordable solid-state dimmable switch. Today, a Lutron switch is usually less expensive than a smart bulb. A switch, however, doesn't give you the color option.

Bulb Adapters

Another option is a Wi-Fi bulb converter such as the Incipio adapter. These adapters allow you to continue to use your existing bulbs.

Figure 6.6   Incipio Smart Light Bulb Adapter

Outdoor Lighting

Outdoor lighting options are neither as plentiful nor affordable as are those for interior lighting. Nevertheless, they will turn on automatically according to a schedule. Some even know when you're away. Our outdoor lights are controlled with a Wemo outlet that integrates with Nest and other systems to automatically control lighting when we leave or arrive home. For holidays I also use Philips Hue outdoor lighting.

LED Light Bulbs

We are gradually swapping out all of our light fixtures in our home with LED bulbs. We have several types of Legrand dimmable Wi-Fi wall switches, and they all work beautifully.

In case you decide on a dimmable wall switch for your LED lights, keep in mind that some LED bulbs do not work well with dimmable switches and you may hear a buzzing noise or see flickering lights. Keep your receipt and packaging in case you run into issues and want to try to return something.

LED Light Strips

A dizzying array of LED light strips is available. Some are low voltage; some have a limited distance or require their own transformer for power. Rather than face the daunting task of figuring out transformers and voltage regulators, we opted for the plug & play Philips Hue light strips for our bedroom and study. The Philips Hue light strip is easily expandable to a maximum of 10 meters or 33 feet. It plugs into a regular power outlet and does not require a transformer and low voltage wall switch. Additionally, it supports 16 million colors.

6.4 Lighting and Electrical Manufacturers

There are quite a few manufacturers of smart lighting and electrical devices. We found several popular and reliable manufacturers. Among them are Wemo, Philips Hue, Qubino, Lutron, and Legrand. Personally, I like the look of Legrand Adorne outlets - as well as the lifetime warranty. I admit, however, that they are a bit pricier than some.

Although I was comfortable planning and buying my Legrand equipment, I chose to have an electrician install the switches and outlets. Electrical switches encompass single-pole, three-way, multiple locations, and low voltage LED. Electricians are up to the challenge of wiring them correctly. I, on the other hand, am not.

Lutron

Lutron is still a family-owned company headquartered in Coopersburg, PA. Lutron has been dedicated to innovative development since 1961. The Caséta starter kit includes a smart bridge and Lutron app and is compatible with several types of connected devices and systems such as:

- Apple HomeKit

- Google Assistant

- Amazon Alexa

- Apple Watch

- Sonos

Philips Hue

Everywhere you look in smart home apps, you'll see Philips Hue lighting. Philips Hue devices require the Philips Hue bridge. You pair the devices to the bridge with the Hue mobile app.

1. Plug in the bridge.

2. Install the Philips Hue app on your smartphone or tablet.

3. Press the button on the Hue bridge to enable the Philips Hue app to discover the bridge and then select Light setup to connect Philips Hue bulbs and light strips.

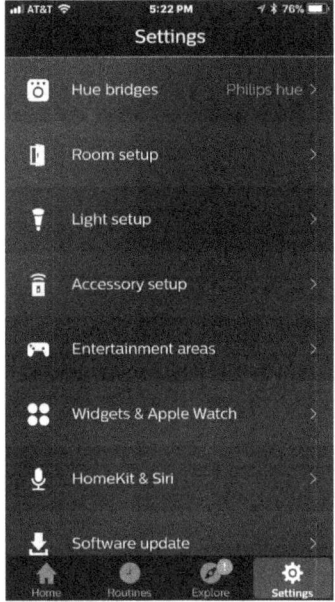

Figure 6.7   Hue Settings

Hue Scenes

The Philips Hue mobile app has a section for scenes that reflect a color palette. Scenes are automatically added to Amazon Alexa anytime you select the option to "discover new devices and scenes." There is one caveat: the Hue app automatically creates scenes in each room. This can confuse Alexa. Renaming scene names for each room to avoid duplicates is a worthy idea.

1.   Open the Philips Hue app on your mobile device.

2.   Tap the room name and go to Scenes.

3. To delete a scene, touch the name for a few seconds to enter edit mode and then click on the **X**.

4. While in edit mode, double-tap the scene and type the new name.

Routines

The Philips Hue app includes routines, a light schedule, and timers that support your daily routines.

Philips Hue Log in

To use the Hue bridge remotely, you must create a Philips Hue account. In the mobile app, select Explore and then log in to your account. You can also access your account from the Philips web site.

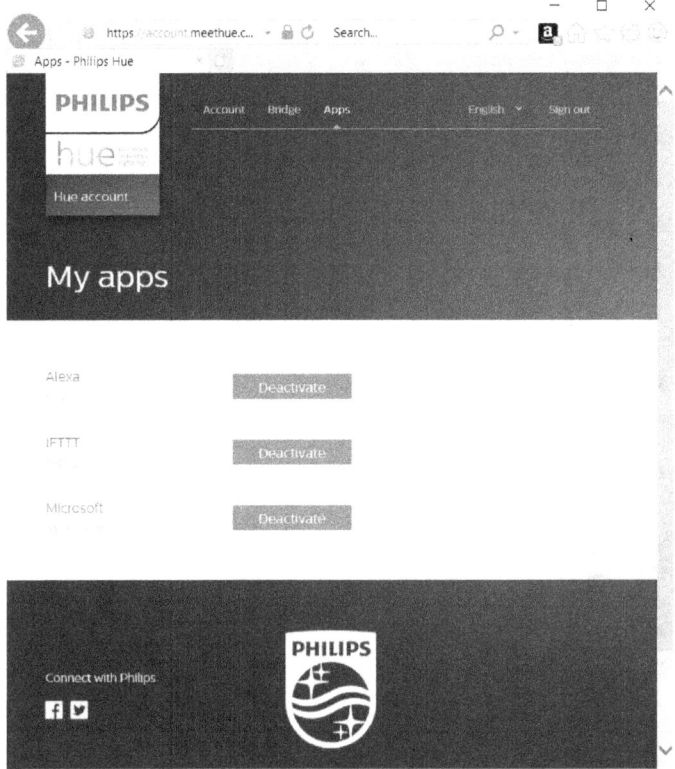

Figure 6.8   Philips Hue Account

Widgets for Apple Watch

To control Hue lighting with your Apple Watch or wearable device, you must create widgets.

1. Open the Philips Hue app on your mobile device.

2. Under **Settings** select Widget Setup.

Figure 6.9   Widgets & Apple Watch

3. Open the Apple Watch app on your smartphone.

4. Scroll down and make sure the Hue app is shown in the section Installed on Apple Watch.

5. On your Apple Watch in the section "Apps," select Hue. You should see your widgets.

Figure 6.10 Hue Widget on Apple Watch

Legrand

Legrand takes IoT seriously, and the Eliot project started in 2015 is an amalgamation of Electricity and IoT. Legrand has several types of Wi-Fi switches, and my personal favorites are in the Adorne collection. The Legrand Hub provides integration with Alexa, IFTTT, and other systems using the ARTIK Connect Cloud service. In the Alexa app, search for the skill called "Samsung's ARTIK Cloud." Samsung's SmartThings app also has integration to Legrand through a Samsung SmartApp called "ARTIK Cloud," as outlined in Chapter 7.

The biggest challenge we faced with Legrand light switches and electrical outlets, was figuring out what to buy. Legrand Wi-Fi switches have a master switch and a remote switch. The Wi-Fi master switch controls the flow of power to the light (on or off). The remote Wi-Fi switch does not work at all unless paired to the master switch. Surprisingly, the wall plates also require a bit of planning, which we've outlined in the next section.

The Legrand Adorne collection has options for both the style and color of your wall plates and optional night lights are available for the wall boxes to light your way in the dark. Legrand has unique pop-out electrical outlets and flashlights. The dimmer switches are impressive. Some have sliders. Others have a light level indicator that shows the light intensity on dimmable lights. As of this writing, the light switch models include motion, soft tap, paddle, and touch switches. Some models of the electrical outlets have USB charging capability. I confess I tried all the styles and love them all.

Legrand also has a Radiant collection which includes the Legrand Radiant Wi-Fi charger, which uses the Qi technology for wireless charging.

Since I signed up for e-mails, Legrand sends me 20% off sales offers regularly. When HGTV featured Legrand, there was a campaign with a national hardware store, and my local store special ordered Legrand Wi-Fi switches for me during the 20% off promotion. The Legrand Adorne collection is guaranteed for life, easy to set up, and after two years still works flawlessly. It also doesn't hurt that they are visually striking and innovative.

The Legrand Lighting Control app is also available on the Apple Watch. The app automatically appears on the Apple Watch home screen when it is paired with an iPhone that has the Legrand mobile app. You don't have to create widgets or worry about extra setup steps - it just works!

Figure 6.11 Legrand App on Apple Watch

Wall Plates

Legrand wall plates fit over your existing electrical wall box, so you don't have to change anything there. If you are adding a new box, we'd recommend deep boxes to allow extra room for the Legrand switches. Legrand switches are fine in regular boxes, it's just easier to work with them if you have more room.

The wall plate kits are more expensive than the decorative wall plate covers because they include the metal frame. To assemble a Legrand unit, first the metal frame screws on top of your existing wall box. The Legrand switches snap into the metal frame, and then the decorative wall plate snaps over the metal frame.

Figure 6.12   Legrand Metal Wall Plate

6.5 A Sample Legrand Installation

This topic walks you through the installation of Legrand switches, programming the switches, and the Legrand hub setup.

Before we program the Adorne switches, we'd like to recommend you keep notes as you go along. You may refer to this later if a surge or something knocks out the programming.

- Which light does the switch control?

- What is the model number of the switch?

- Is this a 3-way switch where you control a light from two locations? If it is a 3-way, is this the master or remote switch?

Fortunately, removing Legrand wall plates is ridiculously easy. The model number of the switch is printed on the front, as shown in the last figure. The model number designates which switch is the master. When programming, you start with the master switch.

Groups combine two switches that control one light, also known as a three-way switch. Wi-Fi switches are similar, except that the process must begin at the master switch. A Wi-Fi master switch is paired with the corresponding remote Wi-Fi switch.

Theoretically, you can program more than two lights in the same group. I actually did this accidentally after a power surge knocked out my programming because I forgot which switch controlled which light. Hopefully, you don't have a clever kid in the house, who thinks this would be a fun April Fools prank.

Initial System Setup

To configure the light switches and outlets, online tutorials and instruction sheets are available from Legrand's web site. My electrician asked me to test the Wi-Fi switches he had just installed, and we literally unpacked the Legrand hub, looked up instructions on my iPad, and not 5 minutes later 3 rooms were programmed. It was by far the easiest smart thing I set up to date.

Add Switches to Your Home ID

Every Legrand home begins with the creation of a Home ID. All Legrand devices are bound to the Home ID. Once switches are "bound" to your home you can create groups, or pair a master Wi-Fi switch with the corresponding remote Wi-Fi switch.

1. Ensure all Legrand switch and outlet status LEDs are solid amber.

2. Press and hold the On-Off button on any switch for 5 seconds. We'll call this particular switch the initiator switch. The LED status light of this initiator switch will flash amber. The LED status light of all other switches will flash green.

3. Press and hold the On-Off button on the initiator switch again for 5 seconds. The status LED of the initiator switch and all other switches will flash green for 2 seconds and then turn solid white.

Groups and Pairing Wi-Fi Switches

To control a light, combine the switches into a group. A light can be controlled by any switch in that light's group.

1. First Ensure the status LED of all potential group members is solid WHITE.

2. Press and hold the On-Off button on any master switch for 5 seconds. We'll call this particular switch the initiator switch.

3. The status LED flashes amber at the initiator switch.

4. The status LEDs of other Legrand switches and outlets flash green.

5. Move to the corresponding remote switch you want to pair with the master switch in step 1. Press and hold the On-Off button for 5 seconds and release.

6. The status LED at the initiator switch flashes green for 2 seconds and turns solid white. The pairing process is complete.

Adding a Switch to an Existing Installation

When adding a new switch to an existing home installation, the switch must be bound to the "Home ID" as outlined earlier. Ensure the status LED of the new device you just installed is solid amber. The LED status light on all other switches should be solid white.

1. Press and hold the On-Off button of any already bound switch for 5 seconds and release. This is now the initiator switch.

2. The status LED of the initiator switch with flash **amber**. The status LED of the new device you just installed will flash **green**.

3. Press and hold the On-Off button of the initiator switch for 5 seconds and release. The status LEDs of the initiator switch and the new switch will flash **green** for 2 seconds and then turn solid white.

Location and Scenes

The Legrand Lighting App has options to create "scenes." For example, you can add all light switches and outlets in the family room to a scene called "family room lights." There are also options to set the location and time zone in **Settings**. The location is used to determine sunrise and sunset for schedules.

Reprogramming Switches and System Updates

Sometimes the switch LED status indicators will flash but recover after a few minutes. No intervention is required. To resolve flashing LED indicators, try resetting the switch. When a switch is not responding correctly, perform a factory reset.

1. Hold the On-Off button 20 seconds.

2. Bind the switch to your existing installation (Home ID), as outlined previously.

3. Add the switch to a group, or pair with a Wi-Fi master or remote switch.

Integration With Samsung SmartThings

Utilizing the "ARTIK Cloud" SmartApp, the SmartThings mobile app integrates with Legrand switches and outlets. After configuration, you can control your Legrand devices, and even control dimmer intensity.

6.6 Fans

While on vacation this year we toured the Angels Envy Distillery in Louisville, Kentucky. The modern two-story distillery has an open floorplan with gleaming copper and wood accents. We were struck by the beautiful ceiling fans. These massive fans are a work of art. Imagine my surprise when I ran across identical fans while searching for a smart fan.

The "Big Ass Fan" company makes gorgeous fans that are perfectly balanced. The company has a line of Haiku fans that monitor room conditions, with a Wi-Fi connection to link to your smart home. Unfortunately, I couldn't justify the price point for a bedroom fan; otherwise, there would be a Big Ass Fan in my bedroom right now.

Ultimately I selected the Dyson Pure Cool Link Air Purifier & Fan, which happened to be on sale at Costco for a great price. The fan comes with a remote control, an app, and connects to Alexa and Siri. The tower fan has no blades and is portable, so I can easily move it to any location in my home. The Pure Cool Dyson technology also delivers cooled purified air.

6.7 Telephone

These days, my communications with the outside world are over a Wi-Fi or cellular network, phone, watch, or iPad. I use my home phone or "landline" for 911 or faxing. With Siri and Alexa handy in just about every room in my house, I also use my virtual assistant to make calls, as shown below.

Voice Assistant Calling

Both my Mac and iPad are linked to my iPhone so that I can use Siri to place FaceTime calls on those devices. Chapter 12 has details on setting up the FaceTime app and placing calls.

Google Home can also make calls, just say "OK, Google, call the nearest donut shop." Google is also experimenting with "Google Duplex." With Duplex, you ask Google Assistant to make a hair appointment or a similar request. I can't help but wonder what happens on the other side of that conversation? Will the receptionist, that answers a phone call from Google, asking to schedule a dentist appointment for John Doe, one day be replaced with automation?

The Alexa mobile app and Echo devices allow you to send messages or place calls to other Alexa mobile apps or

Echo devices in the US, Canada, or Mexico. Chapter 11 has details on Alexa "Conversations." My VoIP provider Ooma also has Google and Alexa skills, as shown in Chapter 6.

VoIP versus a Landline

My husband could not understand why I insisted on keeping a landline phone. I've always felt the quality of a landline signal made it easier to understand conversations. Also, my landline was my safety net for when power and cell towers are down, and I want to call 911. I found comfort knowing my landline was always powered, and the phone company also had backup battery generators.

When AT&T installed its systems at our new home, I noticed the source of my home phone line was the router. Just to be sure I understood what I was seeing, I asked the AT&T representative, and she said my home phone was, in fact, VoIP. I decided to save money and find my own VoIP provider that had 911.

While there are apps like "Whatsapp" that provide VoIP on cell phones, after a bit of research, I decided to purchase an Ooma Telo device. The basic monthly service is free, or you can pay a nominal monthly fee for Ooma Premier. Advanced 911, e-mail, voice-mail, and a phone app are included. The phone app integrates my cellular and VoIP lines and allows me to make international VoIP calls from my smartphone. Ooma Premier supports Google Voice and Alexa, so I can say:

"Alexa, use Ooma to call Michael."

Overall, I've been very pleased with the Ooma service. I'd encourage you to check out all the VoIP providers before making the switch, keeping in mind the following:

- A 911 service requires a registered street address. Not all VoIP solutions include 911.

- Ask if you can use a traditional "desk phone" with the service. I like the convenience of a desk phone with a speaker for conference calls.

- Will the service e-mail you when you have a voice-mail?

- Are there skills for virtual assistants like Alexa or Google Voice?

- Is Voice-to-Text available?

- Does the device support Bluetooth headsets?

- Is Call Blocking or Call Forwarding available?

6.8 Plumbing

Smart home plumbing is not exactly glamorous, but be on the lookout for innovations in showers, bathtubs, toilets, mirrors, and faucets. The HGTV Smart Home series showcases new technology in their yearly Smart Home. The 2018 HGTV Smart Home featured Kohler products.

Based in Wisconsin, Kohler has been a family-owned business for almost 150 years. Kohler's smart home devices are powered by Microsoft Azure. Kohler Konnect™ devices are controlled from a mobile app, hands-free motion control, or voice-controlled virtual assistants.

The Verdera Voice Lighted Mirror with Amazon Alexa has the most promise, in my opinion. The night light or LED makeup lights are unique features. The built-in speakers play music and enable Alexa to read the news, calendar events, and give advice on your morning commute and weather.

Hands-free control of the Sensate Kitchen Faucet is possible with voice or motion control. The faucet even dispenses the exact amount of water you specify. While on the way home from work, start PerfectFill and the bathtub is filled to the precise depth and temperature you request. The Numi® intelligent toilet also has a hands-free operation. Seat warming, lighting, UV cleaning, audio, and more features are included.

Sensors for water leaks or monitoring water usage are available from companies like Phyn or H2Know but are not as well known as some smart home technology.

7. Home Security

In this chapter we discuss

Whether you choose components or an all in one system, when smart devices work together, it's like a blanket of protection around your home. This list is just a few of the many systems available, no doubt there are many more.

- Skylink

- Nest

- SmartThings

- Insteon

- Honeywell

- SimpliSafe

- Wink

- Piper

- Canary

Combining smart home security devices with sound, lighting, and messaging provides the next level of security. Each system has unique features. For example, the Canary system is an all-in-one unit. It includes a high definition camera with night vision, as well as a sensor that monitors temperature, humidity, and air quality. The optional Canary membership adds two-way talk, desktop streaming, and video storage.

7.1 What Can Smart Security Do

Until recently, home security meant keeping burglars out with motion sensors, glass breaks or locks; and of course, smoke and fire alarms. Now with a smart home, there is a lot more you can do.

- View and talk to visitors, workers or delivery folks and unlock doors.

- Monitor water leaks, mold, gas, water flow, or air quality.

- React when you leave or arrive home.

- Turn on sprinklers when a fire alarm activates. My first experience with smart security was an e-mail alert when my daughter arrived home from school and disarmed the system. Depending on your needs, you can configure lights to blink, play loud music, or send custom messages to friends or property managers.

Chapter 13 shows you how to create a SmartApp to trigger an alert when a door is left open for more than a specified time. It has options to send text messages to two contacts, turn on up to three lights (and change colored bulbs to red), and sound a siren.

Imagine you're in another part of the house, and a door sensor uses IFTTT to trigger a call, message or "drop-in" to alert you of an intruder. A cat deterrent could be a Samsung sensor on a cabinet to detect an open door. A motion sensor when a dog gets near the trash can trigger a siren. An alert from a motion sensor in your mailbox means you have mail. The possibilities are endless.

7.2 The Types of Security Devices

There are smart devices to monitor a wide variety of conditions, and with a few key components, you can protect your home and add convenience for a variety of tasks. Here's a list of security sensors and devices.

- Sensors: water leak, glass break or noise, motion, smoke, mold, arrival, gas, air quality, presence or occupancy, faucet water flow, vibration, or temperature.

- Cameras

- Smart doorbell (with camera)

- Sirens

Look for sensors that do more than one thing like the Canary hub. For example, the Samsung multipurpose sensor monitors temperature as well as motion. With this sensor, you could monitor when a door or window is opened, or automatically close the blinds when the sun is shining directly on the windows causing the temperature to change.

Cameras

When considering which camera to buy look at these features.

- Storage (local or cloud)

- Night vision

- Facial recognition

- Speakers

Smart cameras fall into two storage categories - local or cloud storage. The Samsung SmarthThings Hub v3 no longer includes the "video core" module. This means it does not support Dlink or Samsung cameras that connect locally, but the cloud-connected Ring or Arlo cameras do work.

Welcome Home

A key decision point for security is identifying when you are away or arrive home. Ideally, "Away" is defined when everyone in the household is away. "Arrive Home" generally is when anyone in the household comes home.

- Honeywell RedLINK has a wireless entry/exit remote.

- The "Automatic Pro Car" adapter tracks your car's location and uses Geofencing to determine your arrival home.

- SmartThings has an arrival sensor but also uses mobile phones for location tracking.

- Other systems use registered smartphones to identify your location.

7.3 Nest

Google purchased Nest Labs in 2014, and today, there are several new Nest products that also integrate with door locks. In May 2019, Google announced it was merging Nest and Smart Home divisions, and would ship the new smart home hub "Nest Hub Max" in the Spring The Nest Hub Max includes a camera and 10" smart screen, and is similar to Amazon's Echo Show. The Nest Hub Max can function as a security camera, and facial recognition will respond when you're in the room.

At the heart of the Nest Secure Alarm System, the Nest Guard includes an alarm, keypad, motion sensor, and Google Assistant built-in. The Nest Detect Sensors protect doors and windows, while the Nest Hello doorbell includes a camera so you can talk to the person at the door.

- Nest Learning Thermostat

- Nest Protect Smoke Detector

- Nest Cam IQ Security Camera

- Nest Secure Alarm System

- Nest Detect Motion Sensor

- Nest Hello Smart Doorbell

Both the Nest Protect and Nest Detect sense when you walk past and shine a soft white light. This "Pathlight" feature senses movement in the dark and the intensity is configurable. You can also turn of Pathlight.

For security, pet cams, or watching the nursery, Nest Cam IQ cameras are wonderful with innovative features. The Nest Cam includes "Talk and Listen" to scare off intruders. Even if it doesn't scare the intruder to know big brother was watching, knowing you have his photo and the police were on the way would probably motivate him to get the heck out.

> It sounds like something from the future, but Nest cam IQ cameras can use facial recognition to identify if the person belongs in your home, and differentiate between a pet and a person.

Nest has a feature called "activity zones" so you can create alerts around special places like cribs. If the Nest Protect senses carbon monoxide, the Nest Thermostat can automatically turn off your furnace. The new Nest Hello doorbell will stream live video to your smartphone, as well as send and receive audio.

7.4 Samsung SmartThings

The Samsung SmartThings Home Monitoring Kit includes a hub, multipurpose sensors, a motion sensor, and the mobile app. Samsung also makes smart outlets and water leak sensors. The system requires a Samsung SmartThings Hub or the Samsung Connect Home Smart Wi-Fi System PRO which includes the hub functionality in a Wi-Fi mesh router. There is one LAN out port on the device for adding additional equipment.

The SmartThings ecosystem has been around a while, and there is an impressive network of connected devices and SmartApps. Manufacturers like Legrand are implementing IoT in their hardware using Samsung's

ARTIK platform, which is another reason so many things work with SmartThings.

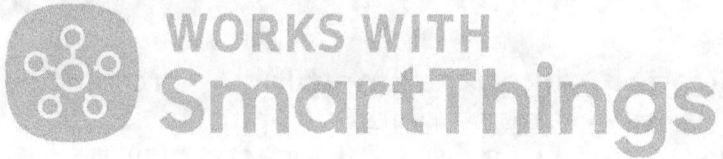

Figure 7.1   Smart Things Compatible Logo

A SmartThings hub works with SmartThings sensors that have ZigBee chips, and will also work with other ZigBee devices. Look for the logo "Works With SmartThings." The SmartThings website has interesting videos on what a smart home can do, as well as a shop. Our experience dealing with customer service was outstanding, and we wouldn't hesitate to buy online again, although you may prefer to see the equipment in person before buying it.

The Samsung SmartThings Multipurpose Sensor detects that doors or windows have been left open, or if the temperature changes, and can react to a change and trigger the Aeotec Siren. The temperature sensor could be used to trigger blinds to open or close.

Initial SmartThings Setup

To get started with SmartThings, you need a hub and at least one sensor. The initial setup is quick, and then you configure the sensors and automations in the mobile app.

1. Launch the SmartThings mobile app.

2. Create a Samsung account and log in.

3. Enter the Welcome Code (found on the box) for the SmartThings hub.

4. When prompted, allow the SmartThings app to discover your devices.

5. Use the option Add Device Manually to add Honeywell, Logitech, sensors, speakers and other devices not automatically added.

If your Samsung motion sensor does not automatically connect, open the sensor unit and press and hold the connect button for 5 seconds.

During the initial SmartThings setup, your smartphone is automatically added as a device. The location of your smartphone is used as a presence sensor to identify when everyone is away. You can view this setting in Marketplace, Sensors, Presence Sensors, Mobile Phones. There are several examples that follow that show how to add additional smartphones, and configure a Goodbye! automation to use smartphones as presence indicators.

It's interesting that the SmartThings app includes instructions on how to set up your Amazon Echo or Tap devices. Scroll down to Voice Control and select the model. Basically, the process involves launching the Alexa app and adding the SmartThings skill.

Smart Home Monitor

In the context of a security system, most of that control is handled by the Smart Home Monitor in the SmartThings mobile app. This is also where you arm or disarm the system.

1.   In the SmartThings mobile app, go to the Dashboard.

2.   Select **Smart Home Monitor**.

3.   Select **Settings** (the gear icon).

Silence an Alarm

Before I explain how to set up alarms, I'd like to take a moment to tell you how to turn off an alarm. I wish I'd been smart enough to learn this **before** I tested my alarms the first time. I'm sure my cats would have been a lot happier too if I'd known how to turn off the siren quickly.

1. Launch the SmartThings mobile app.

2. Go to the **My Home** screen and view your Things.

3. In the figure below the siren shows an alarm. Click on the siren to turn off the alarm.

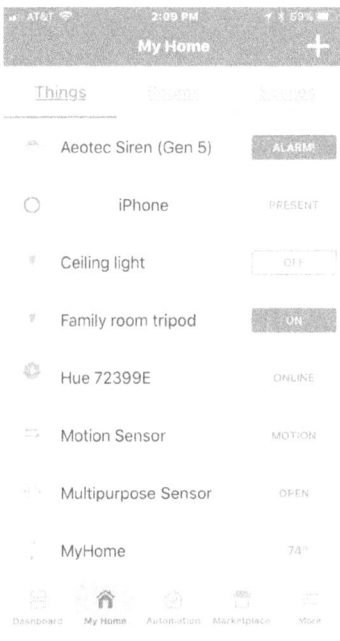

Figure 7.2   Turn off Siren From MyHome Screen

Add a Siren to Smart Home Monitor

Although you may have added a siren device to your SmartThings app, the system doesn't know to use it for alarms until you configure it in Smart Home Monitor, or in an automation in the SmartThings mobile app.

1. In the SmartThings mobile app, go to the Dashboard.

2. Select **Smart Home Monitor**.

3. Select **Security**.

4. Select the sensors you want to use when you are away and click **Next**.

5. Select the sensors for when you are home and click **Next**.

6. Click on Alert with Sirens, and then select the siren(s).

7. This is where you can also set Alert with Light, and even set the color of smart lights.

Modes

Modes are set when an automation runs. So for example, the **Goodbye!** automation can change the mode to Away.

Select More in the bottom right corner of the app to see the current mode.

Add Another Person to Your SmartThings Account

The SmartThings app can include multiple people in your household. You can view this setting in Marketplace, Sensors, Presence Sensors, Mobile Phone. By tracking the location of smartphones, the app can automatically determine when everyone has left your house.

1. Launch the SmartThings mobile app.

2. Select More in the bottom right corner.

3. Select Manage Users, and click on **Add** Users. An e-mail is sent to the user with instructions to install the SmartThings app on their smartphone. The user creates their own SmartThings account and is automatically linked to your home.

4. On the new smartphone in the SmartThings app, go to Marketplace, sensors, presence sensors, mobile phone, and select **connect now**.

5. Now when you set up the Goodbye! automation, you can select multiple phones.

Configure the Goodbye! Automation

The SmartThings app includes a default **Goodbye!** automation you can customize. Let's say you have added everyone's smartphone as a SmartThings device, and you want the Goodbye! automation to run when everyone leaves your home.

1. In the SmartThings app, select Automation.

2. On the Routines tab, click on the gear icon to go into **Settings** for the Goodbye! automation.

3. In the section "Turn off these lights or switches," select lights you want to turn off.

4. Change Smart Home Monitor to **Armed (Away)**.

5. Change the mode to **Away**.

6. Tap Automatically perform "Goodbye!."

7. Tap **Everyone leaves** and select people in your household.

8. If you have a smart thermostat, you can also set the temperature.

Create a Custom Automation

In case you want to create a custom automation, let me show you an example that triggers a siren when the motion sensor detects motion. This scenario is perfect to sound an alarm when a dog gets into the trash can.

1. In the SmartThings app, select Automation.

2. Click on **Add a Routine**.

3. Type a name for the routine and click Next.

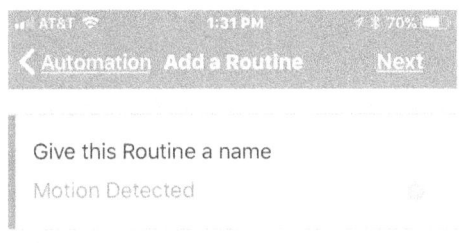

Figure 7.3   SmartThings Add a Routine

4. In the section What do you want to happen? select **Turn on these lights or switches** and choose the Aeotec Siren. Click on **Done**.

5. Scroll down to Additional Settings and tap "Automatically perform Motion Detected" to set the action.

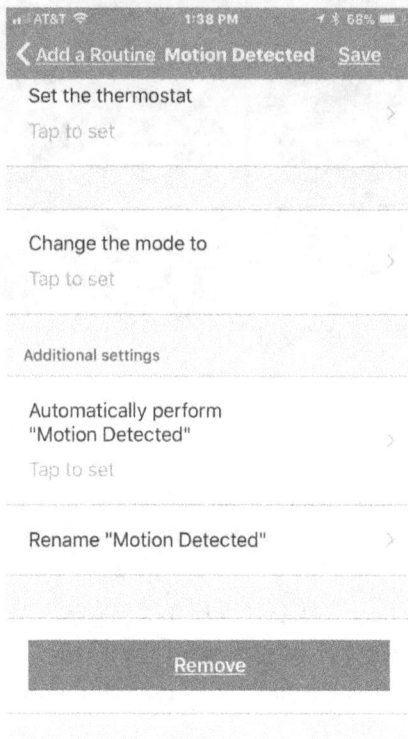

Figure 7.4   Automatically Perform This Action

6. To add sensors scroll down and select **Things Start Happening** and select the motion sensors.

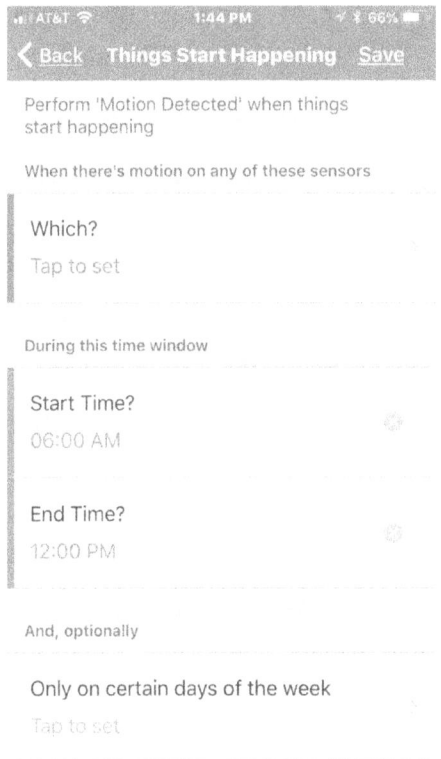

Figure 7.5   Select the Sensors

7. If desired, enter a time window and select particular days for this routine. Click on **Save**.

8. The app returns to the setup screen. Scroll down to Advanced Options to restrict by modes, and add notifications or messages. Click on **Save**.

9. When testing the routine, you can silence the siren from the My Home screen, or disarm the system from the Dashboard.

Marketplace

The "Marketplace" is where you can find add-on applications that interact with SmartThings, or you can write your own as outlined in Chapter 13. So, for example, you can install a SmartApp that alerts you when the door is left open for a period of time.

1. Launch the SmartThings mobile app and go into the Marketplace.

2. Select the tab for **SmartApps**.

3. Select Energy Management.

4. Select **Something Left Open**.

Create a Widget for Your Smart Watch

To control which SmartThings routines are available as widgets, in the SmartThings mobile app, select More and then click on **My Account**.

Use the Online SmartThings App

You can create custom modes, create SmartApps, add Device Handlers, and more in the online SmartThings app at graph.api.smartthings. This is the SmartThings community where folks share code and ideas. Sometimes you don't see your hub listed in the online app, even though you did set it up in your mobile app. If that happens, in the online app, go to My locations, click on your home, and then log in again. This is also where you can add custom modes.

In Chapter 13, I show you how to create a SmartThings SmartApp for when a door is left open. It has options to notify two contacts, turn on three lights (and set the color), and sound a siren.

Integration with Samsung Connect Cloud

Samsung Connect Cloud (which includes ARTIK Cloud) is part of Samsung's unified IoT platform. To control ARTIK devices, you have to install the ARTIK Cloud for SmartThings app. Note this process imports ARTIK Cloud devices to SmartThings, and also sends SmartThings devices you select to ARTIK Cloud. In this example, we'll add Legrand light switches and power outlets to SmartThings.

1. In the SmartThings mobile app, on the home screen, navigate to the **Marketplace**.

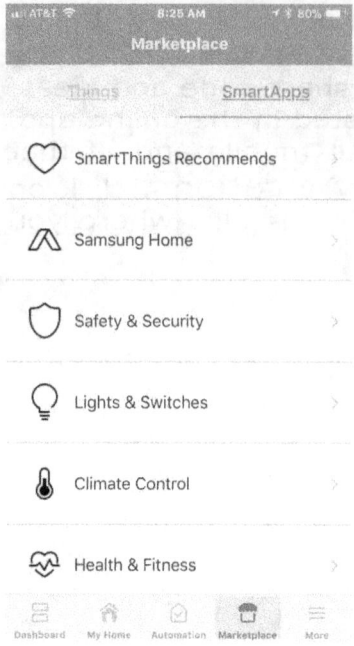

Figure 7.6   SmartThings SmartApps

2. Select SmartApps and click **Samsung Home**.

3. Click on ARTIK Cloud.

4. You are prompted to log in to your ARTIK Cloud account and link it to SmartThings.

5. Click on Synchronize ARTIK Cloud and SmartThings devices.

6. If you want to add your SmartThings devices to ARTIK cloud, select them here, and click Next.

7. Click Save to import ARTIK Cloud devices to SmartThings, as well as import any SmartThings devices you selected in Step 6 to the ARTIK Cloud.

8. You can now control your ARTIK Cloud devices like Legrand dimmable switches from your SmartThings app.

Figure 7.7   Legrand Dimmable Light Switch in SmartThings

7.5 Samsung ARTIK Cloud

The Samsung ARTIK Cloud lets you control your ARTIK Cloud devices, create scenes and rules, and view charts and data logs of what's going on in your smart home.

To see what devices are in your ARTIK Cloud log in to your account at https://my.artik.cloud.

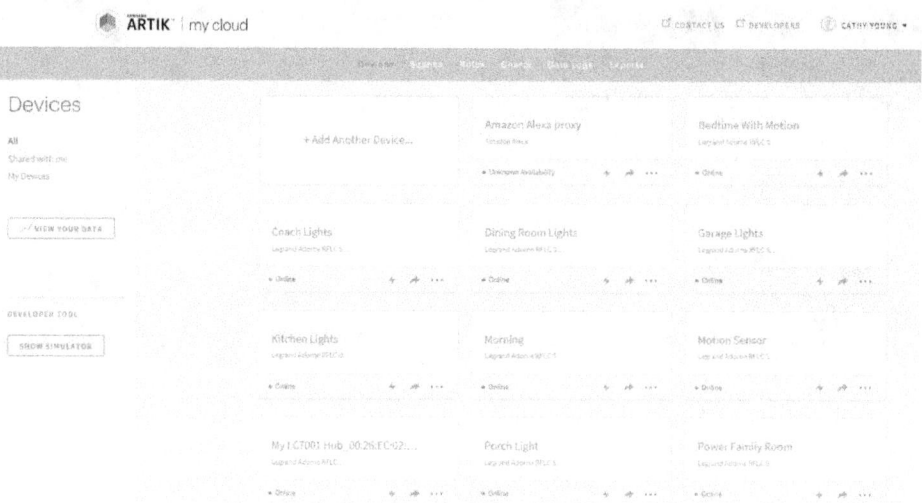

Figure 7.8   ARTIK Cloud Devices

If you're wondering how often you leave your lights on, you can pull up a chart to see the history or export the data.

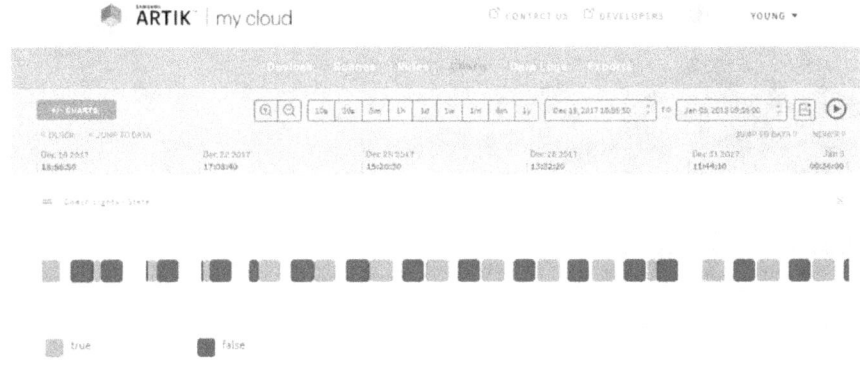

Figure 7.9   ARTIK Cloud Activity Charts

7.6 Door Locks

Initially, we envisioned our door would unlock as we drove up to the garage. For security reasons, though, you must use the manufacturer's mobile app to unlock doors or use a PIN for Kevo integration with Alexa. However, as long as we have our smartphone with the Kevo mobile app open, we can open the Kevo lock with a simple touch.

Figure 7.10   Kevo Lock

Kevo locks utilize the Unikey security platform to encrypt all Bluetooth traffic with military-grade encryption, although the US patent does mention Zywave, ZigBee and other wireless protocols would work equally well. Unikey adds Inside/Outside Intelligence® for an extra layer of security, to prevent unauthorized entry if your mobile device is in range of the door's sensors. Kevo locks are controlled by tapping the lock once, and only unlock when there is a smartphone nearby that has the Kevo app open. The Inside/Outside Intelligence® is important if you have your mobile phone inside your home, and the Kevo app is running. You wouldn't want a stranger to walk up and unlock the door with a tap.

The day after I set up my digital locks, a repairman needed to get into the garage, and I unlocked the door remotely. The next month I accidentally locked myself out of the house. I walked over to a neighbor's house and called my husband to unlock the door remotely. Even better that, my husband didn't laugh at me, and was able to get back to work right away. My list of what my smart locks can do grows daily, and a few examples are shown below.

- Share digital keys with friends or workers.

- Notify you when your child is home from school.

- Unlock the door for deliveries.

- Integrate your locks and thermostats.

- Receive discounts on insurance. (Check with Liberty Mutual).

Our first question when considering smart door locks was what happens when the battery dies, or we don't have our smartphone in hand. After being reassured smart locks still work with an old-fashioned key, we set our worries aside and soon discovered how cool these devices are.

Smart locks integrate with smartphones and may also include a key fob, which may be handy for those without a smartphone. Would this be a child under the age of 6?. Anyway, there are several manufacturers making smart locks that communicate via Wi-Fi, Z-wave, or Bluetooth.

- Schlage

- Kwikset

- August

- Yale

Installation

The deadbolt in your smart lock must be perfectly aligned so that it opens and closes without resistance. This is one area where an experienced carpenter who guarantees the installation is well worth the money.

Initially, our builder had 3 different carpenters try to set up our locks. The deadbolt was installed where it was turning in the wrong direction, which eventually damaged the electronic lock mechanism so that it had to be replaced. Fortunately for us, the 4th carpenter was familiar with automated locks and installed the lock properly. As mentioned later in the section "Deliveries," the "Amazon Key" program is one way to get free professional installation.

Setup

Once the smart deadbolt lock is installed, you are ready to configure it.

1.   On your smartphone, connect to your home Wi-Fi network.

2.   Download the mobile app.

3.   Create an account.

4.   Follow the prompts to connect to your lock.

5.   Create digital keys.

To save frustration when you replace the battery or reconfigure the lock for any reason, make a note of these details.

- The model of the lock (for future software updates).

- How long the battery will last and how to replace it. (Why not ask Alexa to set a reminder in 3 months?)

- How to do a master reset.

- The account login and password.

My Kevo lock was installed in such a way that it would be very difficult to reach all the battery cover screws. Since I know I'll have to replace batteries in the future, I left one of the screws off to make the process easier.

A generic e-mail account for your home instead of your personal e-mail is a good idea. A different account and password for each system provide added security. In any case, I recommend you keep a record of the ID and password for future reference.

Kevo Hub

There's not much setup involved with your Kevo hub, just plug it in, and the mobile app will identify it. The hub is used for remote access, as well as for integration with

IFTTT and other systems. As of this writing, you can only lock or unlock the door with the Kevo mobile app, or the Alexa skill. The lock will provide status to other devices. So, for example, when you unlock the door through the mobile Kevo app, IFTTT can trigger lights to turn on.

Digital Keys

Smart locks also let you create digital keys that you can share with friends, family, or workers. At any time, you can see the status of a key, or delete a key that is no longer needed. This definitely beats driving to the hardware store for a new key.

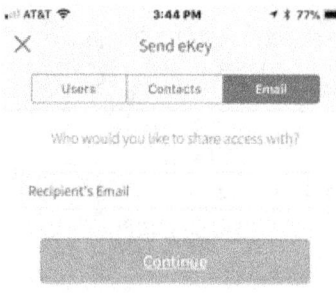

Figure 7.11   Digital Keys

Connect Kevo to Thermostat

The KEVO mobile app has an option to connect to Nest or Honeywell thermostats.

1. Connect to the thermostat account.

2. When prompted "Match Locks" to your thermostat.

3. Set temperatures for when you arrive (unlock the door).

Connect Kevo to Alexa

There is a KEVO skill for Amazon Alexa, and she can easily lock doors. For security reasons a PIN is required when Alexa unlocks doors.

7.7 Deliveries

When I heard Alexa could notify me when packages were due to be delivered, I was intrigued.

"Alexa, where's my stuff?"

Taking it a step further, I wondered if UPS could notify me of any scheduled package. It turns out UPS will send text alerts, and now there is a skill for Amazon Alexa. In addition to text alerts, if you have a UPS Smart Choice account, you can sign a delivery release and provide a garage code for the delivery driver. In addition, Microsoft Cortana can scan your e-mails and use UPS tracking IDs you've searched for to track packages.

At this time, Amazon is offering Prime members "Amazon Key," which includes your choice of a smart lock and a security camera bundled for around $280, with free installation. The idea is that you can see the delivery driver at your door and remotely unlock the door, and then re-lock it once your package is safely inside your house. This is a great way to get a camera and a lock, as well as a guaranteed installation by an experienced professional. The Amazon Key service for deliveries even has an in-car delivery option.

8. Garage, Lawn, and Garden

In this chapter we discuss

Garage

Water Heaters

Irrigation and Garden

Temperature and Weather

Outdoor smart home automation includes irrigation, garage doors, and water heaters. Not as well known are robotic lawnmowers, soil monitors (water, soil PH, sunlight), outdoor lighting, and weather stations.

- Robomow

- Mipow Garden Playbulb or WeMo Outdoor Lighting

- Philips Hue Lighting

- Netatmo Weather Station

- Overhead Storage with Motorized Lifts

- Scotts Gro Water Sensors

Although there have been a few smart soil and water sensors on the market, the ones I saw last year had bad reviews or disappeared from the market. Major manufacturers are entering the market now, and it might be a good time to take another look at this technology.

8.1 Garage

In addition to smart garage doors and keypads, parking aids, and automated car location sensors, storage lifts are useful garage smart devices. The ability to provide a customized garage code or unlock a door for a delivery person or worker means you don't have to wait around all day. A notification that the delivery is complete is a nice feature. The following is a brief list of companies with products for the garage.

- Liftmaster

- MyLifter

- Chamberlain

- Garageio

- Garage Gator

- Skylink Nova

- NEXX Garage

- GoControl

- GogoGate 2

- Insteon

Garage Door Openers

Currently, for a subscription fee, the Chamberlain MyQ Smart Garage Hub is compatible with NEST, Wink, IFTTT and Amazon Alexa, among others.

Skylink is known for manufacturing safety systems. The Skylink Nova will open your garage door when there is a smoke or fire alarm.

Genie garage door openers offer an accessory called the Aladdin Connect system, which includes a garage door controller and door position sensor. Installation is relatively easy and requires running a wire from your existing garage door opener to the new "garage door controller" unit. The garage door controller unit can mount to existing metal brackets, and plugs into a power outlet. The controller does need a good Wi-Fi signal for connection to the internet.

The Alladin Connect app allows you to give temporary access to friends or family. The app can program the garage door to automatically close at a specific time of day, which means I no longer leave my door open all night. The app also alerts you when the door position sensor battery is running low.

When Alladin Connect added integration to Alexa and Google Assistant in May 2019, I was excited. Reviews have been mixed, in part because Alladin Connect uses a PIN for added security. You can disable the PIN by saying "Alexa, tell Aladdin Connect to disable PIN."

Remote Entry Keypads

With the Liftmaster keypad, you enter a code to activate the garage door opener. Although the keypad is not a smart device in itself, there are new ways to take advantage of the technology. For example, if you have a UPS Smart Choice account, you can choose to sign a delivery release and provide a garage code for the delivery driver.

Car Adapter/Sensor

Automatic, Zubie and Hum adapters plug into a car's standard OBD-II port. These adapters link your car to your smart home. The Automatic Pro Car fills an interesting niche. It is similar to the SmartThings, NEST Hello or Honeywell arrival sensors, but does a lot more.

- Crash Alert & Emergency Services

- Automobile Diagnostics

- Parking & Live Vehicle Location Tracking

- Fill Up Logging

- IFTTT to connect to Google Sheet, Concur or Expensify

The company Automatic has an Alexa skill to alert you about maintenance issues or fuel levels, and in 2017, BMW announced its Alexa skill. Edmunds has an Alexa skill that includes recalls, market value, and car shopping activities.

For more information on automotive smart things, check out Chapter 3.

Overhead Storage

Overhead storage of bikes, kayaks, or boxes is not new and is even better when motorized. I love the idea of my bike out of the way, but I am way too lazy to use anything that means I have to do heavy lifting or work pulleys. Garage Gator and GarageSmart sell a motorized lift. The lift raises bikes with the push of a button.

The GarageSmart MyLifter includes an app for your smartphone or tablet. The app uses smart sensors to balance the platform, gauge weight limits and set a predetermined level.

Figure 8.1   MyLifter Garage Storage Racks

Parking Assistants

Both GarageSmart and Chamberlain have laser park accessories. These devices use motion sensors and lasers to help you park. GarageSmart Parking Assist adds a camera, which is useful when you lower your MyLifter overhead storage platform from a remote location. The camera also serves as a security camera in your garage.

8.2 Water Heaters

Smart water heaters adapt to your schedule when combined with NEST thermostats or other systems. Smart water heaters predict when to start heating water, and learn peak water usage times. Today, coordinating water heaters with dishwasher or laundry schedules isn't common, but it is certainly a possibility in the future.

Air Filters

In Chapter 7, we touched on HVAC systems and innovations in smart air filters. Because my HVAC unit is in my garage, I thought I'd mention the Filtrete smart filter in this Chapter also. These smart filters are relatively inexpensive, and the sensor monitors when the filter is clogged. Since I never can remember when to check my air filter, I really appreciate the reminder from the app that my air filter is dirty. The mobile app also keeps track of the filter size and type to make reordering simple.

8.3 Irrigation and Garden

Smart systems that conserve water are a good investment, especially given the cost of potable water today. Schedules and timers have been available for a while, and smart systems also integrate with rain meters or weather forecasts.

Before buying an irrigation system check if your local municipality has a rebate program.

- Rain Bird

- Rachio

- GreenIQ

- Scotts Gro Systems

Smart irrigation also ties into fire alarms, and weather forecasts to automatically adjust watering schedules. Beyond water conservation, it is certainly easier to repair leaks as you walk around your yard. With your smartphone in hand, it's easy to find broken heads. Simply turn zones on and off while walking around your yard .

When gardening, you may also benefit from Plantlink, Scott's Gro water sensors, EasyBloom Soil Monitors, or the Netatumo Weather Station.

8.4 Temperature and Weather

There are several types of smart outdoor temperature controls. Personal weather stations like Netatumo predict and collect weather data. Companies like Honeywell have an outdoor temperature sensor as part of their HVAC offerings. The Samsung multipurpose sensor monitors temperature as well as motion. Automatically closing shades when the sun is shining directly on the windows is a great way to save electricity.

Weather Applets

The IFTTT weather applets are powered by Weather Underground and include several interesting recipes.

- Weather Reports

- Emails about the UV index

- Mobile Notifications of High Pollen Counts

- Alerts When Snow or Rain is Forecast

Grill Temperature Probes

Grill temperature probes pair with a remote, so that you can monitor grill temperature from the comfort of your living room. iTronics manufactures the ThermoPro sensor, which comes with a lifetime warranty. Most probes come with a remote, and a few include a smartphone app.

The Fireboard thermometer has a smartphone app and integration with Amazon Alexa and the Google Assistant, although it doesn't have IFTTT integration at this time. It could be fun to have the lights flash when food is done.

- ThermoPro

- Fireboard

- Tappecue

- Rengard

- Weber iGrill

- Ivation

- Morpilot Smart BBQ

9. Home Entertainment

Home entertainment systems encompass audio and visual components, as well as universal remote controllers. Streaming media devices and smart TVs also fall into this category.

- Universal Remote

- Music and Speakers

- Streaming Media

- Smart TVs

- Casting and AirPlay

- Photo Viewing

9.1 Universal Remote

Universal remotes have been around for years. The latest generation includes features that work with smart home devices.

- Pop Home Switch

- Logitech Harmony Hub

- Caavo Control Center Plus

- Simple Control's Simple Hub

Logitech Harmony Hub

The Harmony hub is a universal remote. This is one device that just keeps getting better. I bought mine years ago, and through the Logitech software updates, it is just as current as any new smart device out there. In addition to a remote, there are mobile and computer Harmony apps. The Harmony Hub works with Amazon Alexa and the Google Assistant. The newer Harmony Express universal remote has Alexa built-in.

Depending on the device or activity, you can configure the app to use voice and text. This makes it easier to enter passwords and information. When linked to Amazon Alexa or Google Assistant, you can also use your voice to control Harmony activities.

Devices include the normal home entertainment things you'd expect like TVs, DVDs, Apple TVs or receivers. Smart home and Wi-Fi devices are added in the Harmony app Home Control section. There are 250,000 supported devices today, and the list is growing daily. And that's not a typo - Logitech really does support over 250,000 devices.

The Harmony custom activities are used to group devices into unique experiences. So, for example, the "dinner time" activity could close blinds and adjust lights. Activities can also be controlled from the mobile app remotely when you are outside your home.

Install the Harmony Mobile App

1. Download the Logitech Harmony mobile app and create an account.

2. Power up your Logitech Hub. If the smartphone app can't connect to the hub, it displays a picture prompting you to press the reset button on the hub to pair the hub. A red light will flash on the Harmony hub. In the app, select Re-scan.

3. When prompted, enter your home Wi-Fi password.

Once the hub is active on your home Wi-Fi network, you can set up devices and activities.

1. Add devices to your Harmony app.

2. Create activities. The default name is usually the model number, but there is an option to rename a device.

3. Sync the Harmony hub with the Harmony app to update your activities.

Gestures

The Harmony app also includes a gesture mode, which supports touch screen gestures. Default gestures include swiping up to turn up the volume, or double-tap to play video. You can also customize the gestures with gesture mapping.

Keyboard and Remote

The Harmony app also supports a smart keyboard and remote. Within each custom activity, you can enable keyboard options.

Use Your Voice or Text Entry

Enable text entry to make it easier to enter passwords and information. The Harmony app connects to these devices with Bluetooth.

1. Launch the Harmony mobile app on a mobile device connected to your 2.4 GHz home network.

    Ensure Bluetooth 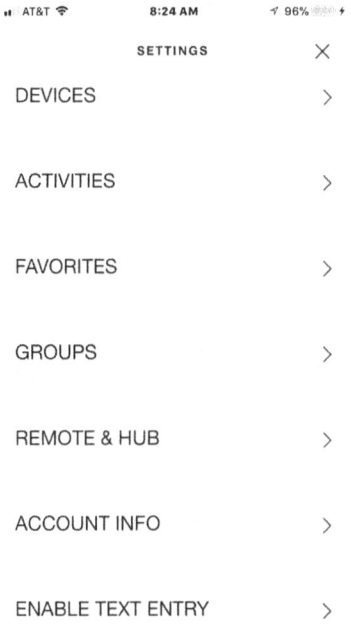 is active on your mobile device.

2. On the Menu   select Harmony Setup, **Add/Edit Devices & Activities**.

3. Select **Enable Text Entry**.

AT&T 🔧	8:24 AM	⚡ 96% 💿 ⚡
	SETTINGS	✕
DEVICES		>
ACTIVITIES		>
FAVORITES		>
GROUPS		>
REMOTE & HUB		>
ACCOUNT INFO		>
ENABLE TEXT ENTRY		>

Figure 9.2   Harmony App, Enable Text Entry

Bluetooth Pairing

1.   To enable Bluetooth pairing, on your Smart TV, go into Settings, choose "Bluetooth," and select **Add a device** to enable Bluetooth pairing.

2.   In the Harmony app, select the activity to complete pairing the Bluetooth device.

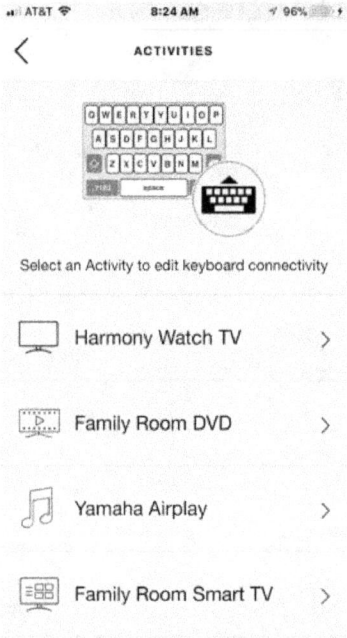

Figure 9.3   Select the Harmony Activity

3. Follow the instructions in the Harmony app to complete pairing the Bluetooth device.

Figure 9.4   Pair the Device

Harmony Activities

After creating an activity, "edit" or "re-run" the activity to change the start sequence, set the startup channel, or add additional steps. This is also where you can add a step to change to a particular channel number under the device action setting. If you don't have favorite channels set up, the app will prompt you to create favorites at this point. When a device needs more time before switching inputs, add a power delay step to resolve the issue. To add a "Wi-Fi" device to an "Activity," use the option to "View your Settings."

Logitech Harmony allows up to 8 devices. Wi-Fi and smart home devices do not count as one of the allowed 8 devices, so this is a good option when available.

To set which device controls volume and channels, or change device inputs, select the "re-run activity" button. These options also configure home control devices, as outlined in the next section.

Home Control Devices

Harmony has home control options for Ecobee, Lutron, Nest, Insteon, Qivicon, Lifx smart bulbs, SmartThings and PowerView, among others. To add home control devices, after you create the activity, edit the activity, select the start sequence, and choose "edit home control."

Favorite Channels

To set up favorite channels, on the main screen, select the star icon, or in Settings select favorites.

Control the Activity

Use the remote to change channels, control volume, and play or pause the video.

In the Harmony app, tap the remote icon . To control the device using touch gestures, tap the hand icon.

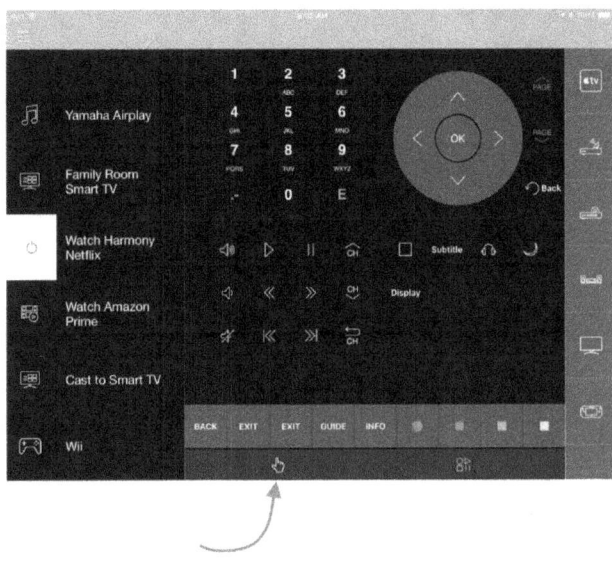

Figure 9.5   Hand Gestures in Harmony App

Mobile devices with small screens typically have more than one page of remote controls. This setting is indicated by an ellipsis, as shown below. Swipe left or right to scroll between pages.

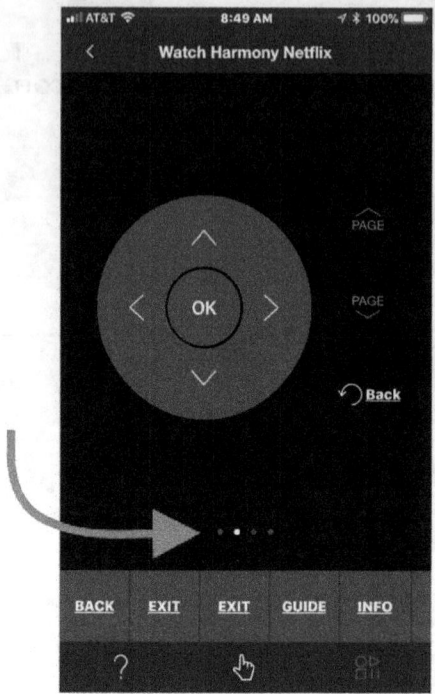

Figure 9.6   Swipe in the Harmony App

Fix Activity

If something doesn't start properly in the Harmony app, from the menu, choose the activity, for example, "Fix Apple TV." The app will automatically give you options to power on devices or change inputs for the selected activity.

Alexa Skill

If you are using Amazon Alexa, add the Harmony skill. In the Alexa app select Smart Home, "Your Smart Home Skills" (in blue), Enable Smart Home Skills and select Logitech Harmony. Follow the prompts to log in to your Harmony account and to connect Alexa. Once connected to your Harmony account, in "Your Smart Home Skills" select the Scenes tab and click on **Discover Scenes**.

See Chapter 11 for more information on Alexa skills.

9.2 Sound Systems

This section is entitled Sound Systems, because with a smart home you may want to add in features beyond just listening to music. For example, you can have your smart lights integrate with speakers and move to the beat, or trigger sound when there is an intruder. In addition to surround sound systems and traditional speakers, the newer smart speakers with virtual assistants are popping up.

There are several approaches to playing music.

- Amplifiers/Speakers

- Smartphone & Tablet Apps

- Smart Speakers - Virtual assistants

- Streaming Media Devices

- Smart TVs

- Casting

- AirPlay from MacBook computers, smartphones or tablets

Originally, I selected my Yamaha amplifier because it had Wi-Fi and Bluetooth connectivity and supported AirPlay. Although the Sonos Wi-Fi speakers have been available for a while and have a wide range of features, I have some 20-year-old Bose speakers I wanted to integrate with my smart home, so the Yamaha amplifier was a good choice.

Compared to the Alexa built-in features, there is more control of the Yamaha amplifier through the SiriusXM skill or the MusicCast mobile app. Controlling music through Alexa is discussed in Chapter 9.

To listen to SiriusXM, I can use several approaches.

1. Open the Yamaha MusicCast app on my smartphone or tablet.

2. Ask Alexa to use the Yamaha MusicCast skill to connect to SiriusXM.

3. Switch the Yamaha input to Bluetooth and ask Alexa to connect to SiriusXM using the Alexa Yamaha skill.

Smart TVs may also have apps for Pandora, iHeartRadio, or other services. My advice would be to experiment and choose your favorite.

Yamaha Amplifier/Speakers

The Yamaha RX-A870 Advantage AV Receiver Tuner includes a MusicCast controller app and integration to Alexa.

"Alexa, ask MusicCast to play music in Family Room Yamaha."

"Alexa, ask MusicCast to mute volume."

"Alexa, ask MusicCast to change to AirPlay."

"Alexa, ask MusicCast to change to HDMI2."

"Alexa, ask MusicCast to change to SiriusXM."

Alexa SiriusXM Skill

There is also an Alexa skill for SiriusXM.

"Alexa, play Comedy Central Radio on SiriusXM."

"Alexa, play SiriusXM Hits One on SiriusXM."

"Alexa, play channel 94 on SiriusXM."

1.   On your smartphone or tablet, first connect to your home Wi-Fi network.

2.   Download the MusicCast mobile app.

3.   Create a Yamaha MusicCast account.

4.   In the Alexa app, add the skill MusicCast and link it to Alexa.

Speakers for Alexa Echo

Alexa has a mini audio jack to connect an external speaker, and Gen 2 Alexa devices will also connect to a Bluetooth speaker. In my family room, I often listen to music or the TV on the surround sound speakers at the same time I talk to Alexa, so in that room, I normally use the built-in Alexa speaker.

To switch between Bluetooth (my surround sound speakers) and the built-in Echo speaker, I say:

"Alexa, connect to Bluetooth."

"Alexa, disconnect from Bluetooth."

Applet TV Music

There are two ways to listen to music on your Apple TV.

- Subscribe to iTunes Match or Apple music.

- Enable Home Sharing and play music from your computer's iTunes library.

Subscription Music Services

If you subscribe to iTunes Match or Apple music, you can play your own saved music.

1. Start your Apple TV and select **Music**.

2. Scroll to select **My Music**.

9.3 Over-the-Top Streaming Media

Over-the-Top, OTT, streaming media devices allow Over-the-Top, OTT, streaming media devices allow you to stream subscription music or video networks and services to your TV. Popular streaming media devices include Apple TV, Google Chromecast, Roku, and Amazon Fire TV. Other OTT providers are OnRewind, Tedial, Dozn, Sportradar, Deltatre, and Maestro. Both Disney and Apple have plans to launch their own OTT network. Today's smart TVs also include support for a variety of streaming service apps.

Over-the-Top streaming media services like Hulu, Prime Video, or Netflix charge monthly fees. Some solutions like "slingtv" or Amazon's "Fire TV" support local channels with antennas. Amazon's Fire TV adds support for video streaming from websites. Antennas are one way to avoid monthly fees and are discussed in Chapter 9.

Your smart TV, Apple TV, or Amazon Fire TV is a central place for videos, Amazon Prime, YouTube, Hulu, and more. You can control Hulu, YouTube, and Amazon Prime videos with your voice using the Amazon Echo Show and Alexa, or other virtual assistants. In 2019 Apple redesigned its TV app and added Apple TV Channels. The new app is designed so you can log in and control everything in one place, the Apple TV app. Chapter 12 has details on the Apple TV app.

"Hey Google, turn on Friends on Netflix with Chromecast."

Amazon Alexa

Amazon Echo devices, Bose soundbars, and other devices that include Alexa support Alexa Skills for watching TV. Look for these Alexa skills.

- Comedy Central

- DirecTV

- Dish TV

- Fire TV

- Game of Thrones Facts

- Harmony

- TV Guide

- Sony's Android TV

- Vizio Smartcast™

With the DirecTV skill, there are a few phrases you may want to try.

Alexa, turn on TVok

Apple TV

The Apple TV is a streaming media device. You can listen to music or watch movies from subscription services (Netflix, Amazon Prime, Hulu) or your iTunes library, and use AirPlay to display photos or videos from your iPhone, iPad or MacBook. The 4th generation or later Apple TV includes the Apple Home app for remote access.

Enable AirPlay

1. Start your Apple TV and click on **Settings**.

2. Scroll down and click on **AirPlay**.

3. Toggle AirPlay on.

4. If desired, rename your Apple TV.

Turn on Home Sharing

Home sharing allows you to use iTunes libraries that have Home Sharing turned on. It does not share files or photos.

1. Start your Apple TV and select **Computers**.

2. Select your computer.

3. Select Music to play music from your iTunes library.

For each computer where you want to share the iTunes library, turn on Home Sharing in your iTunes app.

1. Launch iTunes on your computer.

2. On the Edit menu, select **Preferences**.

3. Check "Share my library on my local network".

Update Your Apple TV

Software updates ensure your Apple TV has all the latest features.

1. Start your Apple TV and click on **Settings**.

2. Scroll down and click on **Software Updates**.

3. Click on **Update Software**.

4. If desired, enable **Update Automatically**.

Sling TV

Depending on your area, Sling TV network Live TV including ABC, CBS, NBC, and FOX. Sling TV offers an integrated sleek HDTV Antenna. Sling is also available on Amazon Fire TV.

Amazon Fire TV

Amazon has an impressive lineup of devices in its "Fire TV" family, as shown below. The Fire TV recast DVR supports external storage with a connected USB hard drive.

- Fire TV
- Fire TV stick 4k
- Fire TV recast
- Fire TV cube (with speaker)

With Fire TV, you can access thousands of channels, apps, and Alexa skills; and use your voice to control your TV with Alexa. Look for Amazon's "Fire TV recast bundle" that includes a DVR, remote, and HD live-air antenna. Depending on availability and reception in your area, an HD antenna is FOX, NBC, PBS, and The CW.

Amazon "Fire TV" combines several streaming media services. With a Firefox or Silk browser, directly accesses millions of websites like Facebook, YouTube, or Reddit.

- Netflix
- Slingtv

- DirecTV Now
- Prime Video
- Hulu
- MLB.TV
- ESPN
- NBA

Local channels and some websites have no monthly fees. Over-the-Top streaming services like Hulu, Prime Video, or Netflix charge monthly fees.

Going a step further, Amazon Fire TV includes playing games and music. Look for games from developers like EA, Disney, and Mojang. A brief list of music providers is shown below.

- Amazon Music
- Apple Music
- Pandora
- Spotify
- iHeartRadio

Google Chromecast

Google Chromecast is available as an app for smart TVs and smartphones, or you can purchase a Chromecast device that plugs into your TV.

In 2018 Chromecast users could not access Amazon Prime Videos, and Echo Show owners were dismayed they could not watch YouTube videos. Google owns YouTube, and there was an unfortunate dispute between Amazon and Google. In 2019 the feud is ended, and now you can watch Amazon Prime, Hulu, Netflix, and other services with Google Chromecast.

"Hey Google, turn on Friends on Netflix with Chromecast."

DirecTV NFL Sunday Ticket

For satellite subscribers, DirecTV offers the "NFL Sunday Ticket." DirecTV offers customers without access to satellite service, like college students, NFL Sunday TickeR.

Hulu Live TV

One choice we considered for NFL football was Hulu with Live TV. This OTT (Over-the-Top) provider has CBS, Fox, and NBC streaming. Additionally, you can stream ESPN. There's no NFL Network, but with its array of channels you'll be able to watch Sunday afternoon and night games, Monday night NFL games and Thursday Night Football matches.

9.4 Smart TVs

Expanding on the concept of streaming media, smart TVs have built-in support for casting and smart apps for music and video streaming media subscription services like these examples.

- Netflix

- Google Chromecast
- Hulu
- Amazon Video
- Pandora

You can control your home entertainment devices using a universal remote like Logitech's Harmony hub. In addition, some smart TVs also integrate directly with virtual assistant's like Amazon Alexa, so that you can control the TV through your voice. My Sony XBR55A1E supports Amazon Alexa and Google Assistant. Google Chromecast will control Hulu, Netflix, and more.

"Alexa, turn on the TV."

"Hey Google, turn on Friends on Netflix with Chromecast."

"Alexa, Change the channel to CBS on Family Room TV."

"Alexa, watch TV."

"Alexa, play TV."

Naming your Speakers and Smart TVs

When you have more than one casting device available, you may want to update the TV's network name to make it easier to locate the correct device. To avoid confusion when using Alexa, Google Home, or other Whole Home Apps, I use specific names.

- Family Room Yamaha
- Family Room Lights
- Family Room Blinds
- Family Room Outlet

The network name is usually configured in the device's system, setup, or settings menu.

- Network Name
- Display Name
- Device Name

I updated my Yamaha amplifier's network name to "Family Room Yamaha" under Setup, Network, **Network Name**. For my Sony TV, the setting was in the "About" menu as **Device Name**. My Vizio TV had the network name under System, **Display Name**. In the Logitech Harmony mobile app, there is also an option to rename each device.

Casting, AirPlay, and Miracast

Casting, AirPlay, and Miracast are technologies to mirror music or videos from your mobile device or computer to your TV. Apple devices (iPhones, MacBook computers) use Apple AirPlay, while the Google Chrome application uses "cast."

Cast Connections

Look for TVs that have the "cast" feature or support Apple AirPlay. Sometimes communication is via the local network (wired Ethernet or Wi-Fi) and other times it utilizes Bluetooth. My older Bowers and Wilkins speaker supports AirPlay through a direct LAN Ethernet connection. My Yamaha amplifier utilizes a direct Ethernet or Wi-Fi connection for AirPlay.

Cast from a Google Chrome Browser

To try casting in a Google Chrome browser, open a YouTube video. In the top right corner of the browser window, click on the Chrome Settings menu and select "cast."

Add the Cast button to the Chrome Toolbar

When you select "cast" from the Chrome Settings menu, the "cast" button will temporarily appear next to the Chrome Settings menu icon in the toolbar. If you want to keep the "cast" button on the toolbar, right-click on the "cast" icon when it appears and select "Always Show Icon."

Cast from iPhone or iPad

While playing music or videos in your music app, swipe up and click on the "cast" icon to send music, images, or video to a smart TV.

When setting up a "cast to TV" activity for your Harmony or other universal remote control, configure the activity to use the TV as the source for sound.

9.5 Photos

Displaying your iPhone photos on your TV is so much fun. I would encourage everyone to try it. Photos in iCloud can be viewed on your Apple TV. Another option is to enable AirPlay and send photos from your MacBook, iPhone, or iPad over AirPlay to your Apple TV.

View iCloud Photos in Photo Stream

From MacBook or iPhone, you can use AirPlay to view iCloud shared photos through the Apple TV.

1. Start your Apple TV and scroll down to **iCloud Photos**.

2. Select **My Photo Stream**.

View iCloud Photos with AirPlay

1.   Start your Apple TV. Ensure AirPlay is enabled.

2.   On your MacBook, iPhone, or iPad open photos and start a slideshow.

3.   Click on the AirPlay icon to send the photos to the Apple TV.

View Photos on Apple TV

When you enable iCloud and set up a shared folder, you can view photos from your phone or MacBook on your Apple TV.

1.   On your smartphone or tablet first connect to your home Wi-Fi network.

2.   In the Photos app, select a photo.

3.   Click on the share icon to open the share screen.

4.   Click on **AirPlay** .

5.   Select your Apple TV.

Figure 9.7   Select the Apple TV

iCloud Photo Sharing is another option instead of AirPlay. Once configured the Apple TV will display iCloud Photos.

1.   Select the photo on your smartphone.

2.   Click on iCloud Photo Sharing   .

3.   Add comments for the photo(s).

4.   Invite people to view the photo(s).

5.   Select the shared   album for the photo(s).

The iOS photos app is where you manage or change your shared photos.

1. On your smartphone or tablet first connect to your home Wi-Fi network.

2. In the Photos app open the shared photo.

To manage iCloud settings on your Windows computer, download and install the iCloud app for Windows.

1. Launch the iCloud app on your Windows computer.

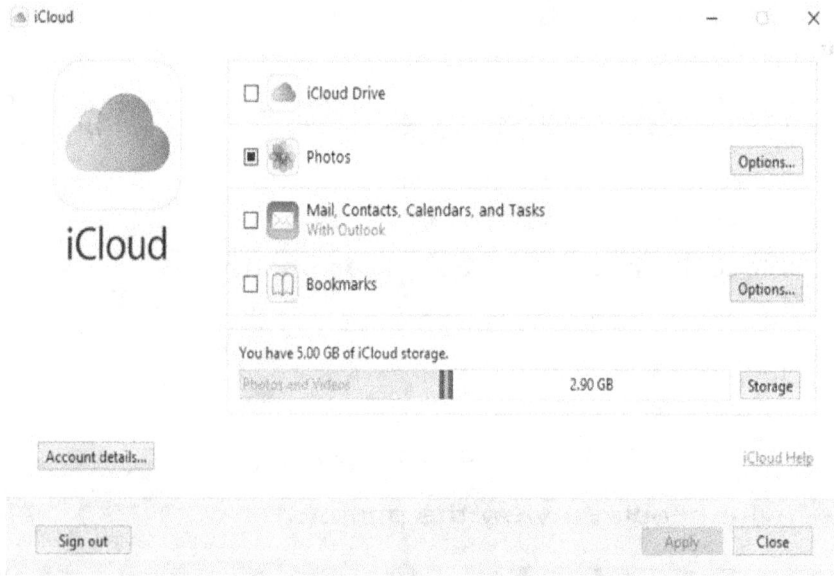

Figure 9.8   The iCloud App

2. Select Photos, and click on **Options**.

3. Scroll down to enable iCloud Photo Sharing.

4. Click **Apply.**

290

10. Introduction to Virtual Assistants

In this chapter we discuss

Overview

Amazon Alexa

Google Assistant

Microsoft Cortana

Apple Siri

Samsung Bixby

Personal virtual assistants are found in smartphones, tablets, smart screens, soundbars, Bose headphones, Ecobee 4 Thermostats, laptops, smart speakers, cars, and smart TVs, to name a few. Amazon Echo,

Google Assistant, Apple Siri, and Microsoft Invoke are examples of smart speakers that have virtual assistants.

Smart screens leverage an Android mobile operating system and include the devices shown below. Some smart screens have cameras. In 2019 Amazon added the "Silk" browser to Echo Show, with integration with Alexa Meal Kits.

- Amazon Echo Show

- Portal from Facebook (with Alexa)

- Lenovo Smart Display

Using virtual assistants requires a fundamental change in the way we interact with the world around us. Adopting a mindful approach can make the transition easier. Each week I set aside a few minutes and ask myself, "Can Siri do this task for me?" Then I spend a few minutes exploring what's possible today. I say "today" because the list of what these virtual assistants can do is changing daily. Microsoft expects Cortana to manage e-mail hands-free in the near future. (Could there finally be an easier way to deal with spam?)

Automobile manufacturers are also adding virtual assistants. BMW, for example, supports Alexa in their newer models and also has an Alexa skill for further integrations with other smart home devices.

While this Chapter is an introduction to virtual assistants, Chapter 11 will focus on setup and using virtual assistants. Detailed Alexa and Siri examples are included, although the same basic principals apply to all virtual assistants. Chapter 11 is a good place to explore what a virtual assistant can do.

10.1 Overview

When working with virtual assistant applications, skills integrate with other systems. Voice control, a mobile app, and a web application are all ways to control a virtual assistant. In addition to voice commands and integrated skills, the virtual assistant apps have features to combine several devices into one command. Look for these terms when using virtual assistant apps.

- Device Groups

- Skills

- Scenes

- Routines

- Shortcuts

- Automations

Each manufacturer has their own interpretation of "scene." Philips HUE lights refer to color modes as scenes. The Hunter Douglas PowerView app uses "scenes" to describe shade settings. For example, a scene called "family room shades" could have three shades preset with tilted vanes.

In 2018 virtual assistants were usually found in smartphones, computers, or smart speakers. Examples in 2018 were Siri, Microsoft Cortana, or Amazon Alexa. In

2019, see virtual assistants are becoming commonplace in automobiles, appliances, thermostats, routers, headphones.

10.2 Amazon Alexa

At this time, the Amazon Alexa platform seems to have the most support in terms of manufacturers with skills or integrated devices. The Alexa virtual assistant is also showing up in these devices.

- Amazon Echo
- Echo Dot
- Echo Spot
- Echo Plus
- Mini
- Echo Show
- Echo Look
- Portal from Facebook
- Martian Passport Smartwatch
- Bose Soundbars and Headphones
- BMW Automobiles
- Ecobee 4 SmartThermostat
- NetGear Orbi Router
- HP and Acer Computers and Laptops
- LG Smartphones
- Moto Smartphones

Alexa's popularity may in part be due to the way Amazon compensates developers for innovative and popular skills. The downside of thousands of skills is it can be difficult to find skills of interest to your situation.

Smart cameras are good for video conferencing, and the built-in cameras on some Echo devices introduce video into the virtual assistant equation. Displaying recipes or song lyrics is a neat feature. What about taking a photo, and searching the Internet for photos that match the picture? Today you can do a Google image search, and there are apps that search images for plants or animals. Asking our virtual assistant to take a photo and tell us what the object is will be the next step.

Galaxy phones with the virtual assistant Bixby allow you to shop for products right when you see them, and Bixby Vision is available in the camera or Samsung Internet apps.

Chapter 11 focuses on setup and using virtual assistants, in particular, Amazon Alexa. The same basic principals apply to all virtual assistants. This is a good place to explore what a virtual assistant can do.

10.3 Google Assistant

The reviews of the Google Assistant suggest it is one of the best virtual assistants in terms of understanding your voice. Google devices include Google Home, Google Nest Hub Max, Google Mini. The Nest Hub Max is a smart screen, similar to Amazon's Echo Show. The Lenovo Smart Display is a smart screen based on the Android mobile operating system that supports Google Assistant. Google Assistant is also showing up in other products like the Ecobee 4 Thermostat.

Google Assistant uses the Google search engine, my personal favorite search engine. Google Home integrates with Google Calendar, Google Maps, and Chromecast. Google Home also remembers your previous questions to give better answers in the future. One unique feature of the Google Assistant is it can understand two commands at once.

Figure 10.1   Google Home

10.4 Microsoft Cortana

Microsoft's personal virtual assistant Cortana is available in Windows 10, a mobile app, or on the Microsoft Invoke. The Invoke is a Harman Kardon smart speaker. On February 16, 2018, Microsoft announced Cortana will work with IFTTT.

During 2019, there are signs that Microsoft Invoke may be moving in another direction. A deal between Microsoft and Amazon means you can open Alexa with

Cortana, and vice versa. Cortana will be part of Xbox, native Microsoft apps, and the Office Suite. Microsoft partners are also building Cortana powered things.

Figure 10.2   Microsoft Invoke

The first time you start Microsoft Cortana on your Windows 10 device you are prompted to log in or create an account. When you next start Cortana, you are prompted for your mobile number. Cortana texts a link to your smartphone to download the Cortana app.

"Hey Cortana, send a text."

Another optional setup step is to add the Harman Kardon Invoke speaker to the Cortana app.

1.   Open the Cortana app on your smartphone or tablet.

2.   Click on the menu and select "Devices," and follow the prompts to add the Harman Kardon speaker.

Cortana works with NEST, Philips Hue, Samsung SmartThings, and a variety of other systems.

Settings

In Settings, you can enable the option "Let Cortana respond to Hey Cortana." There is another option to use Cortana when your device is locked. This is also where you can make sure Cortana can hear you, and quickly set up your microphone if needed.

Skills

Cortana skills are available from the main menu of the Cortana app, in the "notebook" section.

1. Launch the Cortana app on your computer or mobile device. Select the main menu and click on "**Notebook.**"

2. Click on Manage Skills, then click on Connected Home.

3. To enable the service, click on Enable Connected Home. Follow the login prompts.

4. Search for the skill you want, and follow the prompts to link Cortana to your smart device.

Compared to Amazon Alexa Skills, today there are not that many Cortana skills; however the list is growing.

When you search for skills in Cortana, it also finds applications installed on your computer, as well as web apps.

Track Packages

Microsoft Cortana can track packages from specific retailers like Amazon, Target, Walmart, Apple, eBay, or the Microsoft Store. Cortana scans emails for key phrases to locate packages. Once you search for a FedEx, USPS or UPS tracking ID, Cortana tracks it.

1. Open Cortana and select the **Notebook** icon.

2. Select Manage Skills and scroll down to **Add a Package**.

10.5 Siri

Siri is found in Apple devices like the Apple HomePod, the Apple TV, the Apple Watch, the Apple Siri Remote, or the iPhone. Siri is also integrated with Apple apps and can be customized with the Shortcuts app.

Combining Apple's virtual assistant Siri with an amazing speaker, the Apple HomePod is an intelligent home assistant. Apple's HomeKit automation platform works with Philips Hue, Honeywell, August, First Alert,

Lutron, Logitech, and others. Look for this logo to find HomeKit compatible devices.

Figure 10.3   Works with Apple HomeKit

Tip: The 4th generation or later Apple TV includes the Apple Home app for remote access.

The "Home" app is available for your smartphone, MAC, tablet, and Apple Watch. Controlling your smart home with your watch is simple with "Favorites."

Configure Rooms and Devices for Apple Watch

1.   Open the "Home" app on your tablet, smartphone, or MAC.

2.   Double click, or firmly press, on a room. Click on "Settings."

3.   Ensure the toggle "Include in Favorites" is turned on.

4.   Open the "Home" app on your Apple Watch and swipe to control rooms and devices.

Configure the iPad as a Home Hub

Instead of purchasing an Apple HomePod speaker, you can configure some Apple TVs or iPads as a home hub to allow remote access to your accessories.

1. On your iPad running iOS 10.3 or later, go to **Settings**.

2. Scroll down to Home and enable "Use this iPad as a Home Hub."

Invite People to Join Your Home

Apple can identify when everyone in the family has left home if you add members to your home in the mobile app.

1. Start the Apple Home app.

2. Select your home.

3. Invite people to join your home account.

Automation

To create a new Apple HomeKit automation for when people leave, choose the action everyone leaves.

10.6 Samsung Bixby

The Samsung virtual assistant "Bixby" is available today on some Galaxy smartphones. In addition to the usual smartphone features, Bixby has a digital search engine enabling you to shop for products right when you see them, as well as "Bixby Vision" available in camera and Samsung Internet apps.

Samsung connected devices include digital cockpit vehicle displays, TVs, washers, dryers, vacuums, ranges, and refrigerators. The Samsung line of SmartThings includes smart home devices for security, lighting, and more. Available today in some Samsung phones, the Samsung virtual assistant "Bixby" will roll out to Samsung connected devices by 2020.

11. Hey Siri, Google, Alexa!

In this chapter we discuss

Alexa

Google Assistant

Siri

Samsung Bixby

Verbal Commands and Phrases

Interesting Skills

In this Chapter first, we'll look at the specifics of setting up virtual assistants. Next, we'll focus on interacting with virtual assistants with reminders, alarms, skills, and more. I've also included a section on several verbal commands, or phrases, to get you started. The last topic is "Interesting Skills" that explores useful ways to interact with your virtual assistants.

Since I predominantly use Alexa and Siri, you'll notice most of the examples that follow use either Alexa or Siri. While features or verbal commands may vary slightly, the principals are the same whether you're using Samsung Bixby, Google Assistant, Cortana, or some other voice assistant.

11.1 Alexa

An Amazon Echo is one of those cool gadgets that you are excited to buy. Even better than that, unpacking and setup is a breeze. Amazon Echo devices are smart speakers with voice control and include the virtual assistant Alexa. To enjoy all the features Alexa has to offer, configure the Echo with personal settings in the Alexa mobile app. You may be tempted to skip this step since Alexa is impressive right out of the box, but you'll be amazed at all she can do once she knows your location, sound of your voice, and household members. You will also find options to choose your particular music, TV, or calendar services, and configure voice purchasing. A "wake" word is used to communicate with Alexa, and this is configurable. The wake word can vary for each Echo in your home. For example, in the office, you could use the wake word "computer," and in the bedroom, the wake word could be "Echo."

Alexa visually communicates with you by way of a flashing light ring on top of the Echo. We'll discuss the various colors and how they are useful in troubleshooting in a bit. Events, reminders, alarms, calling, messaging, and drop-in all are basic Alexa features we'll also explore.

The next area we cover is Alexa skills, which bring products and services to life. The proverbial phrase "separate the wheat from the chaff" comes to mind when looking at the skills since thousands of skills are available. Amazon introduced Blueprint templates in April 2018 for creating your own personal skills. We'll look at Blueprints and a few interesting skills in a bit to help you get started.

Living with Alexa is complex and wonderful and changing every day. Our list of "Ask Alexa" phrases represents a unique language. Eventually, talking to Alexa will be second nature; for now, we tend to forget some things are even possible. Although far from exhaustive, the "Ask Alexa Phrases" at the end of this chapter contain a list of commands available today.

Echo & Alexa Models

The Alexa virtual assistant is part of the Amazon Echo speakers, Fire HD tablets (7th generation), as well as the newer Echo Spot, Echo Look, and Echo Show. In 2018 PC manufacturers like Acer, Asus, HP, and Lenovo added Alexa for PCs. The Show, Spot and Look also include a camera. The Echo Connect enables these Alexa devices to utilize land line phone connections.

With the Spot or Show, you can view lists, traffic maps, recipes, or song lyrics. With the camera video chats are possible, as well as adding a video when you "drop-in" to other rooms. Remote video makes the Echo Show ideal for a nursery. Depending on the model, the Echo Show may support YouTube, Prime Video, and Hulu.

The Echo Look is a closet assistant for fashion advice, and you can take a video of yourself as a sanity check before leaving the house. The Spot makes a nice alarm clock in addition to the usual Alexa features.

The Echo Look camera also supports visual-based skills. Since you can do a Google image search, it's probably no surprise there are apps to search for plants or animals based on images. Galaxy phones with Bixby allow you to shop for products right when you see them, and Samsung's "Bixby Vision" has a smartphone camera, and Samsung Internet.

With the Vuzix augmented reality glasses you can ask, "Alexa, what is it I'm looking at?" No doubt, sometime in the near future, it will be commonplace to take a photo, and ask our virtual assistant, "What is this?"

Basic Echo Setup

To get started with Alexa plug-in your Echo, follow the instructions in the mobile app to connect to your home network, and you're up and running.

- Download the Alexa app for your mobile device.

- Launch the app and follow the prompts.

Figure 11.1   Connect iPhone to Echo Dot

In Chapter 2, we discussed using a generic e-mail account for your smart home devices. As it pertains to Alexa, however, your personal e-mail makes more sense, because you will be using Alexa to place orders, send texts, and read delivery schedules.

To save frustration if you have to make changes in the future, make a note of details like the account login and password.

The Alexa App

In addition to the mobile Alexa app, there is a web interface at https://alexa.amazon.com. Managing skills is easier through the web interface.

The Light Ring

Other than volume and mute buttons, the only physical characteristic for Echo that changes is the light ring. You will notice when you say the wake word the light ring flashes blue. Other colors indicate what is happening in Alexa's pretty little digital mind.

- A pulsing green light flashes when you are receiving a call or Drop-in.

- If you miss a call or there is a message waiting, the light ring will flash yellow.

- When the light ring is pulsing red, the mute button on the Echo is active.

- When Do Not Disturb is active, the light ring will flash purple.

Personalize Your Echo

To really enjoy all Alexa can do, you need to tell her about yourself, and how you want her to handle privacy issues. These settings are optional but well worth a look. Privacy is particularly relevant if you have a device in your bedroom.

Device Name

When you have more than one Echo, you want to give each device a unique name. When you "drop-in" to other rooms, send messages or place calls between Alexa devices, this is especially useful.

1. Go to the menu and select **Settings**.

2. Select your device.

3. Under the General section, select **Device name**. For example: Alexa-family room.

Device Location and Time Zone

Navigation, traffic, skills like Uber, weather reports, scheduling activities, and Geofencing skills all use location and time zone settings.

Figure 11.2   Set Your Location

1.   Go to the menu and select **Settings**.

2.   Select your device.

3.   Under the General section, select **Device location** and **Device time zone**.

Do Not Disturb

You may want to schedule Do Not Disturb for your bedtime hours if you have an Echo in your bedroom. When Do Not Disturb is active, the light ring will flash **purple**. Otherwise, you may find the Echo flashes all night long.

The Wake Word

The Alexa app supports four wake words: Alexa, Amazon, Echo, or Computer. The last one is a nod to all you Star Trek fans!

The newer Echo models do have the ability to determine which Echo is closest to you, but if you have issues with two Echos in close proximity, try a different wake word for one.

1.   Go to the Menu and select **Settings**.

2.   Select your device.

3.   Under the General section, choose your **Wake Word**.

Household

Alexa uses the concept of households to differentiate between family members. You can add adults to your Amazon Alexa household. Alexa can then identify the particular family member to personalize messaging or music. As of this writing, Alexa doesn't use household information for lists, calendars, or purchasing. For example, you can't have Mom's shopping list and a separate shopping list for Dad.

Figure 11.3   Amazon Alexa Household Profile

1.   Go to the menu and select **Settings**.

2.   Scroll to the Accounts section and select **Household Profile**.

3.   Invite family members to join your household.

Once households are set up, you can switch between Amazon accounts - say, "Alexa, switch accounts."

When you train Alexa to recognize your voice, Alexa can identify the correct person who says, "Alexa, play my messages."

Train Alexa to Recognize Your Voice

Train Alexa to recognize your voice by setting up a **Voice Profile** in the Alexa app. Voice profiles are useful when you have several members in your household, and helps Alexa automatically identify the correct person who says, "Alexa, play my messages."

1. On your smartphone, open the Alexa app.

2. Go to the menu and select **Settings**.

3. Go to the Accounts section, and select **Your Voice**.

4. Select **Begin**.

Traffic

To have Alexa give you traffic information for your daily commute, set up a starting point and destination, in the "Traffic" section of the mobile app.

1. Go to the menu and select **Settings**.

2. Scroll to Traffic and enter the starting point and destination.

"Alexa, how is traffic to the airport?"

"Alexa, what's my commute?"

Speakers for Echo

The Echo has a mini audio jack to connect an external speaker, and Gen 2 Echo devices will also connect to a Bluetooth speaker. In our family room, we often listen to music or the TV on the surround sound speakers at the same time we talk to Alexa, so in that room, we normally use the built-in Alexa speaker.

1.   Go to the menu and select **Settings**.

2.   Select your device.

3.   Under the Wireless section, select **Bluetooth**.

In our home, our surround sound speakers are connected to a Bluetooth amplifier. To switch Alexa between Bluetooth and the built-in Echo speaker, I ask Alexa for help.

"Alexa, connect to Bluetooth."

"Alexa, disconnect from Bluetooth."

Volume and Default Sound

Alexa can set a timer, and we suggest you set the default timer volume to ensure you can hear it over the TV or music. To manage the timer volume, log in to the Alexa app.

1. In settings, select **Reminders & Alarms.**

2. In the TIMERS tab, click on **Manage timer volume** to customize your choices.

This section is also where you can set an audio alert for notification of messages.

Music, Video & Books

Alexa supports several music services. Alexa can control your TV or video if your TV manufacturer or service provider has a skill. Alexa can also read books to you. These settings are found under "Music, Video & Books" as shown below.

1. Go to the menu and select **Music, Video & Books**.

2. Select your Music Service and follow the prompts to link your accounts.

3. Select Audible or Kindle for books.

4. In the video section, select "Fire TV" or your service provider.

To set a default music service select **Choose Default Music Services**. If you have a playlist called "Instrumentals" you can say "Alexa, listen to my playlist

Instrumentals." There are also music skills to connect to media services like SiriusXM.

Amazon's "Whispersync for Voice" switches seamlessly between reading Kindle books and listening to the companion "Audible" book.

Calendars

The Alexa mobile app supports Google, Apple, and Microsoft calendars.

1. Go to the menu and select **Calendars**.

2. Select Google, Apple, or Microsoft and follow the prompts to link your calendar to Alexa.

3. In the section "Alexa will add new events to this calendar," you can set your default calendar.

Configure Alexa with Apple Calendar

Two-factor authentication is used to configure your Apple calendar to work with Alexa. In a browser, visit http://appleid.com and sign in. In the Security section select "Generate Password." In the Alexa app follow the instructions to link your calendar.

Configure Alexa with Google Calendar

To set up your calendar to work with Alexa, download the Google Calendar app and log in. In the Alexa app, under settings, select "Calendar" and follow the prompts to link to your Google Calendar account.

"Alexa, what is my schedule for the day?"

Alexa Purchasing

Enable voice purchasing and set the voice code in the Alexa app. Alexa even remembers past orders to simplify purchasing. A voice code provides an added layer of security. When this feature is enabled, Alexa won't place an order without the code. The first time Alexa responds to a command on a commercial, it can be funny, but after that, you probably want to stop that behavior. The "Alexa Account" section of the app includes purchasing settings.

1.   Go to the menu and select Settings.

2.   In the section Alexa Account select **Voice Purchasing** and add a code.

Amazon offers Prime members the "Prime Now" service to order groceries. The Amazon "Restaurants" service provides food delivery in supported areas. The Amazon Key service for deliveries even has an in-car delivery option.

Events or Appointments

To create an event, say "Alexa, create an appointment." You'll see the appointment in the calendar you selected as your default calendar: Google Calendar, Apple or Outlook.

"Alexa, what's my schedule?"

With Siri devices say:

"Hey Siri, delete my Doctor appointment tomorrow."

Reminders, Alarms, and Timers

Next time I forget a birthday; I'm going to set a reminder for next year to buy a birthday gift, preferably for the week before the event.

"Alexa, remind me soccer is on Tuesday at 6 PM."

Check out the IFTTT applet "Blink your Hue lights when your Amazon Alexa timer hits 0."

Siri reminders are a great way to create app integrations. For example, I have an Apple reminder list called "Grocery." My grocery app is configured to use that reminder list. The list is also shared by my family, so that any family member can see the list on their Apple Watch, iPad, Mac, or iPhone. Details about the Apple "Reminders" app and the "Grocery" app are outlined in Chapter 12, "Apps."

Send Reminders to Phone

To enable notifications on your smartphone of Alexa reminders, enable the "Allow Notifications" setting. On your smartphone, go into iOS settings, select Notifications, select Amazon Alexa, and click on **Allow Notifications**.

Calling & Messaging

Calling and messaging apps are integral to Apple devices, but Amazon Alexa has a full line of features as well. Apps like IFTTT, and other smart home systems, use both calling and messaging to alert you to events. Chapter 13 showcases the IFTTT app.

Apple

The Apple messaging app supports typing or dictating traditional text messages, as well as Apple's "iMessages." Audio clips, emoticons, sending money with Apple Pay, handwritten messages, and sharing a map of your location, are also part of the Message app. At any point, you can tap your contact's name to start FaceTime, or e-mail your friend.

Look at Chapter 12 for details on the Apple "Messaging" app. There are dozens of messaging options, and the next list highlights a few.

- View a Contact's Location
- Start a FaceTime Audio or Video Call
- Save or Share Attachment

- Add Photos
- Camera Effects
- Digital Touch
- Handwritten Messages
- Use Apple Pay to Send & Receive $

Apple's Continuity Platform includes the "Handoff" feature. Handoff is a way to seamlessly switch tasks, like messaging, between your Apple Watch, iPad, Mac, or iPhone. Chapter 5 introduces Handoff.

Amazon Alexa

The Alexa mobile app and Echo devices allow you to send messages or place calls to other Alexa mobile apps or Echo devices in the US, Canada, or Mexico. At this time, the Android Alexa app also supports SMS text messaging.

To add Alexa calling that utilizes your existing land line service, plug the Echo Connect into a land line outlet. If you can normally make international calls, emergency service calls, or call non-Alexa phones, with Echo Connect Alexa can do that for you.

The light ring on the Echo will have a pulsing green light when you are receiving a call or Drop-in on your device. If you miss a call or there is a message waiting, the light ring will flash yellow.

A Voice Profile helps Alexa automatically identify the correct person who says, "Alexa, play my messages."

Learn more about voice profiles in the topic "Train Alexa to Recognize Your Voice."

Enable Conversations on Your Smartphone

The first step to use Alexa conversations on your smartphone is to enable calling and messaging in the Alexa app.

1.   Open the Alexa mobile app on your smartphone.

2.   Open the Conversations tab. Tap the speech bubble icon at the bottom of the screen.

3.   Follow the on-screen instructions to enter and verify your mobile phone information.

Your contacts need to do the same process on their smartphone, and then their names will show on your conversations tab.

Send a Message

Configure Alexa conversations in the Alexa app, and you're ready to send messages. For example, send a quick voice message saying dinner is ready to a contact that has Alexa conversations enabled.

"Alexa, message John."

"Alexa, play my messages."

Hold Calls or Do Not Disturb

If you do not want to receive calls or messages, turn on the Do Not Disturb feature for each Echo device. When Do Not Disturb is active, the light ring will flash **purple**.

"Alexa, do not disturb me."

"Alexa, turn off do not disturb."

1. On your smartphone, open the Alexa app.

2. From the Menu, select the **Echo device**.

3. Scroll down and enable **Do Not Disturb**.

4. Select Scheduled and enter a start and end time if you want to schedule **Do Not Disturb** automatically.

Place a Call

You can place a call to one of your contacts that has Alexa conversations enabled.

"Alexa, call John's Echo."

"Alexa, call John's mobile."

"Alexa, answer."

"Alexa, ignore."

Drop-in

The "Drop-in" feature is available on Echo devices, or smartphones that have the Alexa app. Everyone involved has to enable the "Drop-in" feature, as well as grant each specific contact the permission to drop-in.

Enable Drop-in

Your household members can drop-in to Alexa devices if you enable that setting on your smartphone in the Alexa app. When you drop-in on an Echo device you will hear everything in range of the device and have a two-way conversation.

1. On your smartphone, open the Alexa app.

2. Open the Conversations tab .

3. Go to Contacts .

4. Select **My profile** (your name).

5. Enable Drop-in.

Allow Specific Contacts to Drop-in On You

To allow your contacts to drop-in on your Amazon Echo devices enable it for each contact.

1.   On your smartphone, open the Alexa app.

2.   Open the Conversations tab from the bottom menu.

3.   Go to the Contacts section.

4.   Select the contact.

5.   Enable Drop-in.

Receiving a Drop-in or Call

The light ring on the Echo will have a pulsing green light when you are receiving a call or Drop-in on that device.

"Alexa, drop-in on the nursery."

"Alexa, answer."

"Alexa, ignore."

"Alexa, hang up."

See Recent Drop-ins or Conversations

Use the mobile app to see recent conversations or launch "Drop-in."

1. On your smartphone, open the Alexa app.

2. Click on Conversations 💬 to see the recent conversation history.

Select Who to Drop-in On

Another way to "Drop-in" to an Amazon Echo in another location is through the Accounts section.

1. On your smartphone, open the Alexa app.

2. Click on Conversations 💬.

3. Click on Accounts 👤 to see a list of contacts.

4. Select your profile (your name).

5. Select the Drop-in icon 🏠.

Alexa Skills

Alexa skills connect to other devices, websites, cloud services, and subscription services. When you visit the Skills page on https://alexa.amazon.com, the app suggests skills based on your Amazon purchases.

By setting up groups or routines, you can combine several devices or actions like these.

- MusicCast and a Yamaha Amplifier

- Hunter Douglas Blinds

- Subscription Services like SiriusXM

- Honeywell Thermostats

In the Alexa app, a "Smart Home Group" contains both devices and scenes, and allows you to control several devices.

"Alexa, turn off Smart Home."

A routine performs a series of actions with a single command. The actions could be turning on lights, checking weather or traffic, or adjusting a thermostat.

After you add a Smart Home skill, you can discover the new device and control it with your voice. Just say, "Alexa, discover new devices," or use the Alexa app.

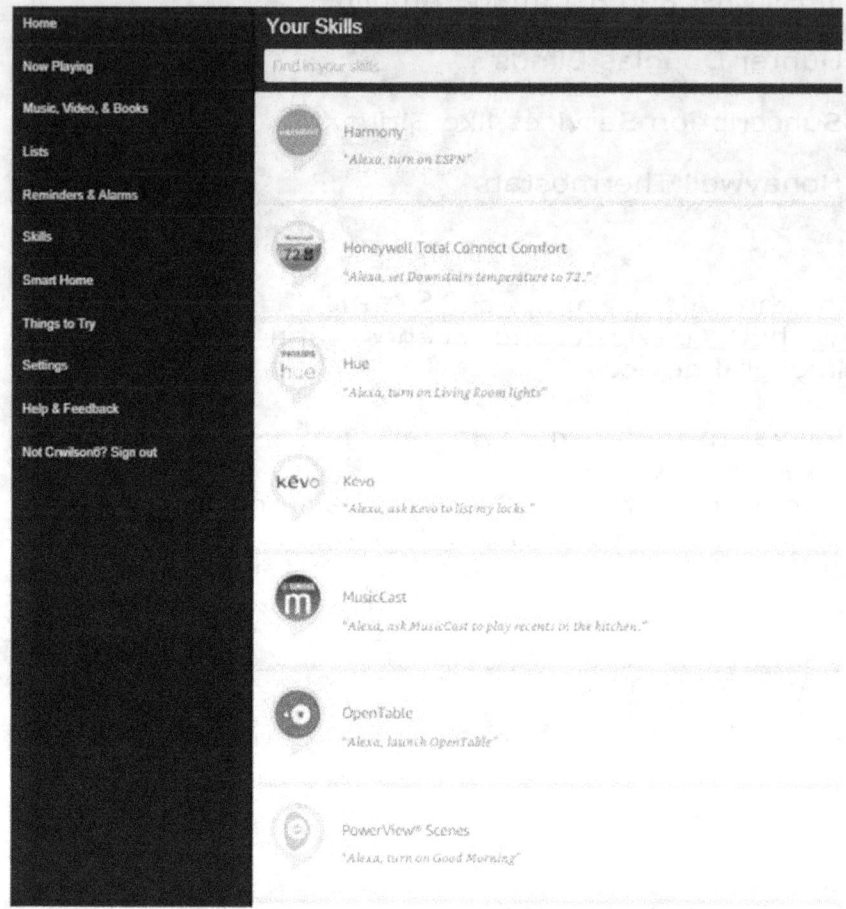

Figure 11.4   Alexa App - Your Skills

1. Open the Alexa mobile app, select the menu, and in the left sidebar click on **Skills**.

2. Search for the skill and follow the prompts to link Alexa. The Alexa app will then switch to the Smart Home screen.

3. Click Discover to locate the devices or scenes. Note that not all devices have scenes.

When your Honeywell thermostat is named "MyHome," you can say "Alexa, set the temperature at MyHome to 80."

Blueprints

Amazon introduced Blueprint templates in April 2018 for creating your own personal skills. Since the initial release of Blueprints, Amazon has steadily added more, such as:

- Houseguest

- Chore Chart

- Whose Turn

- Hallmark Holiday Greetings

- How Many Days (until my vacation!)

The first skill I set up was "Houseguest." I included our smart home phrases, trash days, and TV instructions. Honestly, I thought it was cute, but wasn't sure how useful it would be. My daughter texted me the first night she was house sitting, asking me to turn off the Hue bedroom lights. I forgot to include that command. There is no light switch for the HUE lights behind our headboard, and the lights automatically come on each evening. I learned a lesson from that experience. I need to record all my smart home commands somewhere for visitors too, not just if I sell my house.

The "Hallmark Holiday Greetings" blueprint walks you through the process of creating recording a message and uploading a custom background image. You share your skill with others so they can receive the card through their Alexa-enabled devices. The following list showcases a few Blueprints you may like.

11.2 Google Assistant

Since almost all non-Apple devices run some flavor of Google's Android mobile operating system, chances are those devices will also support the Google Assistant. Look for the Google Assistant in newer models of smart TVs and smart screens.

Activate Google skills is easy. For example, to connect to the skill "Out of Milk" say "OK Google, talk to "Out of Milk."

11.3 Siri

Siri isn't an app you download, but rather is a core part of the iOS operating system on your Apple iPhone, iPad, Apple Watch, or Mac. Siri is a personal virtual assistant, and with iOS 12, Siri is now an intelligent personal assistant. Siri monitors your schedule and calendar, suggesting relevant content throughout the day.

Intelligent Siri will update you on your favorite team's score, display one of your photos from a year ago, or recommend a playlist for your commute Home.

Note: Siri requires an Internet connection. Occasionally Apple's Siri servers are unavailable, so wait a few minutes and try again.

Siri is also perfect for controlling your iPad. You can ask Siri to send messages, place a call, or turn on a setting such as "Do Not Disturb."

Smartphones, tablets, smart speakers, headphones, cars, and more, all have personal virtual assistants. Amazon Echo, Google Home, Apple HomeKit, and Microsoft Invoke are examples of smart speakers that have virtual assistants.

Using virtual assistants requires a fundamental change in the way we interact with the world around us. Adopting a mindful approach can make the transition easier. Each week I set aside a few minutes and ask myself, "Can Siri do this task for me?" Then I spend a few minutes exploring what's possible today. I say "today" because the list of what these virtual assistants can do is changing daily. In this section, we'll look at these topics.

- What can Siri do?

- Enable Siri on Your iPad

- Ask Siri a Question

- Teach Siri About You

- Shortcuts

- Siri Doesn't Respond

What Can Siri Do?

Voice control, a mobile app, and a web application are all ways to control a virtual assistant. In addition to voice commands and app integrations, Siri "Shortcuts" combines several devices or apps into one command.

Enable Siri on Your iPad

In the ASK SIRI section, tap the "Listen for Hey Siri" switch to toggle Siri on or off.

1.   On your iPad, open the "Settings" app.

2.   Scroll down in the left sidebar and tap "Siri & Search."

3.   Tap the "Listen for Hey Siri" switch to toggle Siri on or off. The switch is green when on, and white when off.

Ask Siri a Question

There are two ways to ask Siri a question.

- On your iPad press and hold the Home Button.

- Say, "Hey Siri, call Michael."

Teach Siri about You

The more Siri learns about you, as you interact with her on your iPad, the better her responses will be. In Chapter 4, we discussed "predictive text," where Siri suggests words as you type, based on your previous searches, contacts, etc. Siri learns about you as you use apps like Safari, Photos, or Mail. When you use "Hey Siri," she'll get better at recognizing your voice. Before long Siri will be like an old friend, who knows your likes and dislikes.

Siri Shortcuts

In 2018 Apple introduced Siri Shortcuts were introduced in iOS 12, and already they are hugely popular. With Siri Shortcuts, you record a personal phrase in your app for a particular task. For example, say "Siri, open travel plans." The Siri Shortcut opens the Hotels.com app and displays your hotel photo, address, and check-in time. In this scenario, you recorded a Siri Shortcut in the Hotels.com app named "travel plans."

The list below shows a few apps that have announced plans to support Siri Shortcuts or have them available today. The Siri Shortcuts app shown in Chapter 12 allows you to combine several shortcuts.

- AirBnB

- Amazon Prime Video

- American Airlines

- App in the Air

- Bonvoy (Marriott/SPG)

- Booking.com

- British Airways

- Carrot Weather

- Caviar (Food Delivery)

- Dark Sky Weather

- Dexcom (Blood Glucose Monitor)

- ETA

- Grocery

- Hotels.com

- HotelTonight

- Kayak

- Lufthansa

- Smarter

- Trello

- VRBO

- Waze

I was very excited when Waze introduced a Siri Shortcut, in February 2019. To set up a Siri Shortcut open the Waze app, and search for a location like "Home." Tap the "more" button that looks like an ellipsis or three dots.

Tap "Add Shortcut" and record a personal phrase for Siri to launch Waze.

Earlier, we discussed the "Shortcuts" app for creating your own multi-step shortcuts, or third-party apps that support these "Siri Shortcuts." There is a third choice for shortcuts, found in the "Suggested Shortcuts" screen discussed in the next section.

Suggested Shortcuts

In the Settings app, in the left sidebar, tap "Siri & Search." In the "Suggested Shortcuts" section, in the right panel, tap "All Shortcuts." The default shortcuts for iOS are displayed. Tap any of these shortcuts to record your personal shortcut phrase.

Your Contact Card

Siri will customize your experience by using your Apple ID information in "Name, Phone Numbers, E-mail." Siri also uses information from your personal Contact Card. When you open the Contacts app, your personal contact card is at the top of the list, in the left sidebar.

Siri Phrases

- Text Michael.

- Show me directions to Walmart.

- How far away is Atlanta?

- Call Michael on the speaker.

- Read my last text message from Michael.

- Open the Waze app.

- Show me my timers.

- Show me the weather.

- Play music.

- Play "The Greatest Showman."

Siri Doesn't Respond

When Siri doesn't respond, check your internet connection. Wi-Fi and Bluetooth should both be active on your iPad. To check connectivity on your iPad, press the Home Button. Swipe up to see the Control Center. The status of connectivity is displayed.

1   Turn Siri off and back on.

2   Open "Settings," and in the left sidebar in the "General" section, turn Siri off and back on.

3   Turn off your iPad and turn it back on. Press and hold the Top Button, and touch and drag the slider to "Power Off" your iPad.

11.4 Samsung Bixby

Samsung connected devices include Bixby, as well as Samsung smartphones, tablets, the Galaxy Watch, and TVs. In 2019 Samsung plans to offer the Galaxy Home Smart Speaker. Bixby Vision tries to analyze what's in front of the camera.

Bixby Quick Commands are similar to IFTTT applets that combine multiple steps, events, and devices into one task. Bixby Routines also combine multiple connected things.

11.5 Verbal Commands or Phrases

There are so many Alexa commands that it's easy to be overwhelmed. Here I've grouped some of my favorite commands by the task – what I'm trying to accomplish. In addition to these built-in commands, check out the next section that covers skills you can add.

Deliveries

"Alexa, where's my stuff?"

"Alexa, ask UPS if I have any packages coming."

Do Not Disturb

"Alexa, do not disturb me."

"Alexa, turn off do not disturb."

Drop-in

To listen to an Amazon Echo device in another room, use the drop-in feature.

"Alexa, drop-in on the nursery."

IFTTT Applets

IFTTT applets begin with the phrase "Alexa, trigger."

IFTTT – Legrand Switches or Outlets

"Alexa, trigger turn on kitchen lights."

"Alexa, trigger turn on Christmas tree."

IFTTT – Locks

"Alexa, trigger lock doors."

Lighting

"Alexa, dim HUE lights to 50%."

Locks

The Kevo skill for Alexa can lock or unlock doors. The unlock feature requires an unlock PIN.

"Alexa, use Kevo to lock the family room door."

Listen to Music

"Alexa, connect to Bluetooth."

"Alexa, disconnect from Bluetooth."

Messages and Calling

You can send messages or call smartphones that have the Alexa app, and contacts that have signed up.

"Alexa, call John's Echo."

"Alexa, call John's mobile."

"Alexa, answer."

"Alexa, play my messages."

Music in the Alexa App

The Music, Video & Books section in the Alexa app lists service providers Amazon Music, Pandora, Spotify, iHeartRadio, Deezer, Gimme Radio, SiriusXM, Tunein and

Sonos Speakers. In addition, there are music skills from other manufacturers and service providers outlined in the next section.

Phone Calls

"Alexa, call John's Echo."

"Alexa, call John's mobile."

"Alexa, answer."

Printing

"Alexa, ask My Printer to print my shopping list."

"Alexa, print a hard Sudoku game."

"Alexa, print a Crayola coloring page."

Remember

Alexa can remember random facts for you.

"Alexa, remember Mom likes yellow daisies."

Switch Between Amazon Accounts

"Alexa, switch accounts."

"Alexa, which account is this?"

Temperature

"Alexa set the temperature at MyHome to 80."

Timer

"Alexa, set a pasta timer for 30 minutes."

Traffic

"Alexa, how is traffic to the airport?"

"Alexa, what's my commute?"

TV Commands

"Alexa, turn on the TV."

"Alexa, change the channel to CBS on the Family Room TV."

"Alexa, pause TV."

"Alexa, play TV."

"Hey Google, turn on Friends on Netflix with Chromecast."

12. Apps

In earlier chapters, I've mentioned a few apps that I use with Alexa or Siri for organizing my day. Now, I'll cover some of my favorite apps, and also mention a few categories of apps and the popular apps available today.

12.1 Calendar

The Apple Calendar 29 is the simplest way to display your schedule on your iPad. If you enable Family Sharing for iCloud, it creates a shared family calendar. In this section, we'll look at these topics.

- View Calendars
- Display Month View
- Add an Event
- Change or Share Calendars
- Sync Issues

View Calendars

1. On your iPad, open the Calendar app.

2. Firmly press the screen to see the options "Up Next," "List," or "Today" to change the calendar view.

Display Month View

1. On your iPad, open the calendar app.

2. Along the top of the screen, there are view options for Day, Week, Month, or Year views. Tap the screen to change views. Swipe to scroll through days.

Add an Event

In the top right corner of the app, tap the plus symbol to add an event to your calendar.

Change or Share Calendars

The bottom tab bar has options for the Today view, Calendars, or Inbox. Tap Calendars to see all your calendars.

To add a new calendar, tap "Add Calendar" in the bottom right corner of the pop-up menu. Tap the information symbol next to a calendar to see who the calendar is shared with, and set a color. Swipe to the bottom of the list to delete this calendar.

Customize Notifications

Calendar notifications are customizable, depending on the type of event and notification method. See Chapter 5 on Notifications.

1. Open the "Settings" app.

2. Swipe up and tap on "Calendar."

3. Scroll down and tap one of the options: Upcoming Events, Invitations, Invitee Responses, Shared Calendar Alerts.

Integration with Third-Party Calendar Apps

There are several integration options for third-party calendar accounts.

- Use a third-party app like Tiny Calendar.

- Add your other calendar account to your iPad calendar app.

- Setup the other calendar app to send alerts to your iPad. Every time you create an appointment set a reminder.

Add Accounts to Apple Calendar on Your iPad

1. Open the "Settings" app.

2. Scroll down to "Passwords & Accounts."

3. In the "Accounts" section, tap "Add Account."

4. Select Google and follow the login prompts. If you have trouble connecting your Google account, log in to your Google account from a web browser, and follow the prompts to set up an App password.

Add Accounts to Apple Calendar on Your Mac

You might find it easier to add a Google calendar to your Mac calendar, and then it will be available to your iPad.

1. On your Mac, launch your calendar.

2. On the "Calendar" menu, select "Preferences."

3. On the "Accounts" tab, click the plus symbol in the bottom left corner of the window to add your Google account.

Sync Issues

When your contacts or calendar are not correctly syncing, try a reset.

1.   Open the "Settings" app.

2.   Tap "General" and then tap "Reset."

3.   Tap "Reset Sync Data."

12.2 Contacts

The Contacts app does more than store your contact information. It is the central hub for communication. When you select a contact, you can initiate a message, FaceTime call, or FaceTime chat. You can also send mail, or send money with Apple Pay, or share your location.

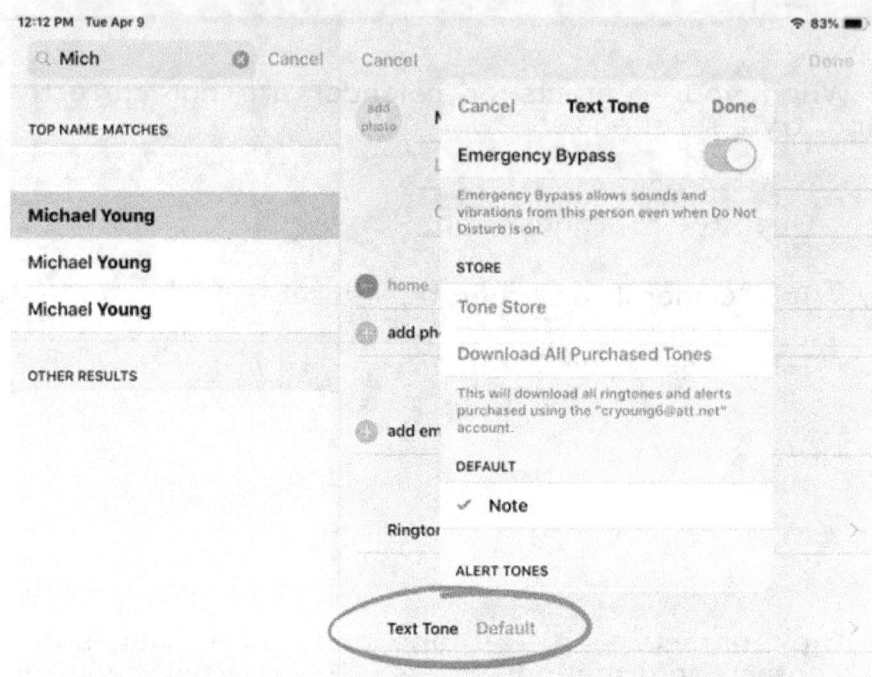

Figure 12.1   Contact Emergency Bypass

Your Contact Card

Siri will customize your experience by using your personal Contact Card. When you open the Contacts app, your contact card is at the top of the list in the left sidebar.

Enable Emergency Bypass

To allow emergency messages for a particular contact, open the Contact in the Contacts app. Tap "Edit" and then tap "Ring Tone" or "Text Tone." Tap "Turn on Emergency Bypass." See Chapter 5 for an example.

12.3 Drafts

The Drafts app is one of my favorite apps for dictation and note-taking. When an idea pops into my head, I tap the microphone to dictate a recording. The screen displays the transcription text of the recording as you are dictating. The Drafts app also works on my Apple Watch, so I always have it handy.

Another option to Drafts would be the Apple "Voice Memos" app with the "Transcribe" app.

On your iPad, open the Drafts app. From the main screen, tap the paper button in the top left corner of the screen to open the "Inbox" that lists your recordings. Tap a recording to see what actions are available. When a recording is open, in the top right corner, tap the "actions" button. Actions include Mail, Message, Share, Google Search, Calendar Events, List in Reminders, Print, and many more.

Actions are customizable and can be reordered. The first action in my app is "e-mail me," which opens an e-mail dialog with addresses I selected already entered.

Add a Custom Drafts Action

1. Open the Drafts app on your iPad. In the main screen, tap the actions button in the top right corner of the screen.

2. In the actions screen, tap the add button in the bottom right corner.

3. Tap the "Add New Action" button.

4. Tap the line under the "Identification" heading and enter a name for your action.

5. Swipe up and under the heading "Steps" tap the line that says "0 steps" to begin entering your steps or commands.

6. On the "Steps" screen tap the add button in the top right corner of the screen that looks like a plus symbol. Select the "Step Type." For an e-mail action, select a contact. You can add a subject and body text, or let the system generate it automatically from your recording.

7. In the top right corner, tap "Save & Exit."

Edit or Delete an Action

1. Open the Drafts app on your iPad. In the main screen, tap the actions button in the top right corner of the screen.

2. Tap to select an action and swipe left to right. Lift your finger, and the edit menu appears. Tap Delete.

3. To change the order of actions, tap to select an action, and drag it to a new location.

12.4 FaceTime

The Apple FaceTime app supports phone calls or video calls. FaceTime supports "Group FaceTime" for up to 32 participants, with the release of iOS 12. Ensure FaceTime is active in the Settings app on your iPad. In the left sidebar, swipe up and tap "FaceTime." Toggle "FaceTime" and " Calls from iPhone" on. If the option is greyed out, try restarting your iPad. On your Mac, open the FaceTime app and go into Preferences. Make sure "Calls From iPhone" is checked.

To start a FaceTime call, tap the profile picture to select a contact. While the contact is selected, tap the information icon to see these choices: Message, Call, FaceTime, or Mail. During a call, tap the microphone button to turn off sound. Tap the microphone again to turn sound on.

During a call, tap the screen to see the controls, then tap "Add Person." While on a call you can also add Camera Effects like stickers. See the topic "Messages" for details on Camera Effects. Switch to the rear-facing camera to share what's around you.

12.5 Files

The Files   app gives you access to your files. With iOS 12, this includes iCloud, Dropbox, Google Drive, Amazon Drive, or other providers. Turn the screen to landscape mode to see the left sidebar with Locations and Tags, as shown below.

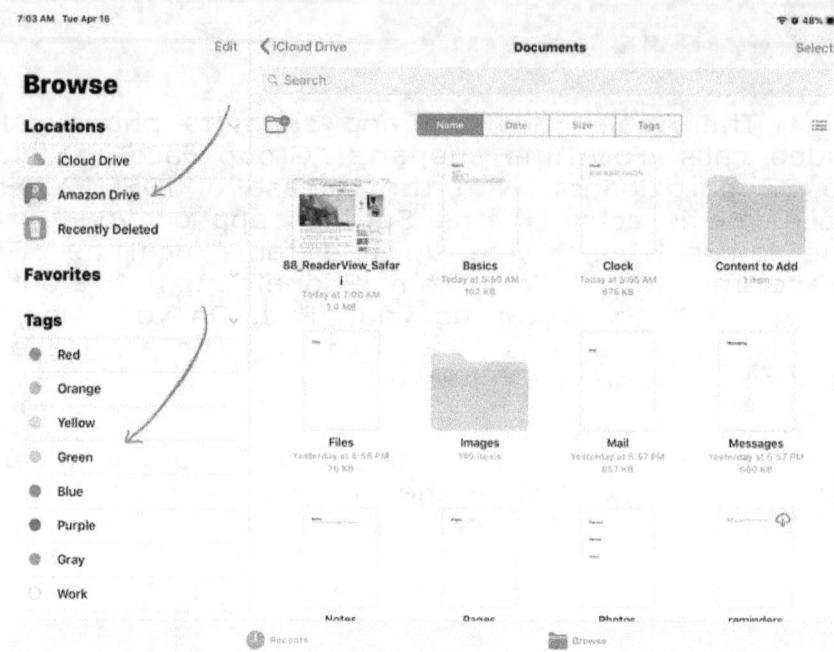

Figure 12.2   The Files App

Browse

Tap "Browse" in the bottom right corner of the screen. A sidebar window opens on the left with choices for locations, favorites, and tags. Locations can include cloud services like these. Swipe up to see more files.

- iCloud
- Amazon Drive
- Dropbox
- Google Drive

Search for Files

In the search bar, tap the "x" button on the right to start a new search. In the main window, touch the screen near the top and swipe down for options like Name, Date, Size, and Tags.

Note: Browse the App Store to find and install third-party apps like Amazon Drive.

Rename a File or Folder

To rename a file or folder touch and hold the file or folder name. This is true whenever you see a file name, whether it's a directory view, or while editing a file. This works on the Home screen, the Pages app, or in the Files app. For example, open the Files app and navigate to the file or folder you want to rename. Tap the filename and then type the new name.

New Folder

When browsing folders and files, touch the whitespace area for a few seconds until a pop-up menu appears. The choices are Paste, New Folder, or Info.

Move, Delete and More

To open a menu with additional commands, touch a folder for a few seconds until a pop-up menu appears. The menu commands include move, delete, favorites, and more.

Move Files and Folders While Scrolling

1. Touch and hold the file you want to move.

2. With the other hand, touch the screen and swipe.

3. Drop the file at the new location.

Copy, Move or Delete a Folder

Touch and hold the file or folder, then choose an option from the pop-up menu.

Share the File with Others

Touch and hold a file, then tap "Share." Select an app like Message or Mail, and the file is "attached" to your message. Select "Add People," and at the bottom of the menu, tap "Share Options." You can set specific access like "Anyone with the link," or "View Only."

12.6 Find My Friends

The "Find my Friends" app is one of the more advanced in terms of features. It shows where your friends are with a timestamp. A great security feature for teenagers, it's also handy when you're at a theme park, trying to coordinate rides or meals.

Say, "Hey Siri. Find Michael."

To add friends to the list, add them to the app.

1. Open the "Find Friends" app.

2. Tap "Add" to invite friends.

3. Press the "Home Button" to open the Home Screen.

4. Tap the "Find Friends" app.

5. Tap the name of your friend to see the time, location, and map of your friend's last known location.

Share Your Location with a Friend

1. Open the Find My Friends app, then tap Add.

2. Type the name of the friend.

3. Tap Send and select how long to share your location.

Get Location Notifications

Have you ever wondered if your spouse has left work yet? I don't want to seem like a stalker and nag my husband to tell me when he'd left work, but it's nice to know it's time to put dinner in the oven. The "Find My Friends" app has this eventuality covered. In the following example, I set up a notification when my spouse leaves a particular location; in this case, work.

1. Open the "Find My Friends" app.

2. Tap the friend you want to track.

3. Tap "Notify Me." Ensure you've selected the choice "The next time Michael: Leaves."

4. Tap "Other" and browse to select a location. Tap "Done" to create the notification.

5. Tap "More," and then tap "Choose Label" and then tap "Custom Label." Type a name for the label.

Arrival

Select a friend in the left sidebar, then tap "Notify Me" at the top of the screen. Tap "Arrival" and follow the prompts. To add a new location on a map, tap "Other." Touch and swipe on the map to find your location, then tap and hold to drop a pin and set that location.

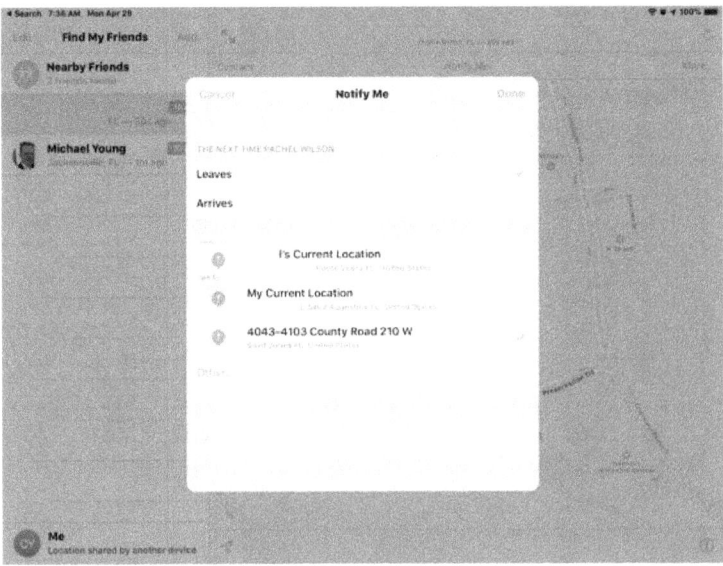

Figure 12.3   Notify Me of Arrival

12.7 Find My iPhone from Your Apple Watch

You may find the Apple Watch Control Center button "Find My iPhone" handy if you tend to misplace your iPhone as frequently as do I! Swipe up on your Apple Watch face and tap the button to sound an alert on your companion iPhone instantly. The blue button has an iPhone with signal bars. At night touch and hold the button to flash a light on your iPhone.

1. Swipe up on the Apple Watch face to open the Control Center.

2. Swipe up and tap the Find My iPhone button.

12.8 Grocery

Grocery shopping moves to the next level with apps like "Grocery." Tap the item to mark it complete. Firmly press the screen to "undo," "add," or switch to a different store. This app knows the route you take through the particular store and learns every time you shop.

The Grocery app uses the iOS reminders lists to store your shopping list. With a combination of iOS "Family Sharing" and an IFTTT applet that automatically links my Alexa shopping list with my iOS reminder lists, I can easily add items to my grocery list with Alexa, Google Home, or Siri. Everyone in our family can access our family shopping list on their Apple device.

Add Items to the List

Add items to your shopping list in your Mac or iCloud "Reminders." If you're like me, you use a virtual assistant to add items to your shopping list. Simply say, "Siri, add corn to my "Family reminders."

If you use another virtual assistant like Alexa, you can link your iOS reminders to the Alexa shopping list with an IFTTT applet, as shown below.

Enable Family Sharing

1. On your iPad, open the Settings app, and tap your name in the Apple ID banner.

2. Swipe and tap "Set up Family Sharing." Follow the prompts to invite contacts to join your family.

Share the List with Your Family

Family sharing is active on my iPad. My "Family" reminder list is shared with both my husband and daughter.

1. Open the Reminders app and tap the "Family" list. Any list would work, but in this example, we're using the "Family" list.

2. Tap "Edit" and then tap "sharing." Select a contact and click add (the plus sign) to send an invitation to join the family.

Use IFTTT to link iOS and Alexa

IFTTT will automatically sync your Apple reminder list when you add an item to your Alexa shopping list. First, enable the iOS and Alexa IFTTT services and link the services to your Apple and Alexa accounts. Second, create an IFTTT applet. Note that IFTTT also has services for other virtual assistants like Google Home or Microsoft Cortana.

1. In a browser, log in to your IFTTT account.

2. Click on "Services." Search for the service "iOS Reminders" and follow the prompts to link your account. Repeat the steps to link your Alexa account to IFTTT.

3. Click on the button to create a **New Applet**. IFTTT stands for "If This, Then That." Begin creating the applet by clicking on "This."

4. Choose the service "Alexa." Click on "Item added to your shopping list."

5. Now you want to select the trigger, which is what you want to happen whenever you add an item to your Alexa shopping list. In IFTTT terms, ask yourself, when I add corn to my Alexa shopping list, do I want IFTTT to do "that?" Click on "that" and select "iOS Reminders."

6. Complete the trigger fields by selecting "Add Reminder to List." Type your iOS list name, in this case, "Family." Click Save.

7. Tap "Settings", the gear button, to rename the IFTTT applet. Click "Save."

12.9 Health and Fitness

CARROT Fit motivates you with a glimpse into your no-exercise future and focuses on 7-minute workouts. The droll verbal abuse and sly humor are unique to this app; squats are called "Territory Markers." The Apple Watch extension adds real-time heart rate data.

Similar to Apple's "Breathe" app, the "Forest-Stay Focused" app has a unique approach to being mindful. Forest is hard to describe so I'd encourage you to check it out. There's a reason it's the #1 app in 113 countries. Headspace:Meditation is another app in this category. Recent research into the neuroscience of mindfulness shows deep breathing reduces stress and has long-term health benefits.

Featured by Apple in "New Apps We Love," Gymatic uses science to identify your exercises automatically, and count your repetitions. The LoseIt! and Yazio apps track exercise and/or calories. The "Utility" Apple Watch face has an option to add the "LoseIt!" complication. The complication shows me how many calories remain in my daily goal. Siri commands are available for the Yazio app. Say, "Siri, add breakfast."

Lifesum has won many awards with its app focused on healthy living that includes diet, exercise, and healthy recipes. Do you have a loved one who forgets to eat regularly? Lifesum diligently reminds you to eat and drink water and warns when your energy level is too low. Lifesum also has complications for your watch face.

You may wonder why the following list of health apps includes Panera. In an interesting twist, when you order a meal from Panera, the calories of your meal are included in HealthKit apps. The adorable characters in Standland make it a contender for the "Stand" activity.

- Calm
- Cardiogram
- CARROT Fit
- CVS
- Daily Yoga
- Forrest
- Gymaholic
- Gymatic
- Headspace (Meditation)
- Lifesum
- LoseIt!
- Map My Run
- My Fitness Pal
- Nike Run Club
- Paddle Logger

- Panera
- Pedometer
- Runkeeper
- Runtastic
- Seven
- Standland
- Streaks
- Strava
- WorkoutDoors
- YogaGlo

Strava is a social network created specifically for athletes. You configure devices like your Peloton bike within the Strava app. The next step is to configure the Strava app with your Apple Watch. Strava also has complications for your watch face.

1.   On your iPhone, launch the Strava app.

2.   Create an account.

3.   Follow the prompts to Connect a GPS watch or computer.

4.   To make changes, click the "More" button. Tap "Settings" and then tap "Applications, Services, and Devices."

5.   Select Apple Watch. The Strava app will walk you through the settings.

6.   In "Settings under Services," tap "Health" to connect with your Apple Health app.

In Chapter 9, I touch on the topic of Sleep. Although the Health app reminds you to set a consistent time to go to sleep, at this time, it doesn't monitor your sleep patterns. To track sleep today, you need a third-party app.

The benefits of quality sleep are you are more focused and have better blood sugar regulation. And most importantly, in my opinion, a fat-burning growth hormone is released while you sleep!

- Auto Sleep
- Sleep ++
- Sleepio
- Sleepmatic
- Sleepwatch
- Pillow

These sleep apps read your recorded health history. Once you have established a baseline of your sleep data, you can experiment with different apps to compare their insights.

12.10 Home App

With the Apple "Home" app   for your Mac, iPhone, and iPad, it is very convenient to control your smart home devices. Rooms and devices set as "Favorites" automatically appear in the "Home" app. In this section, we'll look at these topics.

- Home Automation

- Apple HomeKit Automation Platform

- Configure your iPad as a Home Hub

- Invite People to Join Your Home

- Configure Rooms and Devices for iPad

Because I think home automation is wonderful, I wanted to include a few examples of what home automation can do. Some of these examples use IFTTT and other third-party apps in addition to the Home app. At this point, I wanted to mention some possibilities. If you're interested in learning more, Chapter 7 includes additional information on setting up IFTTT and smart home apps.

- Alert When Doors or Cabinets are Opened

- Arrive Home

- Calendars

- Combine Motion, Lights, and Sound

- Deliveries & Visitors

- Adjust Shades When Temperature Changes

- Close the Garage Door When Severe Weather is Forecast

- Fire Alarm

- Leave Home (or Sleep)

- Refrigerator or Freezer Temperature Change

- Reminder to Buy a Birthday Gift

- Schedule Appliances for Off-Peak Times

- Shopping List

- Sports

- Surveillance

- Timer

- Traffic Commute

- Travel
- Turn on Christmas Lights
- Wake
- Weather

Home Automation

Smart home automation is composed of connected devices, skills, and cloud services. This automation involves more than mere devices in your home since smart home devices interact with the IoT world beyond your home. There are services available today that require only e-mail or text messaging to provide you the exact information you request when you request it. Here is an illustration of this technology: You step off the plane and receive an e-mail with a map of your location because you set up an IFTTT applet to send an e-mail with a map, when you entered the location of Maui, Hawaii. This illustration uses Geofencing and your tablet.

Combining smart devices has the most potential to add value to your smart automation lineup. The ability to combine multiple connected things is starting to appear in virtual assistants and mobile apps.

A few smart home categories include these topics:

- Lighting, Electrical, HVAC and Plumbing
- Security
- Outdoor: Garage, Lawn and Garden
- Home Entertainment
- Smart Speakers and Virtual assistants

- Window Coverings
- Smart Vacuums
- Cooking
- Printing

Apple HomeKit Automation Platform

Apple's HomeKit automation platform works with Philips Hue, Honeywell, August, First Alert, Lutron, Logitech, and others. Look for this logo to find HomeKit compatible devices.

Figure 12.4   Works with Apple HomeKit

Configure Your iPad as a Home Hub

Instead of purchasing an Apple HomePod speaker, you can configure some Apple TVs or iPads as a home hub to allow remote access to your accessories.

1. On your iPad, running iOS 10.3 or later, go to **Settings**.

2. Scroll down to Home and enable "Use this iPad as a Home Hub."

Invite People to Join Your Home

Apple can identify when everyone in the family has left home if you add members to your home in the mobile app.

1. Start the Apple Home app.

2. Select your home.

3. Invite people to join your home account.

Automation

To create a new Apple HomeKit automation for when people leave, choose the action everyone leaves.

Configure Rooms and Devices for iPad

1. Open the "Home" app on your tablet, smartphone, or Mac.

2. Double-click a room. Click on "Settings."

3.   Ensure the toggle "Include in Favorites" is turned on.

4.   Open the "Home" app On your iPad, and swipe to control rooms and devices.

Alert When Doors or Cabinets are Opened

As a tool to discourage our cats from opening (and climbing in) our kitchen cabinets, we use a Samsung sensor to detect when a door is open, and a motion sensor to detect movement. The alerts trigger an Aeotec Siren. The cats do not like the siren. I HATE the siren.

Arrive Home

When you arrive home, have your smart home turn off your security system, adjust the thermostat, open the shades, turn on lights and music, or stop surveillance camera recording.

Calendars

A virtual assistant makes adding events to your calendar a snap, but there are other ways to take advantage of calendar information. An IFTTT applet, for instance, can flash your lights when a calendar event is approaching. Or it can send notifications to remind you of events.

Combine Motion, Lights, and Sound

There are mobile apps that integrate smart lights and music, and the apps trigger lights to move to the beat. Alternatively, sensors detect an event and cause the device to react with sound and lights. Sample applications of this technology include alerts of intruders, fire, or water leaks.

Deliveries & Visitors

A smart home with a camera and smart lock means you no longer have to sit at home all day waiting on a delivery. You can remotely view and talk to visitors, workers, or delivery people and unlock doors.

With a UPS Smart Choice account, you can sign a delivery release and provide a garage code for the UPS delivery driver. UPS will send text alerts to your smartphone.

Adjust Shades When Temperature Changes

Temperatures on windows can change drastically when the sun is shining directly on them. One solution to this problem is temperature sensors and smart shades working together to adjust the shade position automatically as needed.

Close the Garage Door When Severe Weather is Forecast

At our old home, wind-driven rain would pool in one corner of the garage if the door was left open during a storm. Even if you don't automatically close the door when a storm approaches, a friendly reminder that the door is open could be helpful.

Fire Alarm

When a fire alarm is triggered, a smart home automatically turns on lights inside, flashes outside lights for first responders, plays loud audio, opens the garage door, turns on sprinklers and notifies emergency services and contacts.

Leave Home (or Sleep)

It is a bit tricky to define when you have left home. There are automotive sensors, arrival sensors, or location services. The challenge is deciding what defines "away." What if one person leaves and someone else is home that day?

The Apple Home app uses iPhones, registered to family members, to determine if everyone in the family is away. Here are several things your smart home can do when you are away.

1. Close the shades.

2. Adjust the thermostat.

3. Turn off the lights.

4. Lock the doors.

5. Close the garage door.

6. Turn off the TV.

7. Turn off all speakers.

8. Call my cell phone with the weather from Weather Underground and IFTTT.

9. Turn on the security system.

10. Report traffic for your commute.

Refrigerator or Freezer Temperature Change

My kids are grown, so I don't have to worry that they left the refrigerator door open. When on vacation, however, I would appreciate an alert that there was a temperature change at home, or that the freezer lost power.

Reminder to Buy a Birthday Gift

For once, I won't forget to buy a gift, because it is easy to ask Siri to set a reminder for me.

Schedule Appliances for Off-Peak Times

Smart appliances use a schedule and integration with other systems to identify non-peak times of electrical use or to start cycles. Some utility companies, in fact, have conservation programs for electricity use during non-peak times.

Shopping List

One of the handiest things Siri can do is add items to a shopping list. With a smartphone or tablet, you can easily print the list, e-mail a copy, or access the list from the mobile app. In Chapter 7, I outline the "Grocery" app that integrates with family sharing using reminder lists.

Sports

There are IFTTT channels like ESPN that can automatically add your team's games to your calendar. If you're wondering when the next game is or what the final score was, Siri can answer your questions.

Surveillance

Smart cameras and motion sensors provide home surveillance. Another option is to set up your spare smartphone as a surveillance camera with IFTTT and the smartphone app "Manything" to catch your resident cookie thief or the dog getting into the trash.

Timer

Virtual assistants are perfect for setting times for cooking or reminders. Take timers a step further with IFTTT applets to flash lights when the timer reaches zero.

Traffic Commute

Ask Siri for traffic information for your daily commute, or trips to the airport. Create a Siri Shortcut in the Waze app.

Travel

Travel can be grueling, so I'll try anything that makes it less of a hassle. There are travel apps where you enter a destination, and the apps use Geofencing to send you a map of your location when you enter an area. The "Maps" app and Waze app alert you to traffic and road hazards.

Turn on Christmas Lights

Set outdoor lights to be controlled by a WeMo smart electrical outlet programmed to turn on and off at certain times. An interior smart wall outlet is handy for Christmas tree lights.

Wake

Why not take advantage of all your smart devices to kick start your morning routine? The next list includes some ideas for reminders and controlling your home.

- Take medicine.

- Turn on lights and music.

- Adjust thermostat.

- Start heating water for showers.

- Make coffee.

- Read appointments.

- Reminder to allow extra time on your commute if you need to stop for gas.

- Set a timer for 5 minutes before departure time, and flash lights as a reminder to kids that it's almost time to leave.

Weather

The IFTTT weather applets are powered by Weather Underground and include some interesting recipes.

- Send weather reports.

- Send e-mails when the UV Index is high.

- Send notifications of high pollen counts.

- Change the color of lights when snow or rain is forecast.

12.11 Mail

Because e-mail is an integral part of today's smart home and IoT world, I wanted to cover the basic mechanics of an e-mail app. In this case, my examples are based on the Apple Mail app.

In addition to reading mail, you can reply, delete, flag, or mark a message unread. In this section, we'll look at these topics.

- Your Mailbox

- Create an e-mail

- Read and Reply to an e-mail

- Delete an e-mail

- Searching e-mail

- Manage Mailbox Folders

- Set VIPs

- Mail Options

- Recover a Deleted e-mail

- Set Mail Notification Options

- Flag Style

- Signature

- Default Font Size

Your Mailbox

The Mail app displays your mailboxes in the left sidebar, and you read mail messages in the right pane. Your mailbox has several default folders: inbox, trash, drafts, and sent.

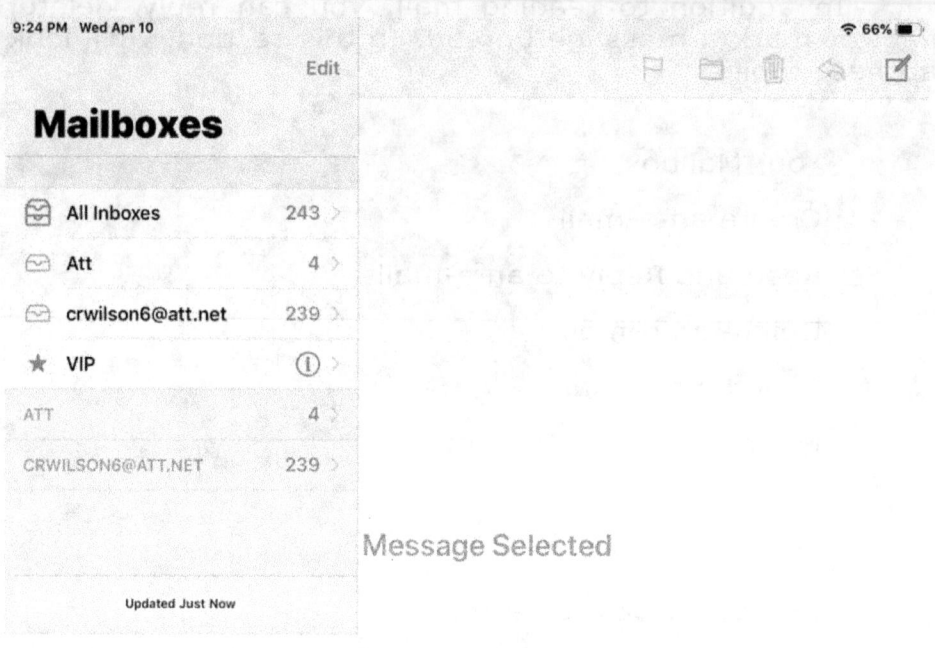

Figure 12.5   The Mail App

The toolbar in the top right corner has these tools.

tia

Flag

Mailboxes

Trash

Reply, Forward, Print

Compose

Create an e-mail

Tap the compose button in the top right corner, to create a new e-mail.

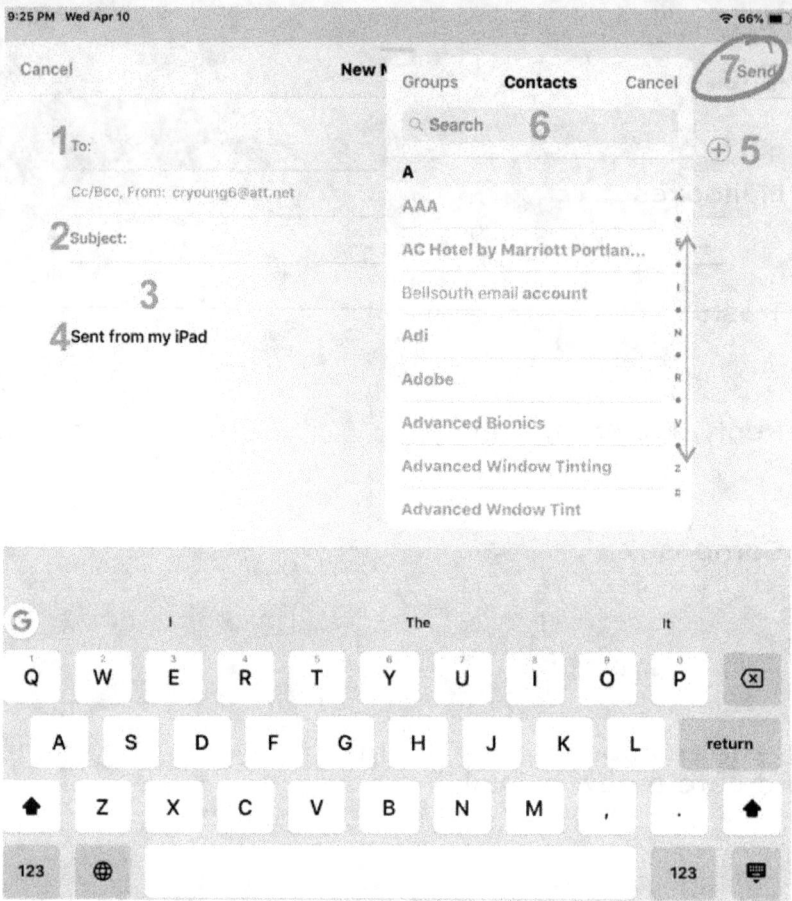

Figure 12.6   Create a new e-mail

1.   Enter an e-mail address. Tap the ⊕ plus symbol to search contacts.

2.   Add a subject.

3.   Type the body of the e-mail.

4.   This is your default signature. Later in this chapter, we'll cover how to change your default signature.

5.   Tap add to open a window to browse your contacts.

6.   To search for a contact name into the name in the Search box.

7.   Tap "Send" when you're ready to send the message.

Read and Reply to an e-mail

1.   On your iPad, press the Home Button.

2.   Swipe and tap "Mail."

3.   Swipe to scroll.

4.   Tap to read the message.

5.   In the top right corner, tap the arrow to "Reply."

Delete an E-mail

To delete an e-mail in your inbox, touch the message in the left sidebar and swipe left. To select multiple messages, tap "Edit," and then tap "Trash."

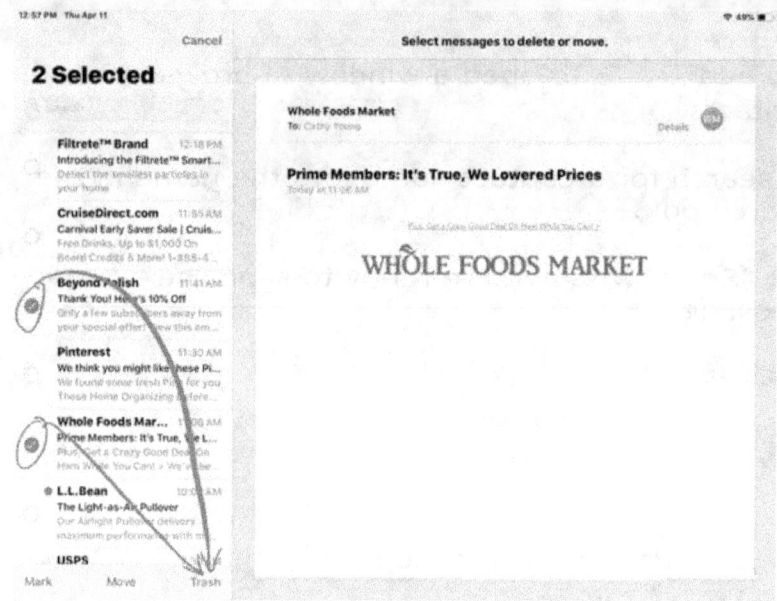

Figure 12.7   Delete Mail

Searching e-mail

To see the "Search" box, touch in the middle of the left sidebar and swipe down.

Manage Mailbox Folders

Each mailbox has several mailbox folders, as shown below in the left sidebar: inbox, trash, drafts, sent.

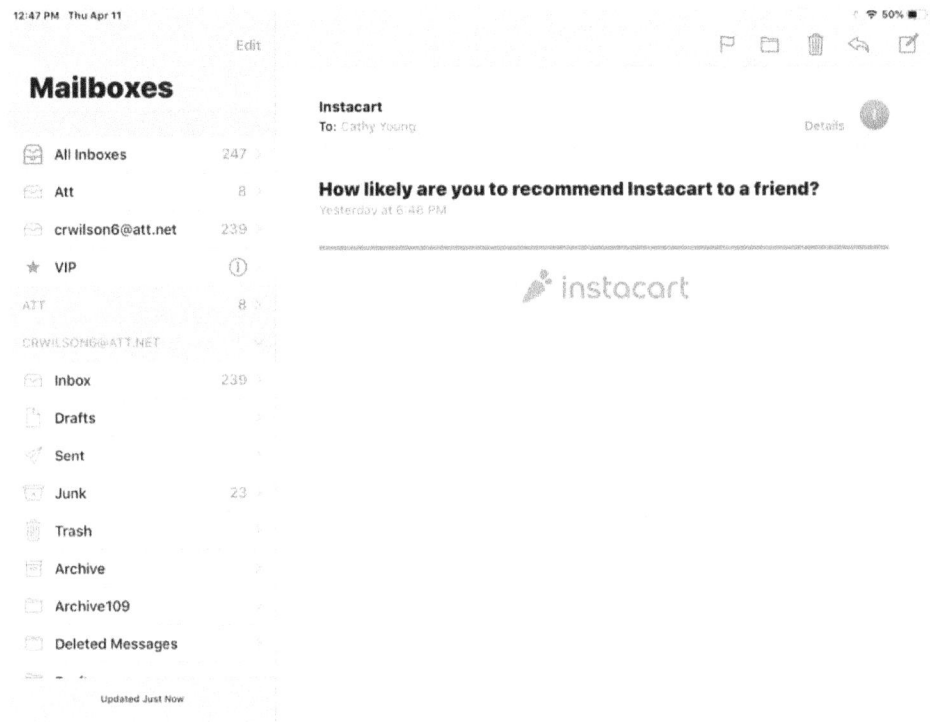

Figure 12.8   Mailbox Folders

Swipe up or down in the left sidebar to see all the mailboxes.

For some mail accounts, you can add a folder within the mail app.

1.   Go to the top level of the mailboxes, and then tap the "Edit" menu.

2.   Tap "New Mailbox" to create a folder.

Mail accounts from ATT.net require you to create mailbox folders within its app or to use an app like Outlook.

3. Tap "Edit" to manage mailbox folders. Tap the folders you want to see in the left sidebar view of the mailboxes, and then tap "Done."

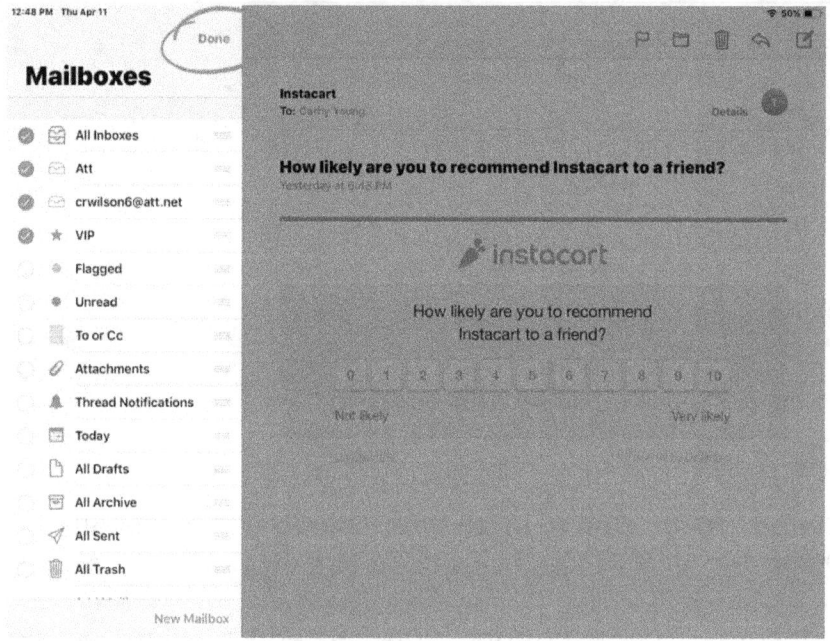

Figure 12.9   Editing Folders

Set VIPs

1. Open the Mail app.

2. In the section Mailboxes, in the sidebar on the left side of the screen, tap VIP.

3. Tap "Add VIP" and choose a contact. If you don't see "ADD VIP" open a mail message from a different contact.

4. Tap "VIP Alerts" to configure notification banners, sounds, and previews.

Mail Options

Select a message and swipe left to see "More" options like reply, forward, mark, notify me, or move the message.

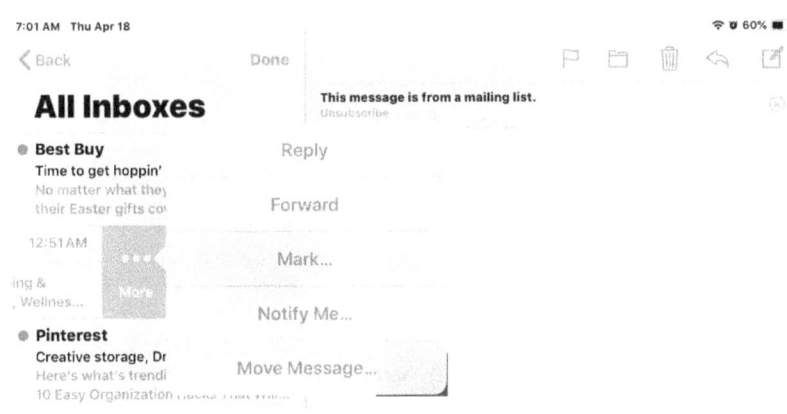

Figure 12.10   More Mail Settings

The "More" choices displayed when you swipe are configurable in the Settings app, in the section "Mail." Tap "Swipe Settings" to choose options.

Recover a Deleted E-mail

Deleted e-mails are in your "Trash" mailbox. In the left sidebar, select your mail account, and then tap the "Trash" mailbox to find your message. If you don't see the "Trash" mailbox, follow the steps outlined earlier to change which mailboxes are displayed.

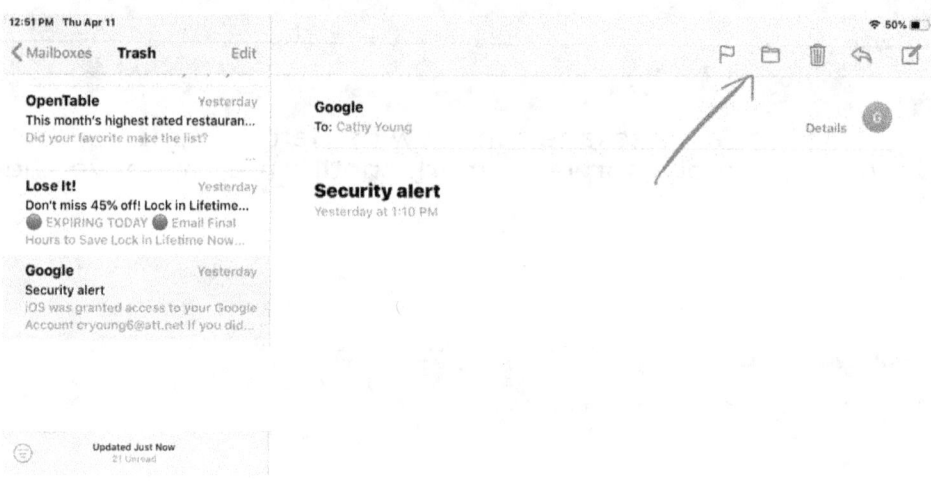

Figure 12.11   Use Folders

Select your message, then move it to another mailbox folder. In this example, we will move the e-mail from "Trash" back to the "Inbox" mailbox folder.

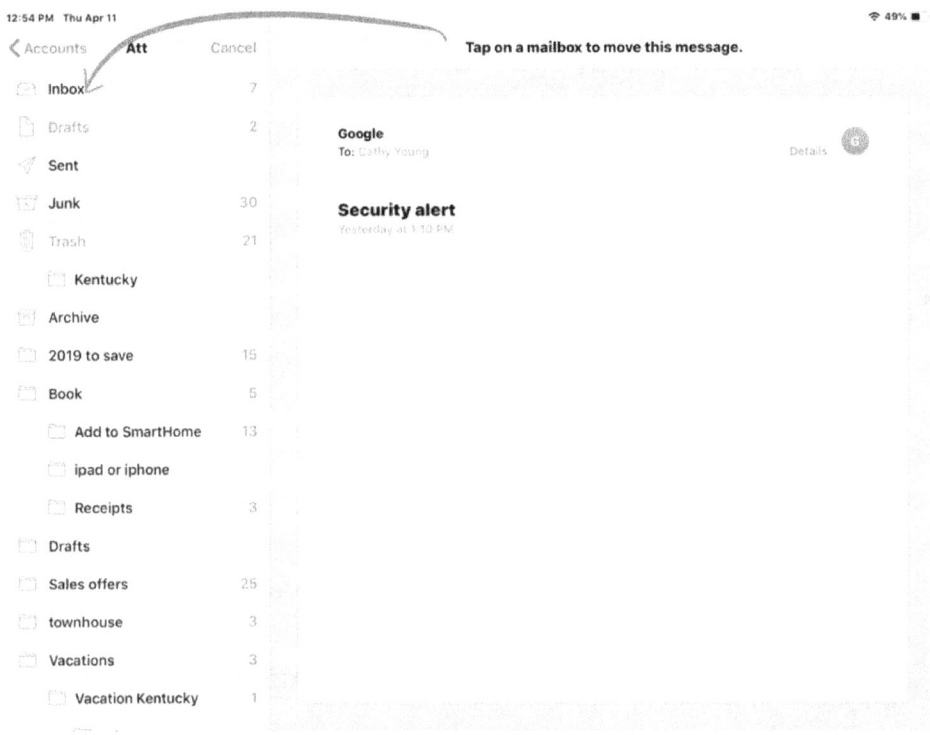

Figure 12.12   Moving E-mails to Folders

Set Mail Notification Options

In addition to notifications for each of your e-mail accounts, you can set preview and other options in the mail settings. For example, the "VIP" option ensures you are alerted only when you receive an e-mail from someone you've marked as important.

1. Open the "Settings" app on your iPad.

2. Scroll down and tap "Mail."

3. Tap "Allow Mail to Access: Notifications."

Flag Style

Use the "Settings" app to set the style for mail flags.

1. Open the "Settings" app on your iPad.

2. Scroll down and tap "Mail."

3. In the "Message List" section, tap "Flag Style."

4. Select the "Flag Style" color or shape.

Signature

In the earlier figure, the default signature was "Sent from my iPad." To change your signature open the "Settings" app. In the left sidebar, tap "Mail" and then in the right panel tap "Signature" and choose the options you want. The default signature is "Sent from my iPad."

Default Font Size

To adjust the font size for e-mails, open the Settings app, and tap "Display & Brightness." Tap "Text Size" and use the slider to select the size you want.

12.12 Maps

Earlier when we discussed Location Services and Geofencing, we touched briefly on maps. The Apple Map app is linked to many of the other Apple iOS apps, and I use this cross-platform app every day. A few of my favorite features follow.

Have you wondered what the ⬆️🛡️ Map application can do? If you're not familiar with the Maps app, you're in for a surprise.

* Show your location on the map.

* Search for a business, then tap to create or update a contact card.

* Search for a business and see the location on a map. Siri will also prompt you with step by step directions when navigating.

The Maps app is integral to iOS apps. Apps like Messages, Mail, Contacts, and Safari will open the Maps app when you tap an address. Both the "Find My Friends" and "Find My iPhone" apps have a map window. In this section, we'll look at these topics.

- Navigation

- Find an Address for a Contact

- Searching for a Location

- Zoom In or Out

- Pins

- Tab Views and Traffic

- Map Notifications

Navigation

Press the Home Button to open the Home Screen, swipe, and tap "Maps." A map opens, and a blue dot indicates your current location.

Tap the "Location" button in the top right corner of the screen, to center the map with your location in the middle of the screen. Pinch the screen to zoom in, or spread your fingers to zoom out. The top of the map is North. Tap the location symbol again to return to North at the top of the map.

Touch the screen with two fingers and rotate your hand to turn or rotate the map.

To measure distances between two locations, I use a third-party app like Google maps.

Find an Address for a Contact

To find the address of a contact, open the Contacts app. Tap the address, and the Maps program opens to that location. In the left sidebar, tap "Directions." An overlay panel opens. At the bottom of the panel in the tab bar, tap "Drive," "Walk," or "Transit.

Searching for a Location

The sidebar on the left side of the screen has search options. Tap a button to find nearby food, drinks, shopping, travel, services, fun, health, or transport.

In the following example, after searching for "Sherwin Williams," the options in the sidebar on the left change. Tap the phone number to call the business, or tap the web site to open the page in Safari.

Swipe up in the sidebar to see additional options like "Add to Contacts."

Figure 12.13   Searching Maps

For directions to a particular location, tap "Directions," then scroll down and choose Drive, Walk or Transit, then tap Go.

Zoom In or Out

Use two fingers to pan or zoom on the map. You can also Double-tap and hold, then drag up or down.

Pins

To add a pin, tap the map and hold till you see a pin, then release. Tap the pin to see details about the address including latitude and longitude information. You can also share or favorite the location. Tap "Edit Location" to position the pen at an exact location.

Tab Views and Traffic

Tap the info button to switch between Map, Transit, and Satellite views. The "Map" view has an option to toggle on "Traffic." When the "Satellite" view is active, you can also tap "3D" in the top right corner of the screen, to change to a 3D map rendering.

At the bottom of the tab view are options to add a place, or mark your location. When done, tap the "x" in the top right corner of the screen.

To find the current location of a contact, use the Find Friends or Messages app.

Map Notifications

1. Open the "Settings" app.

2. Tap "Notifications."

3. Swipe up and tap "Maps."

4. Tap to enable "Allow Notifications," "Show Previews," or select a Banner Style.

12.13 Messages

Messages between apps and devices are a core part of your Internet of Things, so I wanted to cover how to use a Message app. In my case, I use Apple's Message app. Once I got started writing, I had a difficult time deciding how much information to include. The end result is I covered everything I could think of. You can just ignore the parts you're not interested in.

Apple's Messages app supports typing or dictating traditional text messages, as well as Apple's "iMessages." Audio clips, emoticons, sending money with Apple Pay, handwritten messages, and sharing a map of your location, are also part of the Message app. At any point, you can tap your contact's name to start FaceTime, or e-mail your friend. In this section, we'll look at these topics.

- iMessage
- iPhone Text Messages on This iPad
- Create a Message
- Dictate
- Read a Message
- Deleting Messages
- View a Contact's Location
- Start a FaceTime Audio or Video Call
- Reply to a Message
- Save or Share Attachment
- View a Message Timestamp
- Add Photos
- Markup a Photo
- Emojis
- Camera Effects
- Digital Touch
- Full-screen Effects
- Handwritten Messages
- Invisible Ink Effects
- Use Apple Pay to Send & Receive $
- Deleting Messages
- Options

- Message Alerts
- Blocked Contacts

The following is a list of the controls and icons we'll be discussing with a brief description as a reference.

 New Message

 Globe (Select Keyboard)

 Camera

 Handwriting

 Pencil

 Activity (Screen Effects)

 Camera effects

 Microphone

 Eraser

Lasso (to move the object)

Highlight

Signature, Text Boxes, More

More

Markup

Digital Touch

Animated GIFs

iMessage

iMessages allow you to send to an e-mail address if that contact has an Apple device. Apple iMessages include Digital Touch and other Apple features. Blue bubbles indicate iMessages, while regular text messages are green. In the U.S., **business chat** messages are dark gray. The bubble with three dots means the other person is typing. iMessages can include the following features, as well as content from other apps like Carrot Weather or Drafts.

- Photos
- Digital Touch
- Videos
- Handwriting
- Camera Effects
- Dictation
- Apple Pay to Send Cash
- Bubble Effects
- Invisible Ink
- Full-Screen Effects

Note: In the Settings app, in the "Mail" section, you can choose how long to keep messages. Your message history is also stored in iCloud.

iPhone Text Messages on This iPad

Open "Settings" then tap "Messages." Toggle "iMessage" on or off. In the section "Send & Receive," verify your Apple ID and SMS phone number.

Setup Your iPhone

You may see a pop-up to automatically setup iPhone text message forwarding to your iPad, as shown below.

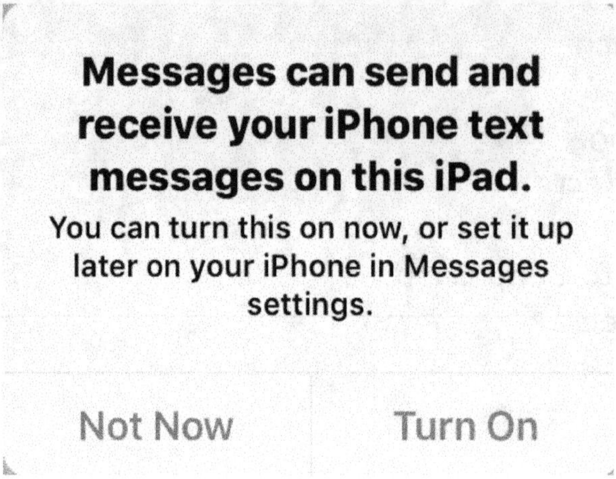

Messages can send and receive your iPhone text messages on this iPad.

You can turn this on now, or set it up later on your iPhone in Messages settings.

Not Now   Turn On

Figure 12.14   iPhone Text Message Forwarding

To manually set up text message forwarding on your iPhone, use the Settings app as outlined below.

1.   On your iphone, open the "Settings" app and tap on "Messages."

2.   Tap "Text Message Forwarding" and select your iPad.

3.   Your iPhone must be on and connected to a Wi-Fi or cellular network.

Create a Message

1.   Press the Home button to open the Home Screen.

2.   Swipe and open the "Messages" app.

3.   Tap the "New Message" button.

4.   Choose a contact , type a phone number, or dictate a phone number.

5.   Type your message and add content

6.   Touch the Share button for a few seconds to add Effects.

7.   Digital Touch , animated GIFs, Photos, and more are available in the App Drawer. The App Drawer is below the text area. The next section includes instructions to mark up your photos.

7. When done, tap the Share button 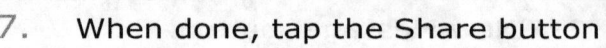 .

Compose
New Message

The App Drawer

Figure 12.15   New Message

As you write, Siri will suggest predictive text options, as outlined in Chapter 4. Tap a suggestion and then tap "Send" to send the message.

Dictate

Tap the microphone button , dictate your message, then tap "Done." You can also verbally add punctuation. For example, "Did it arrive question mark." The dictation tool is many apps. Chapter 3 has additional information on Dictation.

Read a Message

Open the "Messages" app and tap your friend's name in the left sidebar. Swipe up or down in the right panel to see previous messages from that contact. If you swipe up, you'll see all images or attachments ever sent in this conversation.

At the top of the screen, tap your contact's name to see options for Audio, FaceTime or their Info. Info about your contact includes their current location if they are sharing their location with you. There are also options to Hide Alerts or Send Read Receipts.

- Reply
- Details
- Send Location
- Choose Language

Deleting Messages

To delete a message, select the message in your inbox, and swipe left. Click on the trash can symbol. To delete several messages, tap "Edit" to select multiple messages, and then tap "Delete."

View a Contact's Location

While reading a message, tap the contact's photo, in the middle of the page at the top. Tap the info button for location and alert options.

Start a FaceTime Audio or Video Call

While reading a message, tap the contact's photo in the middle of the page at the top. Tap the Audio button to start an audio-only call. Tap the FaceTime button to start a video call.

Reply to a Message

Select a message and tap one of the buttons to reply. Tap the microphone to dictate your response.

Save or Share Attachment

Tap a photo, contact, or attachment to open it.

In the top right corner, tap the ⬆️ Share button for options to save or forward the photo or attachment.

View a Message Timestamp

To see when a message was sent, touch the message bubble and swipe left.

Add Photos

Tap the Camera control 📷 to take a new photo.

To select an existing photo, tap Photos in the App Drawer, at the bottom of the screen.

Markup a Photo

Tap the Markup control when viewing a photo to draw, highlight, or add lines, chat bubbles, text boxes, and a signature. The markup toolbar appears along the bottom of the screen with the pencil, pen, highlighter, eraser, and lasso drawing tools. Markup is discussed in Chapter 4.

Emojis

Emojis are tiny symbols. In addition to Emojis, you can reply with a sticker. Stickers include handwritten responses. Tap the emoji button, swipe, and tap "Stickers."

Camera Effects

Camera Effects are new in iOS 12 and include tools for drawing, adding text or stickers, and more. You will only see Camera Effects when you are using the Messages or FaceTime app with your camera.

When you tap the Camera Effects button, a toolbar opens in the bottom left corner of the photo. The choices are:

- Apply a Filter
- Add a Text Label
- Add Stickers (if available)
- Add a Shape

1. Tap the camera  when creating a message to see Camera Effects in action.

2. Take a photo, and the editing window opens, as shown below.

Figure 12.16   Camera Effects in Messages

Photo editing tools are located along the right edge of the screen.

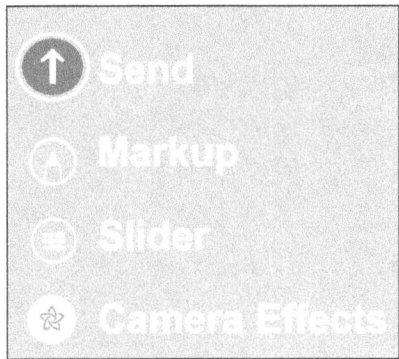

Figure 12.17 Camera Effects Toolbar

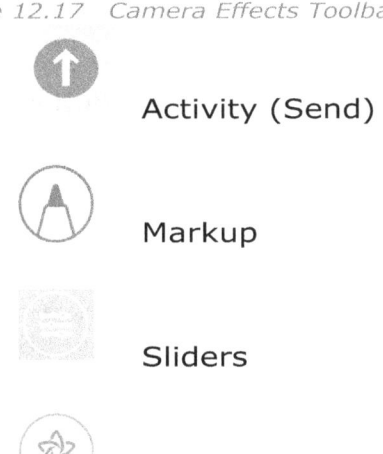

Activity (Send)

Markup

Sliders

Camera Effects

Tap the Camera Effects button to open the Camera Effects toolbar. The Camera Effects toolbar is displayed in the bottom left corner of the screen.

Figure 12.18 Camera Effects Toolbar

 Shapes

 Text Label

Filters

Digital Touch

Digital Touch is a fun way to include animation or sketches in your messages. Digital touch is only available if the recipient also has an Apple device with iMessages set up.

When you send friends a Digital Touch message, they also receive a Haptic (wrist tap) response if they are wearing an Apple Watch. This is a new take on the idea of reaching out and touching someone.

1. On your iPad, press the Home Button.

2. Swipe and then tap "Messages."

3. Start a new conversation or continue an existing conversation.

4. Tap the button for Digital Touch in the App Drawer at the bottom of the screen.

To Show Emotion Try These Digital Touch Options.

Send a Kiss: Tap two fingers on the screen.

Send your Heartbeat: Touch two fingers to the screen until you see and feel your heartbeat.

Break a Heart: Touch two fingers to the screen until you see and feel your heartbeat, then drag down.

Show anger: Touch and hold one finger on the display till you see a flame.

Sketch: Draw on the screen.

Full-screen Effects

Screen effects include balloons, confetti, and fireworks, to name a few.

1. Type your message normally.

2. Firmly press the "Activity" button to open the Effects menu.

3. At the top of the screen, the "**Send with effect**" tab menu has "Bubble" or "Screen." Tap "Screen" and then swipe left or right to choose one of these "Send With" options.

- Love
- Confetti
- Spotlight
- Balloons
- Lasers

- Fireworks
- Bubbles
- Shooting Star
- Celebration
- Echo

In the example below, "Balloons" are selected.

Figure 12.19   Balloon Effects

Handwritten Messages

Use the handwriting tool  to send animated handwriting. Turn the iPad, so the screen is in landscape mode. Select the handwriting tool, located side of the space bar of the on-screen keyboard. The tool is only available in iMessage conversations.

Figure 12.20   Handwriting

Invisible Ink Effects

The  Activity menu opens Effects that include a Bubble Effect for invisible ink, as well as Slam, Loud, and Gentle options.

1. Type your message normally.

2. Firmly press the "Activity" button to open the Effects menu.

3. Tap "Invisible Ink." The message is blurred until the recipient swipes on the bubble.

Use Apple Pay to Send & Receive $

With Apple Pay, you can send or receive money. Apple Pay is available on your iPad if you've enabled "Apple Pay Cash" in your Apple Wallet app on your iPad. If you've added "cash" to your account, you can send cash to friends or family in a message.

1. On your iPad, press the Home Button.

2. Swipe and tap "Messages."

3. Start a new conversation or continue an existing conversation.

4. Tap the button for Apple Pay in the App drawer at the bottom of the screen.

5. Select an amount to send using the plus or minus symbol.

6. Tap "Pay."

Options

Force touch the screen to view the message options. The "Details" option displays contact information. The Details option has choices to phone, text, or e-mail the contact.

- Reply
- Details
- Send Location
- Choose Language

Message Alerts

Message alerts can be set never to repeat, repeat once, twice, three times, five times, or even ten times.

Blocked Contacts

To block messages from a particular phone number open "Settings," swipe up in the left pane and tap "FaceTime." Tap "Blocked" and add a phone number. The phone number is blocked in both FaceTime and Messages. Swipe left on a phone number to remove it from the list of blocked contacts.

12.14 Music

With the Apple Music   app, you can listen to songs, albums, playlists, or artists. There are two options for playing music: either stream music over Wi-Fi or cellular or download music to your iPad.

Your "Library" can also include songs from your personal iTunes music library on your computer. This includes CDs that you own or any source that doesn't use copy protection. We'll cover how to sync these types of songs later. We cover these topics in this section.

- Play Music
- Radio Stations
- More Song Options
- Use Audio Output with iPad
- Change Volume with the Volume Buttons
- Create a Playlist
- Add Songs You Already Own to Your Library
- Sync iTunes Library With iPad
- Download Music
- Check Available Space

Play Music

1. On your iPad, press the Home Button.

2. Swipe and tap "Music."

3. Tap the Library button in the bottom left corner of the screen. The "Library" Menu is displayed in the top left corner of your screen.

4. Tap the Library menu to select a sorting method. Select one of the options: Recently Added, Playlists, Albums, Songs, etc.

6. Tap a Song.

7. The "Player" opens. Tap the arrow to play the song. Tap the bars to pause the song. Tap the back arrows to skip to the previous song, or tap the forward arrows to skip to the next song.

Figure 12.21   Playback Controls

9. Tap anywhere in the slider bar to move to that location in the song.

10. Tap the more button ● ● ● to add the song to a playlist, see lyrics, share a song or more.

Radio Stations

The Music app has Radio stations like "Beats 1." You can also search for songs or artists. If you subscribe to Apple Music all those songs are available when you search.

More Song Options

When listening to music, tap the 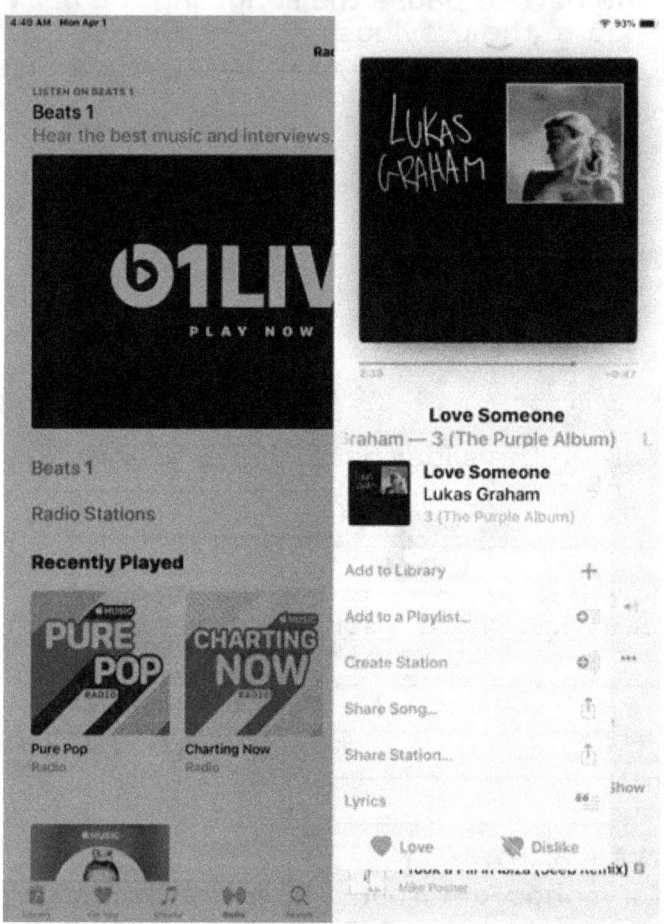 "More" button to see options for that song. The More button looks like 3 dots. Options include adding to your library, a playlist, viewing lyrics, and more, as shown below.

Figure 12.22   More Song Options

Use Audio Output With iPad

To stream music or videos to your favorite speakers, AirPods, or headsets, use the Control Center.

1. Swipe down from the top right corner of the screen to open the Control Center.

2. Tap the "Audio Output" button. Select an output device.

Change Volume With the Volume Buttons

Use the audio volume buttons on your iPad to adjust the volume. Control music, podcasts, or hearing aid volume. If you have Bluetooth speakers or a headset connected to your iPad, this is a simple way to adjust the volume.

Create an iTunes Playlist

Open iTunes and on the "File" menu select "New" and then select "Playlist."

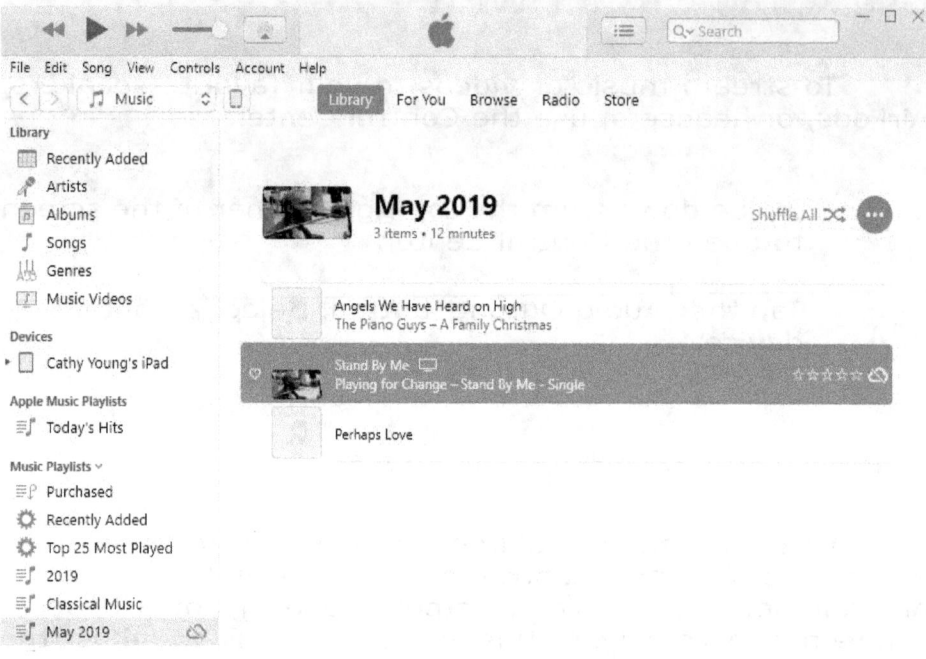

Figure 12.23   Create a Playlist

Add Songs You Already Own to Your Library

Open iTunes and on the "File" menu select "Add to Library." Browse to the folder with your music files. You can add songs you've purchased that do not have music protection software or WAV files from CDs.

Sync iTunes Library With iPad

At any given time you can sync music from iTunes with your iPad, or use iCloud Music Library, but not both at the same time. Typically I use iTunes to sync music I already own, and then I turn "iCloud Music Library" back on.

1. On your iPad, in the "Settings" app, select "Music" in the left sidebar. Ensure "iCloud Music Library" is not enabled.

2. Connect your iPad to your computer with the lightning to USB cable. On your computer open iTunes.

3. Follow the prompts to allow both devices to communicate. In iTunes, a small iPad button is displayed at the top of the screen, underneath the menu bar. Select your iPad.

4. In the left sidebar, select "Music" and check "Sync Music." Choose playlists, artists, or your "Entire Music Library."

5. In the bottom right corner of the screen, click the "Sync" button. The status bar at the top of the screen displays sync progress. Click "Done" when finished.

Download Music to Your iPad

To listen to music on the go when you aren't connected to Wi-Fi or Cellular download albums or playlists to your iPad.

1. Open the "Settings" app.

2. Swipe to scroll down in the left pane and tap "Music."

3.   Scroll to the "Downloads" section and tap "Automatic Downloads."

Check Available Space

Music files can use up a lot of storage space. In case you're wondering how much space is used by music files, on your iPad open the "Settings" app to see detailed information.

* The count of songs on your iPad.

* The total capacity.

* The available capacity.

1.   Open the "Settings" app.

2.   Swipe to scroll down and tap "General."

3.   Tap "About" to see available capacity.

For specific details about the size of songs by artist, in the left sidebar of the Settings app, scroll down to "Music" and then tap "Downloaded Music."

12.15 Notes

The Notes app ⌐▢⌐ is used for checklists, notes, and sketches. You can even "trace" an image when you place a piece of paper on the screen, and trace the image details with your Apple Pencil. This section outlines these topics.

- Create a Note
- Collaborate
- Selecting Text
- Creating Checklists
- Formatting Text
- Lock, Search, Lines & Grids
- Scan and Sign
- Markup
- Sketch
- Ruler
- Add Images, Equations and Drawings
- Add Tables, Charts, Shapes
- Pin Note to the Top of the List
- Lock, Delete, Folders
- Rename a Note

Tap the arrow   in the top left corner of the screen to see your folders. Tap the double arrows, at the top of the page in the left corner, to expand your drawing area. Drag text from a web page into Notes. **Tip:** Turn your iPad to landscape mode to see additional features.

When the Lock Screen is active, tap the screen with your Apple Pencil to use Instant Notes. The Chapter 4 topic "Lock Screen" has details on setting up Instant Notes.

Create a Note

Open the Notes app. Tap the add button in the top right corner of the screen.

Collaborate

Tap the Collaborate button. In the top right corner of the screen, to invite others to collaborate and work on your file.

Selecting Text

Tap on the on-screen keyboard to type, or switch keyboards. Chapter 4 has the details on working with the keyboard.

The gestures you make with your finger are also available with your Apple pencil. Selecting objects and text is easier with the pencil's greater degree of control.

Creating Checklists

Tap the checklist button, in the top row of the keyboard on the right side. A sample checklist is shown below.

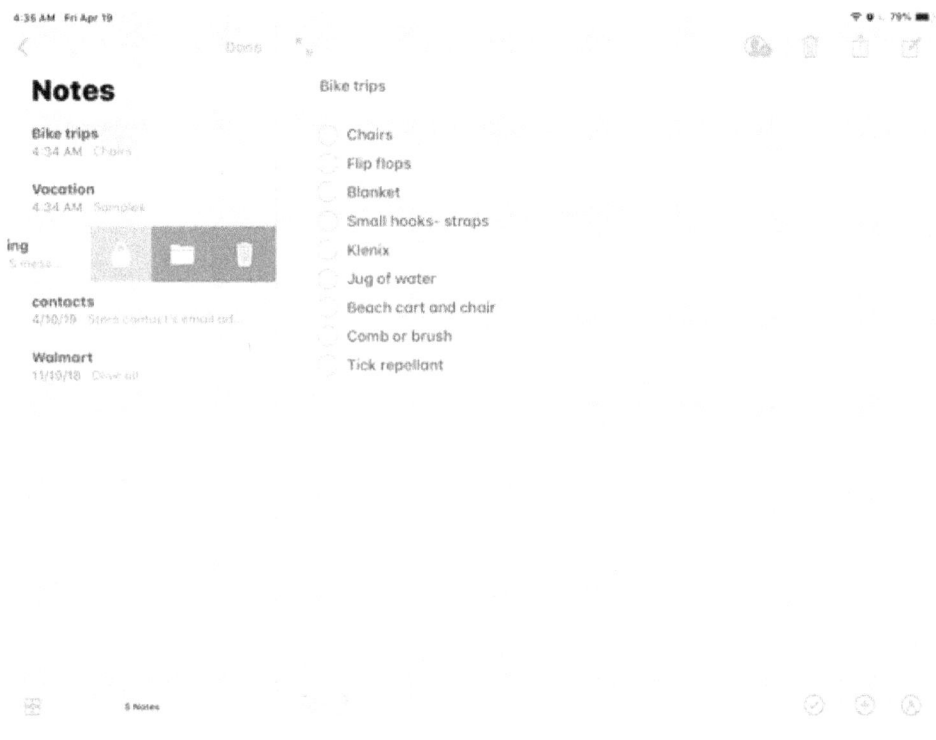

Figure 12.24   Checklists in Notes

Formatting Text

On the on-screen keyboard, in the top left corner, tap "Aa" to format text quickly.

Use the format painter button to update styles, fonts, color, and more for the selected text. You can even add a bullet list of items, as shown below.

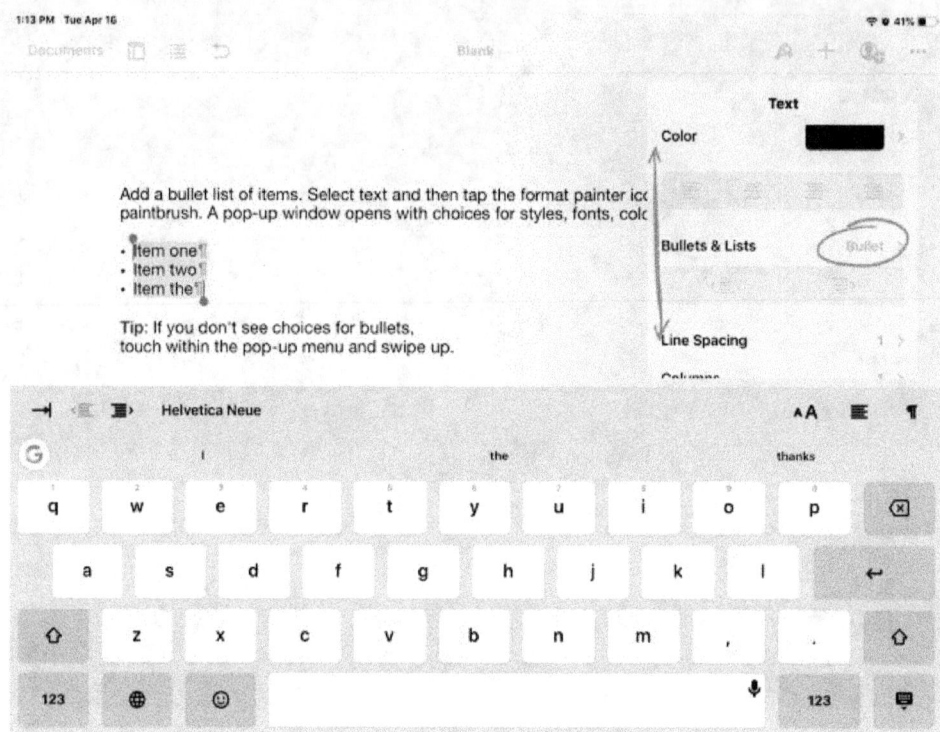

Figure 12.25   Format: Bullets in Notes

Tip: If you don't see choices for bullets, touch within the panel, and swipe up.

Lock, Search, Lines & Grids

The Share button has the usual Activity View choices, as well as the "Find in Note" search feature. The search feature also searches handwritten notes. I also like the "Lock Note," and "Lines & Grids" settings.

Notes Action Extensions

These are several action extensions unique to the Notes app.

- Find in Note
- Lock Note
- Lines & Grids

Tip: When the Activity View is open, swipe left and right in the tab rows to view more buttons.

Scan and Sign

It's very easy to scan a document, and then add your digital signature.

1. Tap the plus button and select "Scan Documents."

2. Tap "Keep Scan" in the bottom right corner. Tap Save to add the scanned image to the note.

3. Tap the scanned document in the Note, then tap the Send button to save it as a PDF file. Open the new document.

4. Select the markup tool, and sign your name.

Markup

The markup tool has controls for the pen, pencil, colors, and more, and is discussed in Chapter 4.

Sketch

Draw your own sketches in the Notes app.

1.   Tap the plus button.

2.   Tap "Add Sketch" in the menu panel.

3.   Select the markup tool and sign your name.

Ruler

After you create a sketch, tap the sketch on the page. Touch the screen for a few seconds with two fingers. While touching the screen, rotate your hand to reposition the ruler, as shown in Chapter 4 in Figure 4.20.

Tip: Although you can draw on the page with markup tools at any time, the ruler is only available when you add a "Sketch" to the note as shown above.

Add Images, Equations and Drawings

Tap the add button to open a menu with a tab view of choices. You can add videos, images, drawings, equations, audio, and more when editing a document. The tables button is the first button in the tab view. The tab view includes these four options.

- Tables

- Charts

- Shapes

- Files (photo, video, drawing, equation)

Resize Image

Tap the image on the page and drag a corner edge to resize the image.

Delete or Move Image

Touch and hold to delete the image, or drag the image to a new location on the page.

Format Image

Tap the image and tap format in the top right corner. Tap "Arrange" to turn on text wrap, move from back to front, and more.

Smart Annotations

In 2018, Apple announced a new version of iWork with Apple Pencil support. iWork apps include Pages, Numbers, and Keynote. Smart annotation anchors comments and proof marks to the original text so that document changes occur around the smart annotations.

To erase all smart annotations at once, click "Erase All" in the top left corner of the screen.

Add Tables, Charts, Shapes

Tap the Add ✚ button in the top right corner of the screen, then tap the tables button at the top of the menu. The tables button is the first button in the tab view. Tap a cell in the table to see format options.

Pin Note to the Top of the List

To keep a note at the top of the list, swipe left to right on the note in the left sidebar, and then tap the pin button.

Lock, Delete, Folders

To lock, delete, or move a note to a folder, in the left sidebar swipe right to left on a note.

Rename a Note

Touch the page and swipe down to see the Suggested Title, or Edit the Note title.

12.16 Numbers

The Numbers app is a spreadsheet app for crunching numbers.

Create a Document

1. Open Numbers. Tap the add button in the top right corner of the screen. Swipe to see the available templates, then tap to choose a template.

Formatting

Tap the format painter button to add tables, format cells, add conditional highlighting, or arrange objects.

Totals

Tab a cell and enter a formula. To total five rows of numbers in column A, type "**=sum(A1:A5)**."

Collaborate

Tap the Collaborate button. In the top right corner of the screen, to invite others to collaborate and work on your file.

Add Images, Equations and Drawings

Tap the add button to open a menu with a tab view of choices. You can add videos, images, drawings, equations, audio, and more when editing a document. Swipe left or right to see more options. The tables button is the first button in the tab view. The tab view includes these four options.

- Tables

- Charts

- Shapes

- Files (photo, video, drawing, equation)

Tap the image on the page and drag a corner edge to resize the image.

Touch and hold to delete the image, or drag the image to a new location on the page.

Tap the image and tap format ![icon] in the top right corner. Tap "Arrange" to turn on text wrap, move from back to front, and more.

Smart Annotations

Smart annotation anchors comments and proof marks to the original text so that document changes occur around the smart annotations. To erase all smart annotations at once, click "Erase All" in the top left corner of the screen.

12.17 Pages

Apple's Pages app ![icon] is a powerful word processor. In this section, we'll look at these topics.

- Create a Document
- Formatting
- Collaborate
- More Options
- Add a Page Break
- Add Images, Equations and Drawings
- Rename a Document
- Use the Pencil in Pages

Create a Document

1. Open Pages. Tap the add **+** button in the top right corner of the screen. Swipe to see the available templates, then tap to choose a template.

Tip: In the Pages app, you can triple-click on a paragraph to select the paragraph.

Formatting

On the on-screen keyboard, in the top left corner, tap the text button "AA" to format text quickly.

Tap the format painter button to update styles, fonts, color, and more for the selected text. You can even add a bullet list of items as described in the earlier topic "Notes." Swipe up or down in the panel to see more settings.

- Font
- Appearance
- Line Spacing
- Superscript or Subscript
- Bullets
- Styles (also used for Table of Contents)

The format painter is also used to format images.

Select an image, then tap format in the top right corner. Tap "Arrange" to turn on text wrap.

Table of Contents

Tap the Table of Contents button in the top left corner of the screen. The table of contents is based on style headings in your document.

Collaborate

Tap the Collaborate button in the top right corner of the screen, to invite others to collaborate and work on your file.

More Options

The More button, located in the top right corner of the screen, is shown below. The More menu includes share, export, print, change tracking, and many more options. Swipe up and down in the panel to see additional choices.

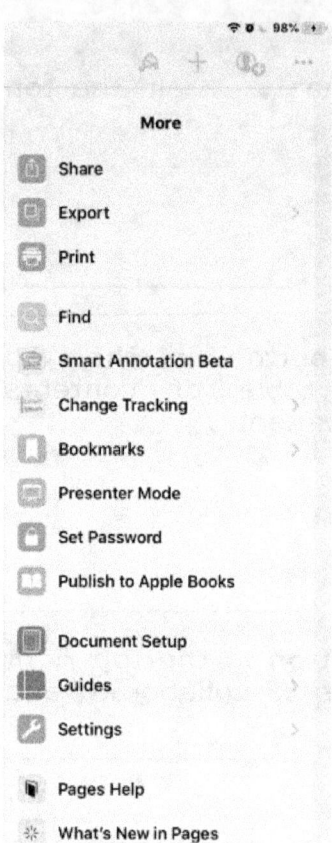

Figure 12.26   More Menu in Pages

Share: The Share ⬆ button opens the Activity View, as outlined in Chapter 4. The three rows include AirDrop, Share extensions, and Action extensions. Swipe left and right in the tab rows to view more buttons.

Document Setup: Tap More than tap "Document Setup." Drag the double lines to change the margins. In the top right corner, tap the button to change orientation.

Add a Page Break

On the on-screen keyboard tap the page break button, that looks like a paragraph mark, to insert a page break into your document.

Add Images, Equations and Drawings

Tap the add button to add videos, images, drawings, equations, tables, audio, and more when editing a document. Swipe left or right to see more options. Tap the image on the page and drag a corner edge to resize the image.

Touch and hold to delete the image, or drag the image to a new location on the page.

Tap the image and tap format in the top right corner. Tap "Arrange" to turn on text wrap, move from back to front, and more.

Rename a Document

Along the top of the screen, tap the document name in the middle of the page. Enter a new name for your document.

Use the Pencil in Pages

Open the Pages app and tap the screen with your Apple pencil. When prompted to "Add Drawing" tap OK.

12.18 Photos

The Photos app   is home to camera photos, screen captures, and images you save from apps. You can organize your photos in albums, edit, delete or search for photos.

There are two options for backing up and syncing photos with other devices. At any given time you can have one or the other active, but not both at the same time.

- iTunes
- iCloud Photo Stream

You can also use iTunes on your computer to sync photos with your iPad, as outlined in Chapter 9.

If you enabled "iCloud Photo Stream," your images are also copied to iCloud, and available from any of your Apple devices. Chapter 9 has instructions on using iCloud.

In this section, we'll cover these topics.

- Search Photos
- Viewing Photos
- Editing
- Markup

- Photo Albums
- Sharing or Deleting Photos
- View Photos on Apple TV

The Photos app opens and displays your albums. Swipe up or down to browse through photo albums. The "Today" and "All Photos" albums display recent photographs. The navigation tab bar along the bottom of the screen includes these options.

- Photos
- For You
- Albums
- Search

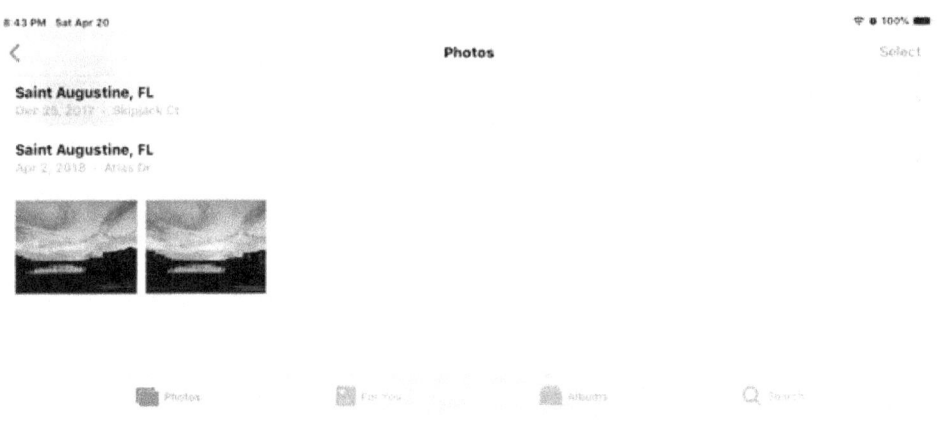

Figure 12.27   The Photos App

Tap the Share button ⬆️ , in the top right corner of the screen, to send a photo in a message or as a mail attachment. Likewise, tap the share button when in Messages to save the image to your Photos, or to use the image as wallpaper. While browsing in Safari tap to select an image, then choose "Save Image."

For details on photo editing, see the earlier topic "Camera."

Search Photos

Photos are grouped into "albums" like "All Photos" and "Favorites." You can also create your own albums to organize photos.

The "Search" feature is a cool way to locate photos. Tap "Search" in the bottom tab bar and enter a phrase or name. In the following example, I searched for the phrase "fountain," and Siri found images going back ten years that I'd forgotten about!

Figure 12.28   Search for Photos with Fountains

Identify People in Photos

Siri will try to identify people in your photos automatically. To see people already identified, follow these steps.

1. Tap "Albums" in the bottom tab bar.

2. Swipe to see "People & Places."

To add a contact from existing photographs, follow these steps.

1. Open a photo and swipe up to see a thumbnail image of people in the photo. In the example below, the section "People" has two thumbnail images of people in the photo.

2. Tap the thumbnail of the person you want to identify, and tap "Add Name" at the top of the screen to enter a name.

Figure 12.29   Identify People in Photos

Viewing Photos

When browsing albums, tap a photo to select it. In the top right corner of the screen, there are buttons to mark the photo as a Favorite or Send, Delete or Edit the photo.

The Share ⬆ button opens the Activity View, as outlined in Chapter 4. There are three tab bar rows in Activity View. The first row is "AirDrop."

The second row under AirDrop displays Share extensions. The Share extensions displayed relate to tasks specific to the current content. In the Photos app, share extensions include options like these.

- Share with Messages
- Share with Mail
- Shared Albums

The third row in the Activity View displays Action extensions which include these options and more.

- Copy
- Slideshow
- Airplay
- Add to Album
- Use as Wallpaper
- Save to Files
- Assign to Contact
- Print

Tip: When the Activity View is open, swipe left and right in the tab rows to view more buttons.

Editing

Keep in mind when editing, that after making changes, there is a "Revert" option, in the top right corner of the screen, to undo any changes you've made. Once you tap "Done," the "Revert" option is no longer available.

 Send

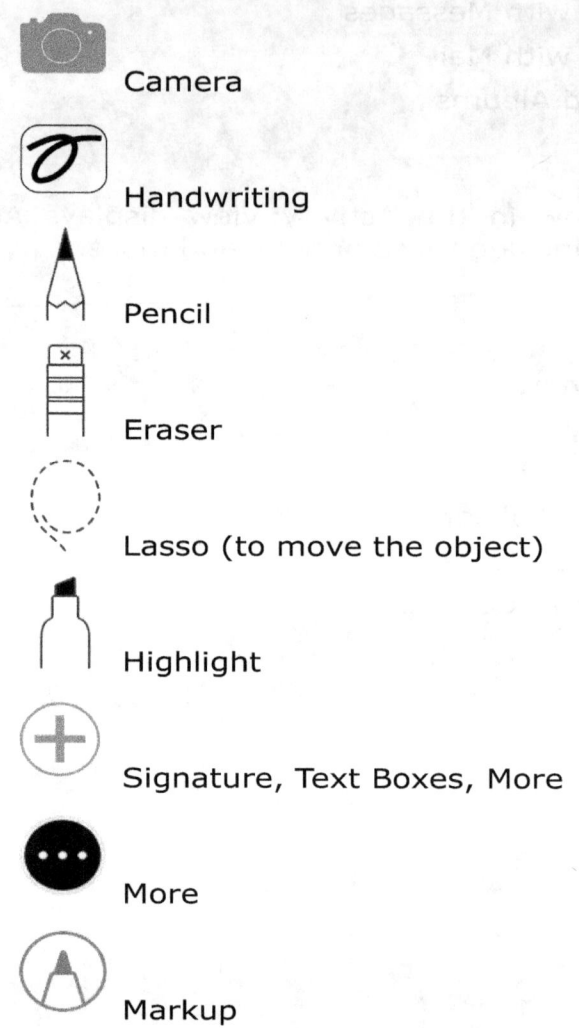

Camera

Handwriting

Pencil

Eraser

Lasso (to move the object)

Highlight

Signature, Text Boxes, More

More

Markup

Download third-party extensions for editing photos in the App Store. A few apps to explore are shown below.

- Afterlight
- Annotable
- Camera+

- Effects Studio
- Fotograf
- Fragment
- Half Tone 2
- infltr
- Litely
- Pixelmator
- Pixlr
- pizzaz plus
- Polarr
- Quick
- SKRWT

Markup

Tap any picture and then tap Edit. A toolbar opens along the bottom edge of the screen with photo tools.

1. Open a photo and then tap the 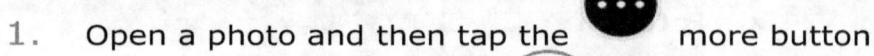 more button.

2. Next, tap the markup tool 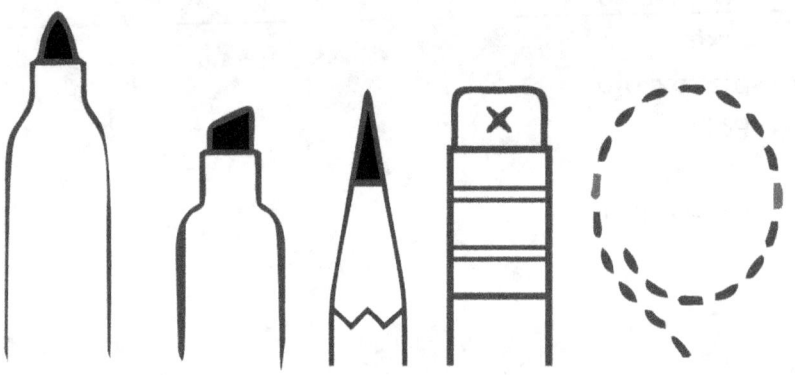. On the left tap to select a tool, and on the right side, tap to select an ink color.

Figure 12.30   Markup Drawing Tools

3. Tap the more button on the right side of the toolbar tap to open the popup window with the options shown below.

Tip: The text boxes and signature features are wonderful for filling out documents and signing them. We actually signed our taxes from our accountant this way last week, as shown in Chapter 4. Why didn't I do this before?!

- Text boxes
- Signature
- Magnifier
- Square

- Circle
- Bubble (Comment)
- Lines

4. Notice the "undo" and "redo" controls that appear in the bottom left corner of the screen.

Crop and rotate: You can adjust the size of the photo by cropping it. On the left side of the screen, there is a dial showing degrees for rotating the photograph, and to adjust the tilt, or straighten the image.

Tap the square button to crop or rotate. A bounding box is displayed. Touch a corner edge and drag it, to resize or crop your photo.

Filters: Filters adjust color. Tap the color tone button that looks like 3 circles.

Camera effects are only available from within the Messages or FaceTime apps. Camera effects include tools for drawing, adding text or stickers, and more.

Photo Albums

Photo albums are used to organize your photos or to share photos with friends. When you enable iCloud, you can see albums on different Apple devices, including PCs with iCloud installed.

Add an Album

Open the "Photos" app on your iPad. Along the bottom tab bar, tap "Albums."

In the top left corner, type ✚ "Add." Select "New Album" or "New Shared Album." The Photos app prompts you to select photos to add to your new album. Tap to select photo(s). Swipe to scroll through your existing photos to select additional photos. When you've selected all your photos for the new photo album, tap "Done" in the top right corner of the screen.

Add Photos to an Album

To add new photos to an existing album, open the album and tap "Edit" in the top right corner of the screen. The top menu now has an option to "Add" a photo. Browse and tap to select photos and then tap "Select." Continue browsing and swiping to see more photos. When you're finished selecting photos tap "Done" in the top right corner.

Sharing or Deleting Photos

To add or remove photos from your album, tap "Select" in the top right corner of the screen. The top menu changes, and options for "Send," "Trash," and "Add To" appear on the top left side of the screen.

Note: Photos are copied and added to albums. The original photos are still in the original location.

View Photos on Apple TV

When you enable iCloud and set up a shared folder, you can view photos from your iPad or MacBook on your Apple TV.

1. On your tablet, first, connect to your home Wi-Fi network.

2. In the Photos app, select a photo.

3. Tap the share button to open the Activity View.

4. Tap **AirPlay**.

5. Select your Apple TV.

iCloud Photo Sharing is another option instead of AirPlay. Once configured the Apple TV will display iCloud Photos.

1. Open the Photos app and select the photo(s).

2. Tap the Share button.

3. Click on Shared Albums.

4.   Add comments for the photo(s).

5.   Invite people to view the photo(s).

6.   Select the shared   album for the photo(s).

To manage iCloud settings on your Windows computer, download and install the iCloud app for Windows.

1.   Launch the iCloud app on your Windows computer.

2.   Select Photos, and click on **Options**.

3.   Scroll down to enable iCloud Photo Sharing.

4.   Click **Apply.**

12.19 Reminders

Initially, I didn't use the Apple   Reminders app that much, and then I realized I could use family sharing with reminders, to sync my grocery list.

The Grocery app outlined earlier uses the iOS reminders lists to store your shopping list. With a combination of iOS "Family Sharing," and an IFTTT applet that automatically links my Grocery shopping list with my iOS reminder lists, I can easily add items to my grocery list with Alexa, Google Home, or Siri. Everyone in our family can access our family shopping list on their Apple device. I'm particularly fond of the Grocery app because while I may forget to bring my iPhone to the grocery store, I will probably be wearing my Apple Watch with the Grocery app installed.

Enable Family Sharing

1. On your iPad, open the Settings app, and tap your name in the Apple ID banner in the left sidebar.

2. Swipe and tap "Set up Family Sharing." Follow the prompts to invite contacts to join your family.

Share a Reminder List

Family sharing is active on my iPad. My "Family" reminder list is shared with both my husband and daughter.

1. Open the Reminders app and tap the "Family" list. Any list would work, but in this example, I happen to have a "Family" list.

2. Tap "Edit" and then tap "sharing."

3. Select a contact and click ✛ "Add" to send an invitation.

12.20 Safari Web Browser

The Safari 🧭 web browser app is used to browse the web. In this section, we'll cover the topics shown below.

- Browse the Web

- Address bar

- Tools

- Bookmarks

- Reading List

- History

- Favorites

- Reader View (Hide Ads)

- Action Tools

- Reading Web Pages

- Web Forms

- Mobile vs. Desktop Versions of a Site

- Autofill

- Tabbed Windows

- Split View

- Block Pop-ups

- Malware and Viruses

Browse the Web

Open Safari, and type a search phrase in the "Web Address Bar," at the top of the screen. As you type in the address bar, the "enter" key on the on-screen keyboard changes to a "Go" button.

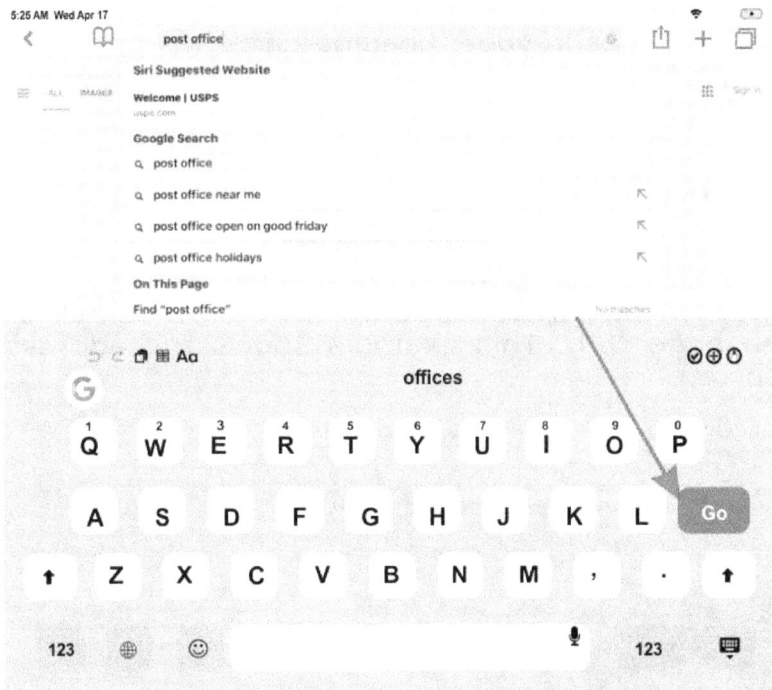

Figure 12.31   Search Safari

1. Open Safari and type "post office" in the search bar at the top of the screen, and then tap "Go" on the on-screen keyboard.

2. Tap on any of the web pages in the search results.

You can create "links" to web pages and save the links in several ways, which we'll discuss in the next sections.

- Page icons on your Home screen
- Bookmarks

- Favorites
- Web Pages in your "Reading List"

Address bar

The address bar is located in the center of the Safari app at the top of the screen. Type in this box to search or enter a web page URL. This example shows the address bar for "msn.com."

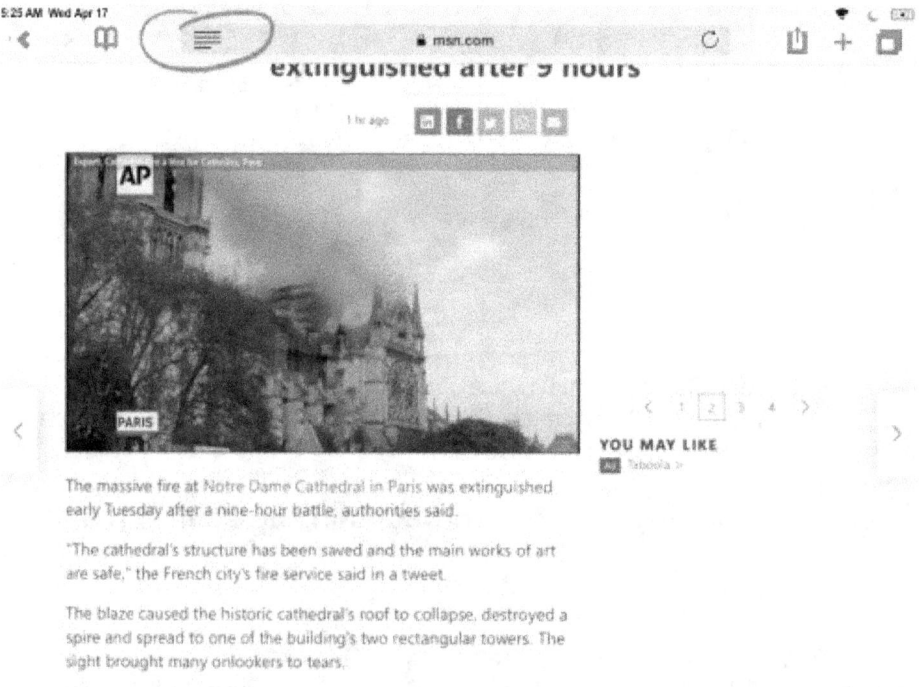

Figure 12.32   The Safari Web Browser

Tap on the address bar to display the on-screen keyboard and type in the address bar. Notice when typing in Safari, the on-screen keyboard "enter" key changes to a "Go" button. To clear the address bar tap the X.

Tools

Navigation tools are on the left side of the screen, to the left of the address bar.

Figure 12.33   Safari Navigation Tools

As you navigate between multiple pages by searching or clicking links on web pages, the "Back" and "Forward" tools will turn blue. Click on a tool to move forward and backward between the pages you've visited.

Reader View   is available for some web pages and is outlined later in this chapter.

Bookmarks

Tap the Share   button to open the Activity View, with options to create a bookmark or favorite this page. When your iPad is in landscape mode, the bookmarks tab opens. The tab view, at the top of the left sidebar, has the choices shown below.

- Bookmarks
- Reading list
- History

To view bookmarks , tap the Bookmark button in the top left corner of the screen.

Close the Bookmark Sidebar

Tap the bookmarks button, to the left of the URL address bar, to close the bookmarks sidebar.

Reading List

Web pages you've marked to read later are stored in your "Reading List." First, tap the plus symbol in the top right corner of the screen. In the left sidebar, tap "Reading List" in the tab view. The Reading List button looks like glasses.

To remove a web page from your reading list, touch the item and swipe left.

History

The web pages you have viewed are stored in your "History." To clear website browsing data, open the

Settings app, and in the left sidebar tap "Safari." Swipe up on the right side of the screen, and tap "Clear history and website data."

Favorites

Tap the Share button to open the Activity View with options to create a bookmark or favorite this page.

The Add button also opens a sidebar for Bookmarks, your Reading List, and History, and also displays your Favorites.

To delete a "favorite" link touch the button for several seconds and release. A panel appears with choices to "Edit" or "Delete."

Tip: If you want the "favorites bar" to be visible, open the Settings app, and in the left pane tap "Safari." Swipe down and enable the "Favorites Bar."

Reader View (Hide Ads)

Some sites will offer a "Reader" view as indicated by a small button to the left of the address bar. This removes the clutter of ads, navigation, and pop-ups and only shows relevant text and images.

Tap the "Reader" button to enable reader view. Tap again to return to normal viewing.

Note: If you don't see the button, Reader isn't available for that page.

Action Tools

At the top of the right side of the screen, there are several action tools, as shown below.

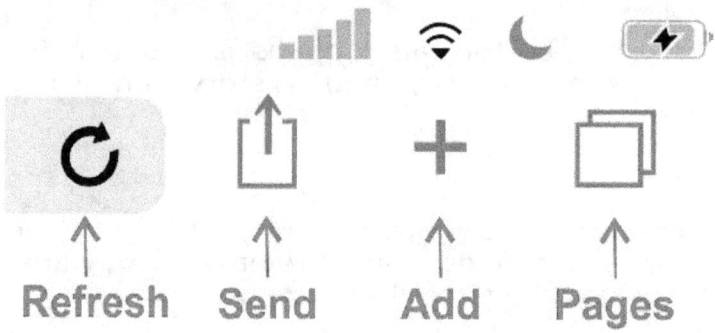

Figure 12.34   Safari Action Tools

The "Refresh" button appears on the right edge of the address bar. Tap this button to reload content with the latest information from the web site. This is handy for news web sites that are continually changing their data.

The Share button is part of the Activity View functionality. Chapter 4 has information on the Activity View.

The Add button opens a sidebar for Bookmarks in the left sidebar, your Reading List, and History. Your Favorites are displayed in the right pane.

History is a list of all the web pages you've ever browsed. This history list can be erased in the Settings app, in the "Safari" settings.

Tap the "Pages" button to switch between pages or open a new page. A page is simply a browsing window. At any given time you may have several "pages" open in Safari.

Reading Web Pages

Touch the screen and swipe up or down to view a web page. A vertical indicator bar on the right shows your relative position on the page, as you swipe up and down.

Pinch the screen to change the zoom magnification on the page. Double-tap a photo to zoom in on the photo. Double-tap again to return to the normal zoom level. Links to other information may be underlined or a different color text. Tap on the link to go to that location.

Tap the "Appearance" button in the top right corner of the screen to adjust color, fonts, etc.

Navigating Around a Web Page

To go back to the top of a web page, double-tap the top edge of the screen.

Searching Within a Web Page

Open any website and tap the URL at the top of the window. Tap the "x" to clear the URL. Type your search "phrase" in the address bar, then tap "Go" on the on-screen keyboard. Scroll down to the bottom section that says "On This page," and click on "Find phrase."

In this example, I'm searching for the phrase "full moon" on the web page.

1. Open Safari and type "When is the next full moon" in the search bar at the top of the screen, and then tap "Go" on the on-screen keyboard.

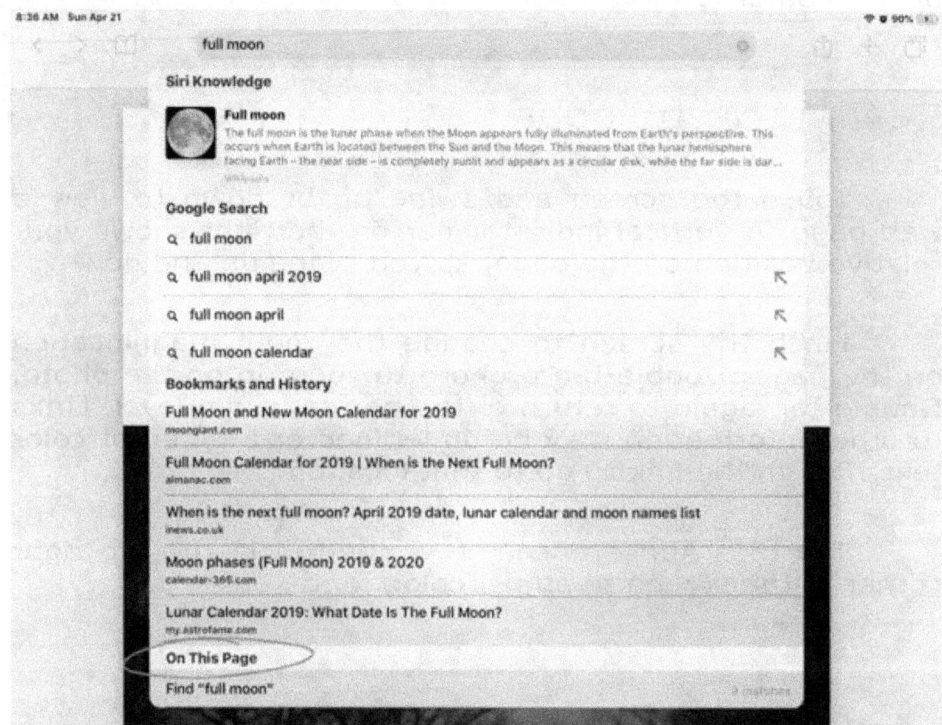

Figure 12.35   Search Within a Web Page

2. Tap on one of the web pages displayed in the search results.

Save Images from Web Pages

While browsing in Safari tap to select an image, then choose "Save Image."

Web Forms

Sometimes web pages will display text entry boxes where they are partially hidden by the on-screen keyboard. Touch the area above the keyboard, and drag your finger towards the top of the screen. The web page is recentered, and the text box should be visible. See the example in Chapter 4 in the topic "Swipe to See a Text Entry Box."

Mobile vs. Desktop Versions of a Site

Often, a web site will identify your device automatically, and present a "mobile" web site version of the site, without the full functionality of the desktop site. To see the full desktop version of a site, instead of the mobile version, tap the Share Button, then tap "Request Desktop Site."

Autofill

When enabled, autofill will auto-populate your name and address, in web forms that support this feature.

1. Open the Settings app. In the left sidebar, scroll down and tap Safari.

2. In the right pane, in the "General" section, tap "AutoFill."

3. Select your Settings for contact and credit card information. To use your contact information, select "My Info" and then choose a contact card.

Add Shortcuts for Web Pages to Your Home Screen

Use the Share control to add a web page shortcut to your Home Screen. In the Share pop-up menu, in the bottom tab bar, swipe left and tap "Add to Home Screen."

Share a Web Site

To share a link to the website, tap the Share button in the top right corner.

Tabbed Windows

Tap the plus symbol, located in the upper right corner of your screen, to open a new tab or browser window. The title of the tabbed window looks like the top of a file folder. Each tabbed window has a brief description with a small "x" on the left. To close a tabbed window, tap the "x," or swipe left on the tab.

Tap the pages button or tab heading to switch between tabbed windows.

Pinch three fingers inward to collapse all tabbed windows into small "preview" windows. This is similar to the view of the App Switcher discussed in Chapter 3.

View the Tab's History

Tap the back $\langle$ or forward $\rangle$ buttons in the top right corner of the screen to move through page history.

Reopen a Recently Closed Tab

Touch and hold the plus button $\oplus$ in the top right corner, then choose from the list of recently closed tabs.

Split View

To see two pages on the screen at the same time, rotate the iPad to change the display to **landscape orientation**. There are several ways to open a second page in Split View.

- Touch and hold the Pages icon in the top right corner of the screen until a panel opens with tab options. Tap "Split View." Make sure the display is in landscape orientation.

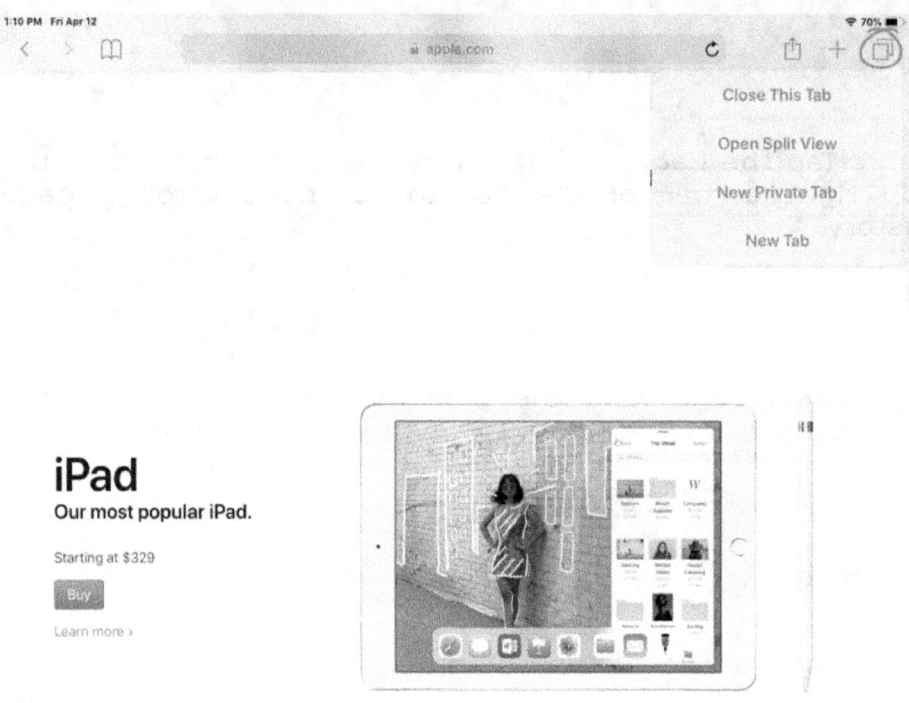

Figure 12.36   The Pages or Tab Panel

- Open a link in Split View: Touch and hold the link, then tap "Open in Split View."

- If you're using a smart keyboard, press CMD + N to open Split View.

- Touch a tab heading, and drag all the way to the left edge or right edge of the screen. Swipe again to close split view and go back to tabs. You can also tap and hold the "Pages" button in the bottom toolbar, and select "Merge All Tabs" from the panel that opens.

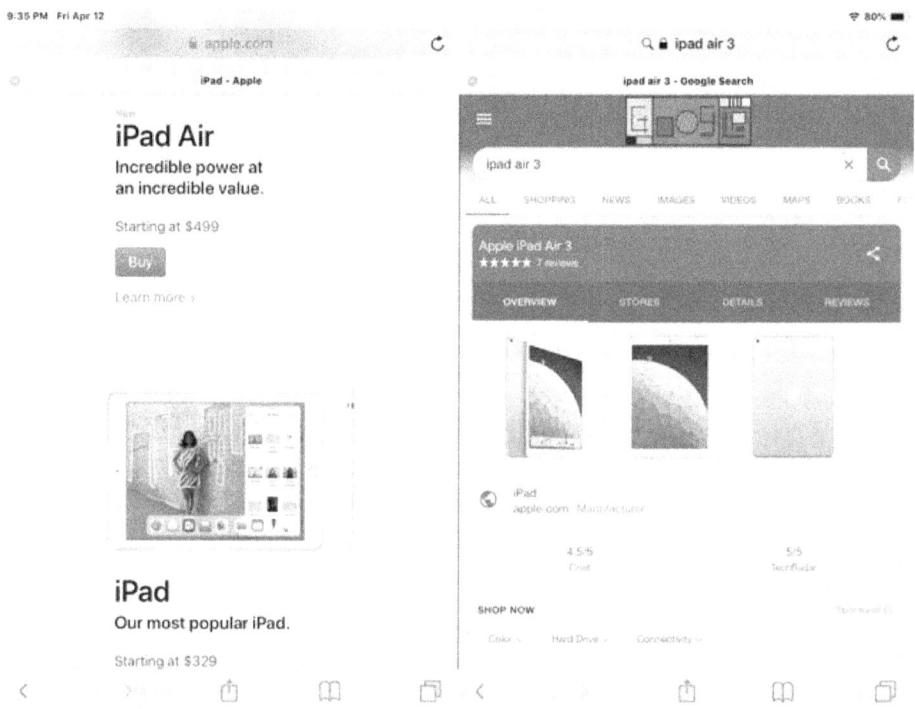

Figure 12.37   Safari Split View

Note: If you have locked the orientation in Control Panel, the screen will not rotate.

Change Sides

To move a web page from one side to the other, touch the tab bar and drag it to the other side of the screen. The split views change sides.

Block Pop-ups

Go to Settings > Safari, then turn on Block Pop-ups.

Malware and Viruses

To get rid of annoying pop-ups from Malware, swipe up on the screen to close Safari. Malware or Viruses are malicious web code designed to capture your personal information. Do not click on the red "X," which is often part of the Malware app.

12.21 Shortcuts

With the new Apple "Shortcuts" app introduced with iOS 12, you can build shortcuts to perform many routine tasks. Think of shortcuts as macros or quick commands. With Siri Shortcuts, you record a personal phrase in your app for a particular task. For example, say "Siri, open travel plans." The Siri Shortcut opens the Hotels.com app and displays your hotel photo, address, and check-in time. In this scenario, you recorded a Siri Shortcut in the Hotels.com app named "travel plans."

The list below shows a few apps that have announced plans to support Siri Shortcuts or have them available today.

- AirBnB

- Amazon Prime Video

- American Airlines

- App in the Air

- Bonvoy (Marriott/SPG)

- Booking.com

- British Airways

- Carrot Weather

- Caviar (Food Delivery)

- Dark Sky Weather

- Dexcom (Blood Glucose Monitor)

- ETA

- Grocery

- Hotels.com

- HotelTonight

- Kayak

- Lufthansa

- Smarter

- Trello

- VRBO

- Waze

You can add your shortcuts to your Apple device "Today View," or ask Siri to run a shortcut. Third-party apps are starting to appear with the "Add to Siri" button to create custom shortcuts. The next section, "Add to Siri," has a few examples.

Shortcuts are listed in the Settings app, in the "Siri & Search" section. The next topic, "Suggested Shortcuts," explains these settings.

Download the new Shortcut App from the App Store. The scripting features of the Shortcuts app pass text, URLs, clipboard contents, and other actions between applications. The following is a brief list of tasks to inspire you.

- Send E-mails

- Make Phone Calls

- Search Local Businesses

- Find Music

- Record Audio

- Ask for Scripting Input

- Get Current Weather

Create a Shortcut

Open the "Shortcuts" app and tap "Create Shortcut." In the left sidebar, swipe up. In the Music section, tap "Get Playlist." Enter your options and tap "Done." To rename the shortcut, in the Library tap the shortcut, and then tap the Settings button in the top right. In the pop-up menu, you can set the button, name, Siri phrase, and more. Swipe up and tap "Add to Home Screen."

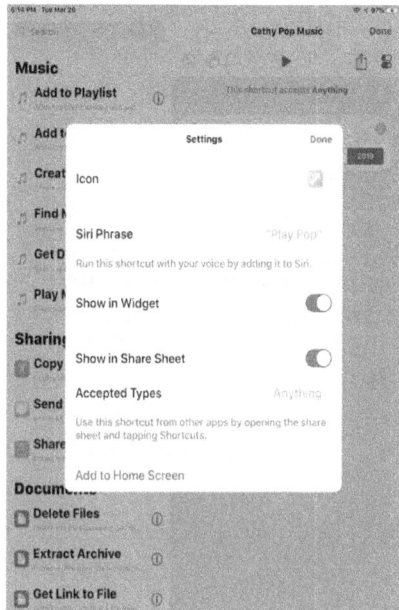

Figure 12.38   Creating a Shortcut

Favorite Shortcuts

In Shortcut Editor, tap the name of the action you want to mark as a favorite.

Waze

When Waze introduced a Siri Shortcut in February 2019, I was very excited. To set up a Siri Shortcut, open the Waze app, and search for a location like "Home." Tap the "more" button that looks like an ellipsis or three dots. Tap "Add Shortcut" and record a personal phrase for Siri to launch Waze.

Earlier, we discussed the "Shortcuts" app for creating your own multi-step shortcuts, or third-party apps that support these "Siri Shortcuts." There is a third choice for shortcuts, found in the "Suggested Shortcuts" screen discussed in the next section.

Suggested Shortcuts

In the Settings app, in the left sidebar, tap "Siri & Search." In the "Suggested Shortcuts" section, in the right panel, tap "All Shortcuts." The default shortcuts for iOS are displayed. Tap any of these shortcuts to record your personal shortcut phrase.

View and Rerecord Shortcut Phrases

Shortcuts are listed in the Settings app, in the "Siri & Search" section. At the top of the screen, tap "My Shortcuts" to view and edit your shortcut phrases.

12.22 Smart Home

The Apple Home app is available on all Apple devices, including the Apple Watch. Many smart home apps like the Neato robot vacuum app and the Legrand Light Control app work perfectly on the Apple Watch.

Legrand encompasses smart lighting as well as electrical outlets. The Honeywell Total Connect Comfort app for thermostats also supports the Apple Watch. Hunter Douglas PowerView shades, Neato, and Legrand all work with the Alexa digital assistant. I prefer tapping my watch compared to talking to Alexa in certain situations, especially if I'm trying to be quiet. For further information on smart home technology, check out our book, "Smart Home, Digital Assistants, Home Automation and the Internet of Things."

Although I love my robotic vacuum George Jr., sometimes it's not a good time for him to vacuum. With a tap on my watch, I can direct George, Jr. to try again later. Our original Neato robot "George" didn't survive all the cat hair at our house. We're hoping George, Jr. has a long and productive life.

Figure 12.39   The Neato App

SmartThings is Samsung's solution for home automation. The SmartThings hub uses the ZigBee protocol to control lighting, security, sensors, sirens, and cameras, to name a few. In the SmartThings mobile app, select "More" and then click on "My Account" to create widgets for your Apple Watch.

An unusual smart app is "Eve for Subaru." Combined with an IFTTT applet, the Subaru app controls over 400 smart home devices.

Some third-party apps require you to create a "Widget" for your Apple Watch. In the figure below, I am creating a widget in the Hunter Douglas app "PowerView."

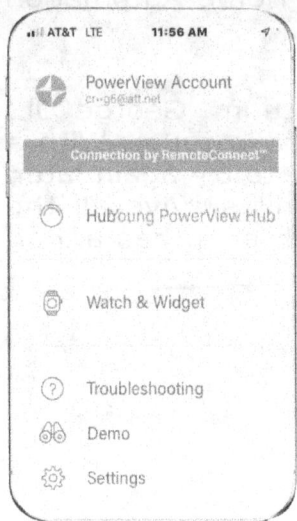

Figure 12.40   Creating a PowerView Widget

12.23 Sports and the Great Outdoors

Picture a beautiful, cool, sunny day. A gentle breeze blows as you prepare to tee off, but you're wondering just how far that green is. A glance at your Apple Watch, and you are all set. The Golf Shot AR has real-time distances to the green, hazards, and over 40,000 worldwide courses. The Golf Shot integration with your Apple Watch is like having a pro caddie on your wrist.

With Sky Guide on your Apple Watch, all you have to do is open the app and hold your watch to the sky. With the screen facing you, Sky Guide will automatically recognize the constellation patterns and orient the screen properly. Sky Guide will show you the constellations that have always been right in front of you, but you never knew existed. Sky Guide can send you a notification on your

Apple Watch when an event is about to happen in the skies above your location.

There are so many apps in this category, I decided to break them down into sports and outdoor. This list of sports apps is the tip of the iceberg. I'd encourage you to search the app store for sports of interest to you.

- 365Scores
- College Hoops
- Cyclemeter
- DraftKings Fantasy Sports
- ESPN
- Football Live
- Golf Shot
- Komoot
- MLB at Bat
- MyScorecard
- NFL Sunday Ticket
- Onefootball - Soccer Scores
- PitchersPal
- Slopes
- The Score

The following is a brief list of apps that you may find interesting for outdoor activities.

- AllTrails
- Big Year Birding
- GAIA
- Gardenia
- History Here
- Santa Fe Botanical
- Sky Guide
- Sunrise Sunset
- Topo Maps
- Trails
- ViewRanger

12.24 Transcribe

Apps like "Transcribe" have action extensions that work within the Voice Memos app.

12.25 Travel

Apps like Hotel Tonight and Hopper find the best rates for hotels and flights. While traveling third-party apps can handle activities like directions, currency exchange, reservations, translation, and locating local events and restaurants. Check out a few of these apps to see if they would fit your lifestyle.

- App in the Air
- BMW Connected
- Citymapper

- ELK
- ETA
- Glympse
- Hilton Honors
- Hotwire
- iTranslate
- Lyft
- Magic Guide to Disney World
- Marriott
- Microsoft Translator
- New York Subway
- Poison Maps
- Toyota Vehicle Remote

App in the Air includes airport maps, live updates, reminders when to head to your gate, wait times for security, and more.

12.26 The TV App

The Apple TV app integrates all your streaming media apps and TV providers with a single sign-on. The new TV app, introduced in 2019, includes Apple TV Channels to simplify account logins. Initially, the app is available on iPhones, iPads, and some Apple TVs. There are plans to add the app to Macs and smart TVs, beginning with Samsung models.

In the Settings app, I added "DirectTV" as my TV Provider in the left sidebar. Open the "Settings" app, then swipe down to "TV Provider" in the left sidebar. Select "Direct TV" or your provider.

Download Shows

In case you're going on a long trip, where you won't have Internet access for long periods, you can download shows you purchased from iTunes.

Tap the More ● ● ● button, on the right side of the screen, when browsing videos. Third-party providers like Amazon Prime, Netflix, and DirecTv may also have an option to download some shows.

Amazon Prime

Browse and select a show, then tap the button. For example, "Download Season 1."

Netflix

Along the bottom of the screen tap "Downloads" to see the content you can download for offline viewing later. Tap to select, then swipe up on the list of episodes. On the right side of the screen, tap the download button to download the episode.

DirecTv

Open the DirecTv app on your iPad and tap the "Playlist." Follow the prompts to activate your DVR for downloads. Tap "On DVR" in the top left corner of the screen to see your DVR recordings. Select a recording and tap the green download button. In the pop-up window, tap "Download & Go." The DirecTV must be open to complete the download.

Subtitles

The "Audio & Subtitles"  control is available when watching videos. Tap the screen to see the playback controls.

Figure 12.41 Playback Controls

On the right side, tap the "Audio & Subtitles" control. You can also turn subtitles on in the Settings app. In the left sidebar, tap "General" and in the right pane tap "Accessibility." Swipe to scroll down to the "Media" section and tap "Subtitles & Captioning."

12.27 Water Sports

Paddle Logger is an interesting app for those who like to be out on the water. I had no idea what SUP and OC meant until my daughter bought a stand-up paddleboard. I still have no idea what OC means, but I do like to Kayak. Sailors will appreciate Waterspeed, an app dedicated to water sports. Real-time speed, direction, distance, heart, weather, and stats make this a popular app.

Please keep in mind Apple's guidance on water resistance and avoid scuba diving, water skiing, or high-velocity water.

- Paddle Logger
- Sail Buddy
- Waterspeed

12.28 Weather

CARROT Weather frequently rates as one of the best weather apps. You can choose between an amusing "snark" version or a traditional "boring" announcer.

- CARROT Weather
- Dark Sky
- Night Sky
- Sunrise Sunset

13. IFTTT

In this chapter we discuss

Create a Simple Applet (Recipe)

Combine Several Actions

Applets Worth a Look

The IFTTT platform is a free web-based service which is fast becoming an integral part of smart homes. Vendors of smart home devices and systems are using IFTTT to create applets for their products. Rather than reciting the long list of what works with IFTTT, it would be simpler to give the short list of what doesn't.

Devices on IFTTT are either a "trigger" or an "action device." Due to security concerns Kevo locks can only trigger an action. For example, when you lock the door it could trigger the lights to turn off.

IFTTT also integrates systems for delivery information, weather, pollen counts or location (Geofencing), and then controls your smart home devices (lights, thermostats, sprinklers). With IFTTT you can also send emails, message notifications, or communicate with your digital assistant(s).

When you visit the IFTTT web site you can search for existing applets (recipes) you can reuse, or create your own. You'll see these common services used in many of the applets.

- Location

- Date and Time

- Calendars

- Notifications

The funniest applet I've seen was entitled, "Blink the lights when the cookie jar defenses are breached." I assumed it used a motion sensor attached to the cookie jar, but in actuality it uses the "Manything" mobile app. The Manything app uses the camera on your smartphone or tablet as a surveillance device. Combined with a stand you can catch the thief (or pet) in the act! Can you imagine the look on your child's face when the Alexa voice says, "I see you, put that cookie back," when no one else is in the room!

I've included no tips on troubleshooting IFTTT applets because frankly these recipes have worked perfectly for me every time. This is high praise indeed considering all the integrations available.

13.1 Create a Simple Applet (Recipe)

When creating your applet recall that IFTTT stands for, "If This, Then That."

1.   Login to IFTTT and click on **New Applet**.

2.   Choose a service.

3.   Choose a trigger.

4.   Complete the trigger fields.

5.   Click on the Plus symbol to fill in "that." This is the action.

6.   Choose an action service and save the applet.

13.2 Combine Several Actions

IFTTT has a Maker tier that allows you to combine multiple services and triggered actions. You can sign up for free at IFTTT.

1. Login to the Maker tier, or login to IFTTT and select My Applets. Click on **New Applet**. There is a choice to Build on the Platform that takes you into the Maker tier.

2. Choose a service.

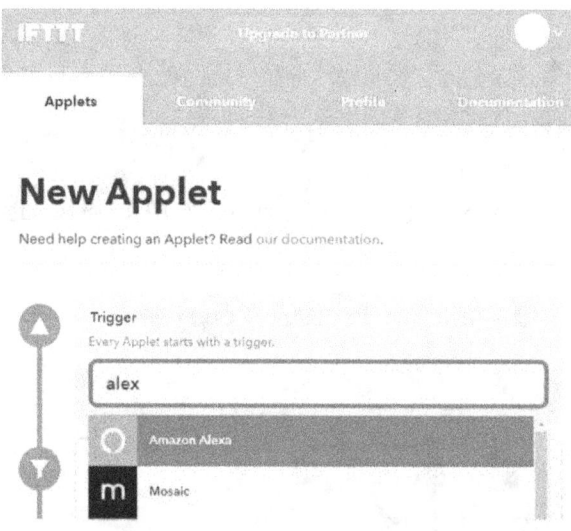

Figure 13.1   Choose a Service

3.   Choose a trigger.

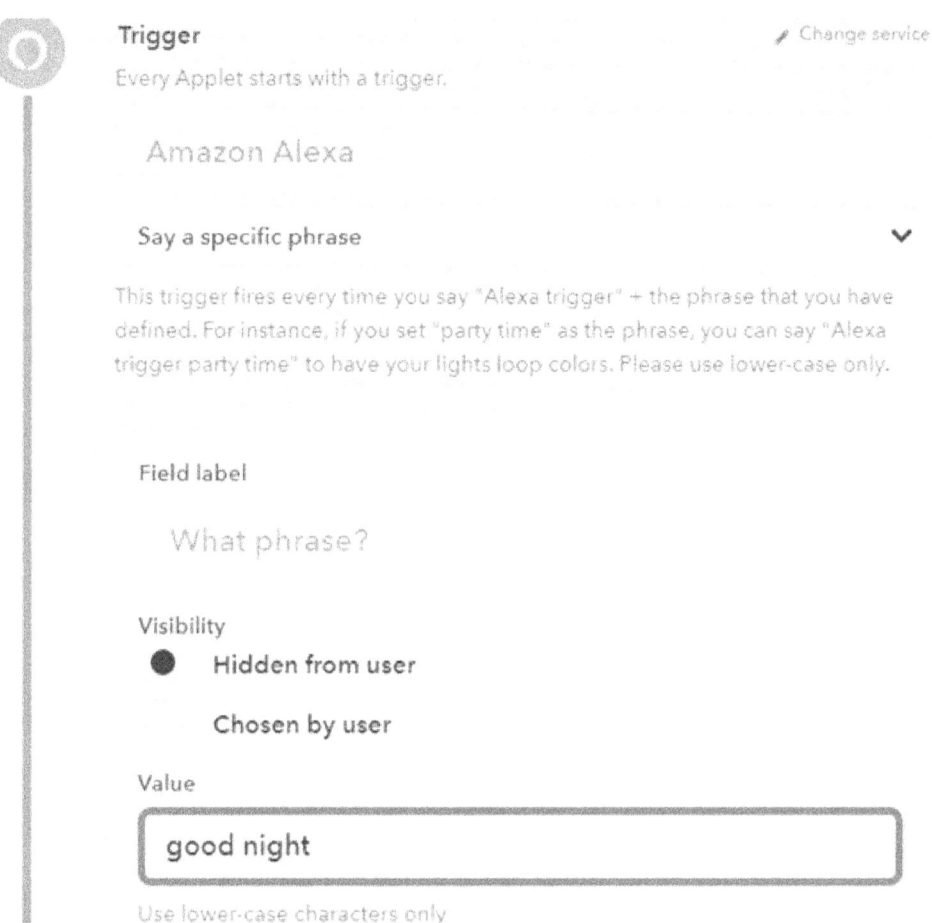

Figure 13.2   Choose a Trigger

4. Now fill in "that" – the action.

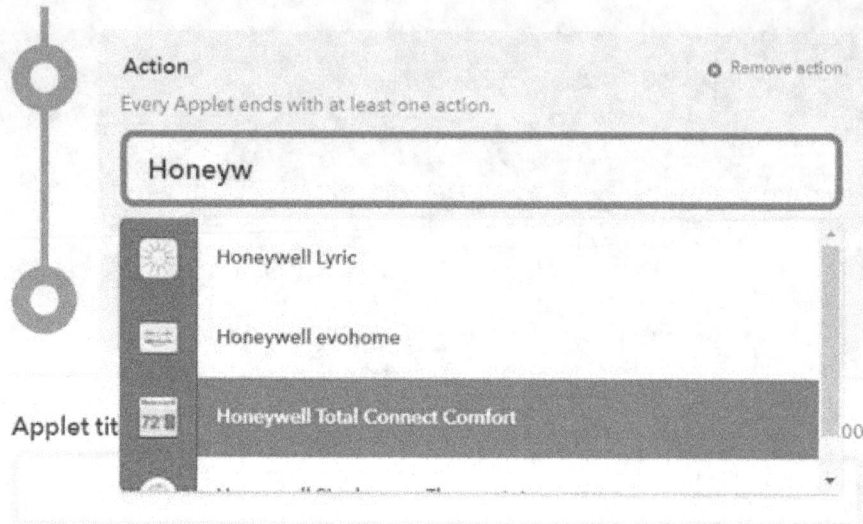

Figure 13.3   Choose an Action Service

5.   Complete the action fields.

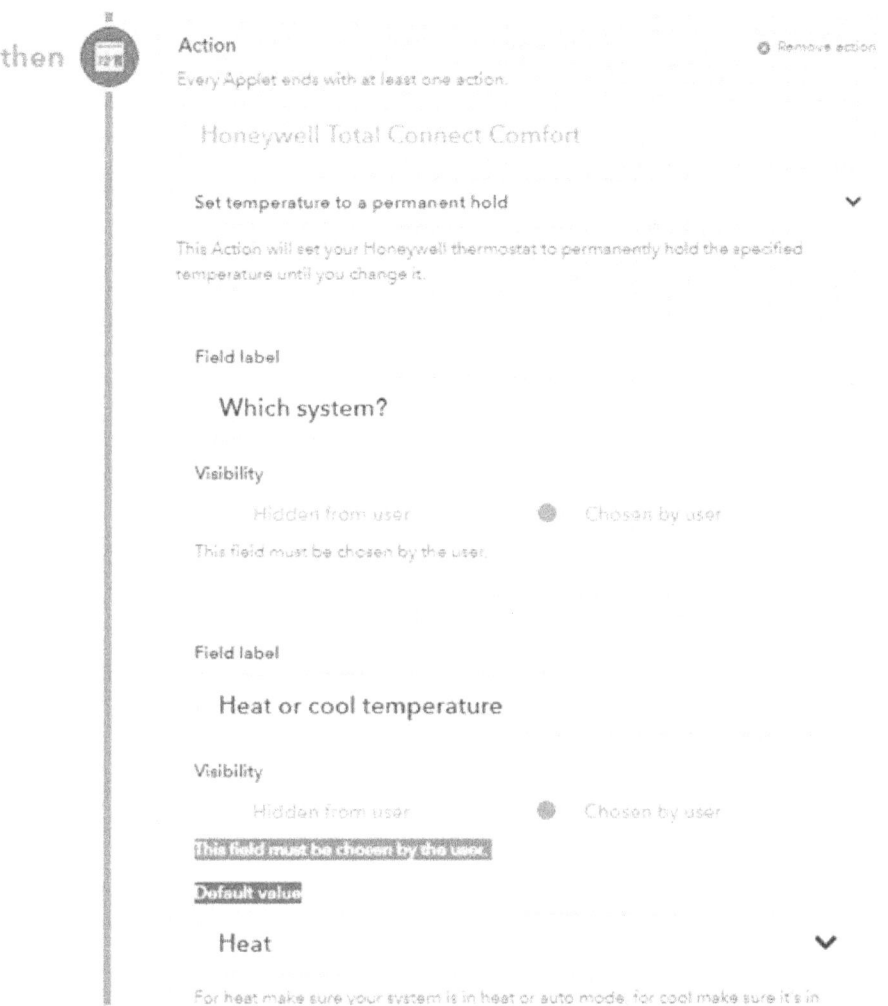

Figure 13.4   Complete Action Fields

6. Complete remaining action fields.

Field label

Target temperature

Visibility

● Hidden from user   ○ Chosen by user

Value

Amazon Alexa/72

Temperature in degrees e.g. 71   Add ingredient

Field label

Temperature in

Visibility

○ Hidden from user   ● Chosen by user

Default value

Fahrenheit   ⌄

then ◯   Add action

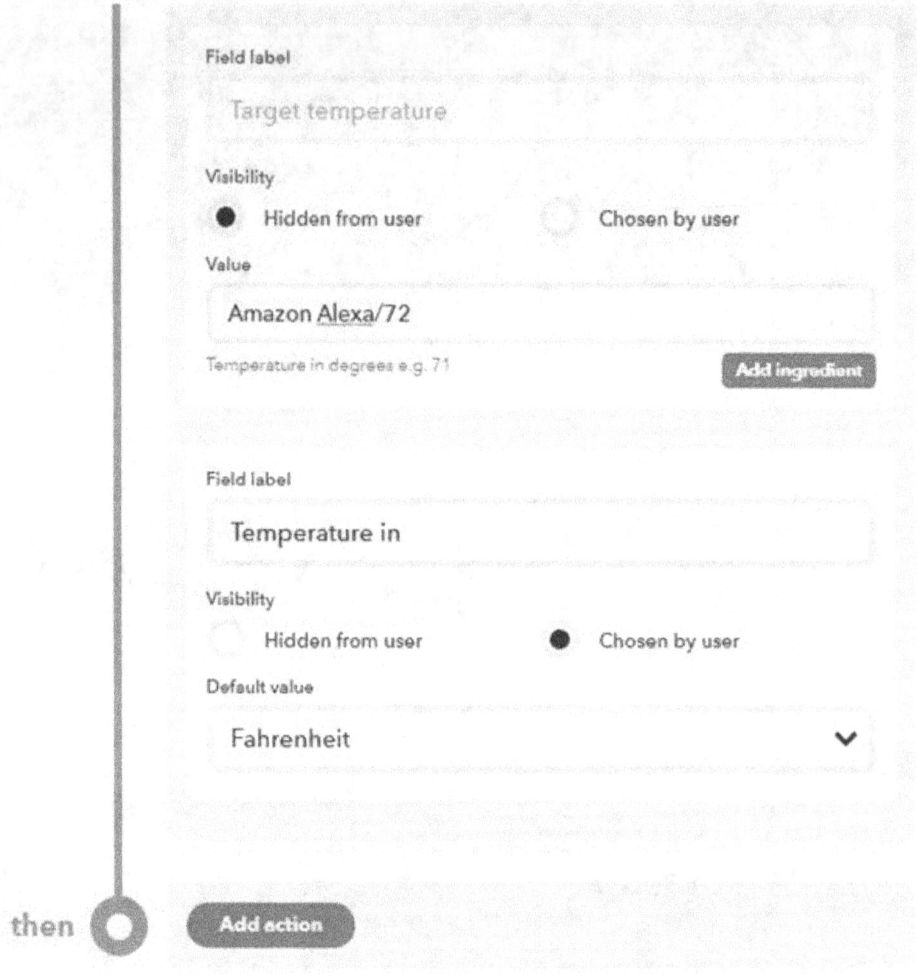

Figure 13.5   Complete remaining Action Fields

7. Repeat to add more triggers and actions. Then fill in a description and save your applet.

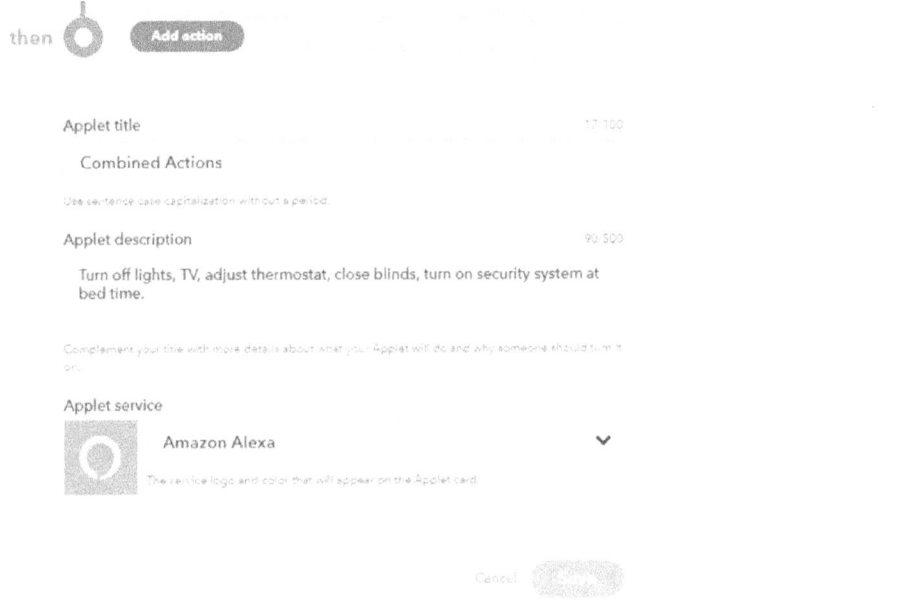

Figure 13.6   Name the Applet

The Applet is private (only you can use it) until you click on Publish.

13.3 Applets Worth a Look

Throughout the book I've mentioned some unique IFTTT applets. When looking around the IFTTT web site you may want to check out a few of these.

- Blink your Hue lights when your Amazon Alexa timer hits 0.

- If tomorrow's forecast calls for rain, then change color on the color hue bulb.

- Turn off lights and close blinds at bed time.

- Turn on "Manythings" camera if motion is detected.

- Blink the lights when the cookie jar defenses are breached.

- Get a mobile notification from ESPN with your team's final score.

- Get alerts when your favorite musician is playing in your city.

- When you arrive in San Francisco send yourself a map of BART.

14. Day to Day & Troubleshooting

In this chapter we discuss

Troubleshooting Overview

Matching Names to IP Addresses

It Stopped Working

Why is the Connection Slow or Intermittent?

Troubleshooting Apple TV

Troubleshooting Amazon Alexa

Troubleshooting begins the moment you unpack a new device. This is the time to document model information and settings. There are always going to be times when you need to make a change or fix a device configuration. The more information you have documented, the easier this process will be. As a side note, after spending a lot of time and money on a smart home, documentation is a selling point if you ever put your house on the market.

Having a list of devices ensures you don't miss updating the Wi-Fi network password on any device when you replace an ISP router. Typing the Wi-Fi network password for every smart home device is time-consuming, and leaving out a smart device (or two) adds to that chore.

The checklist from Chapter 2 can be expanded to include your specific configuration details about login information, bridges or hubs, and automations.

- Scenes

- Schedules

- IFTTT Recipes (Applets)

- Device Groups or Routines

- Skills

- Widgets (Apple Watch)

Knowing the date the device is added to your smart home is useful in troubleshooting. For example, your network starting behaving erratically on April 1st. On the same day you plugged in a new device. Chances are the new device is the problem.

I keep harping on a checklist because smart devices working together can become complicated. Take for example, my IFTTT applet "Goodnight."

1. Alexa needs to login with my Amazon account and password.

2. Alexa needs the IFTTT skill that logs in to my IFTTT account and password.

3. IFTTT is connected to my accounts like SmartThings - the systems that trigger an action. IFTTT prompts me to log in to each connected account with that particular account ID and password.

    *   Honeywell
    *   Samsung SmartThings
    *   Philips HUE
    *   Hunter Douglas PowerView
    *   Logitech Harmony

4. My IFTTT applets need to know what device name I gave my lights, thermostat(s) or scenes for each service.

Anyway, you get the idea, this can be complicated. A handy reference is invaluable for the devices, bridges, hubs, accounts, and automations you setup.

14.1 Troubleshooting Overview

The key to troubleshooting is isolating which part of the functionality is not working. For example, when my blinds don't work with Alexa, these are the steps I take to troubleshoot the problem.

1. What did Alexa actually hear?

2. Rename the device or scene using different words. For example, the scene name could be "close blinds" instead of "shut blinds."

3. Make sure the device itself has a different name than the scene.

   - The device "Family Room Left Side" is the actual blind.

   - "Family Room Blinds Scene" is the scene for all the blinds in the family room.

4. Does the same command work in the native application? For example, "Close all blinds" works fine from within the Hunter Douglas PowerView app.

5. Does the same command work when you say "trigger Close All Blinds" using your IFTTT recipe?

6. If the command works in IFTTT (using the trigger in Step 5), then Alexa did understand the command. If the command also works in the native app (Step 4), you know the problem is the interface between Alexa and the manufacturer's cloud service.

Sometimes the simplest course of action is to go back and check the basics. I become cranky when something stops working. It takes me longer than it should to go back and check the basics.

- When did the problem start?

- When was the last day I added something new?

- Is the cable OK?

- Is the network or Wi-Fi OK?

14.2 Matching Names to IP Addresses

Routers associate MAC and IP addresses to device names. Realistically, you may never have to worry about what devices are connected to your router unless of course you just want to identify intruders or someone surfing on your network. In the event you need to troubleshoot a device, your router can be a source of information about how a device is connected (wired Ethernet vs. Wi-Fi), as well as the signal strength.

For instructions for your particular router, try searching the Internet for the model of your gateway router. Look for instructions to open the router and gateway application in your browser.

Once connected, a status screen should show your connected wired and Wi-Fi devices with dynamic or static IP addresses. Dynamic IP addresses are assigned by the router and can change over time, where static addresses are always the same.

In the following abbreviated example of my home network, you can see that the Logitech Harmony hub and Alexa speakers are connected to the 2.4GHz Wi-Fi network. The "Time Capsule" has a wired Ethernet connection. This table also shows the signal strength of Wi-Fi connections.

Device IP Address / Name	Status	Connection		Radio, Type, Name
192.168.1.65 / viziocastdisplay	off	Ethernet		
192.168.1.66 / GatewayF103A0	on	Ethernet		
192.168.1.67 / MBP	on	Wi-Fi	▮▮▮	5 GHz, Home, ATTfUin
192.168.1.70 / unknown7c72e4903eac	on	Ethernet		
192.168.1.71 / iPhone	off	Wi-Fi	▮▮	5 GHz, Home, ATTfUin
192.168.1.72 / android-8be1f1910d4366ff	off	Ethernet		
192.168.1.76 / unknown0026743f742d	on	Ethernet		
192.168.1.77 / Philips-hue	on	Ethernet		
192.168.1.78 / ipad-2017	on	Wi-Fi	▮▮	2.4 GHz, Home, ATTfUin
192.168.1.79 / iPhone	off	Wi-Fi	▮▮▮	2.4 GHz, Home, ATTfUin
192.168.1.81 / amazon-5b66dc083	on	Wi-Fi	▮▮▮	2.4 GHz, Home, ATTfUin
192.168.1.83 / amazon-db934d353	on	Wi-Fi	▮▮▮	5 GHz, Home, ATTfUin
192.168.1.84 / 2018smarthome	on	Wi-Fi	▮▮▮	5 GHz, Home, ATTfUin
192.168.1.85 / ipad-2015	on	Wi-Fi	▮▮▮	5 GHz, Home, ATTfUin
192.168.1.87 / Laptop	on	Wi-Fi	▮▮	5 GHz, Home, ATTfUin
192.168.1.89 / Apple-TV-3	on	Ethernet		
192.168.1.120 / DIRECTV-HS17-266B3AC6	on	Ethernet		
192.168.1.121 / HarmonyHub	on	Wi-Fi	▮▮▮	2.4 GHz, Home, ATTfUin
192.168.1.126 / Time Capsule	on	Ethernet		
192.168.1.138 / Air4920	on	Ethernet		

Figure 14.1   IP Assignments in Router Tables

Some devices have a friendly name that you can recognize like "Apple-TV-3," while others require a bit of detective work to identify. The first place to check for a name is the device's mobile app, which may provide the IP address, as well as a way to change the network name.

When I don't recognize a device name, I power off the device, and then power it back on, while watching my router connection tables. Let's say there are two devices I don't recognize. I turn off one and watch the list of connected devices in my router. After a few minutes, a device should drop off the list, and I've found a match. When I turn the device back on, it shows up in the router connection tables again, and I know I'm looking at the right device.

Another method I've used to identify an IP address is typing the address in a browser. For example, I type http://192.168.1.254 to see if an application will launch. This is how I found a forgotten label printer.

14.3 It Stopped Working

If a device previously connected and it then stops working, check that your router, Wi-Fi repeater, or network switch are OK. A simple test is to open a browser on your smartphone or other device. The test device should only use Wi-Fi (not cellular service). Go to a popular website like CNN, Google, or MSN to validate that your connection is working.

Another thing I always check is the cable because cables go bad over time. When you haven't changed anything, and the device stops working, troubleshooting can be frustrating. Consider investing in quality cables, as outlined in Chapter 3.

Over time, it's not at all uncommon for a smart device to lose its setup information. For example, my smart vacuum will stop working from time to time. Unplugging it doesn't do anything, but if I reset it to the default settings and rerun setup its fine again.

14.4 Why is the Connection Slow or Intermittent?

When you experience intermittent issues or general slowness, go back to basics and test your network connectivity or batteries.

- Have you added a new device lately?

- Can you connect to a printer or computer within your home network without any problems?

- Can you connect to a popular web site – CNN, Google, or MSN? Open a browser on your smartphone or other device where it is only using Wi-Fi (not cellular).

- When connecting to a website outside of your home, are sites slow?

- Check batteries.

Search the internet for "Speedtest" to check your ISP speeds or go to http://speedtest.att.com.

AT&T has a mobile app for its ISP customers called "Smart Home Manager." The app has an option to rename a device with a friendly name. There are several tools for testing network bandwidth and Wi-Fi signals.

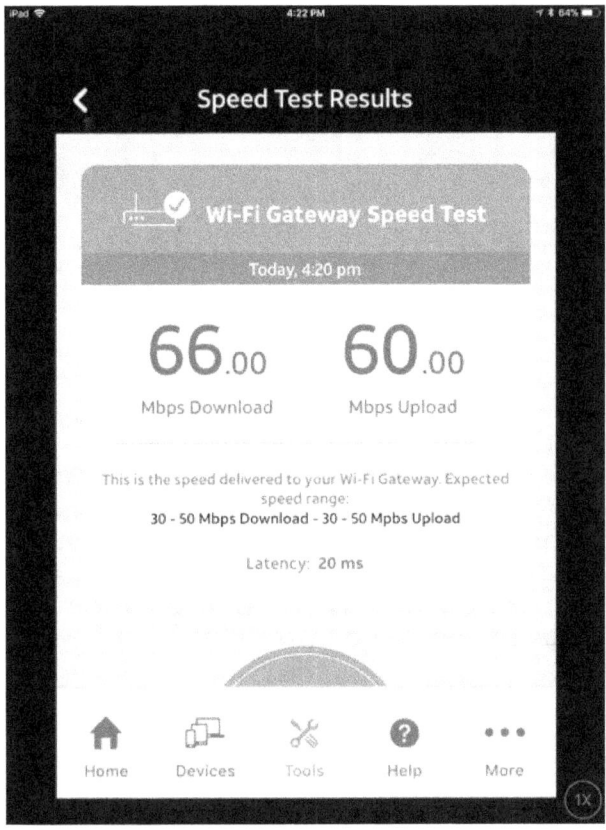

Figure 14.2   AT&T Smart Home Manager Speed Test Results

14.5 Troubleshooting Apple TV

When you have problems with your Apple TV, a software update may resolve the issue.

1.   Start your Apple TV and click on **Settings**.

2.   Scroll down and click on **Software Updates**.

3. Click on **Update Software**.

4. If desired, enable **Update Automatically**.

14.6 Troubleshooting Amazon Alexa

Alexa issues are usually around commands, differentiating devices and scenes, or network connectivity. Alexa sometimes has trouble understanding what you say. Occasionally she is confused about which command you want. When this happens, go back to the original device's mobile app, and rename the device or scene. Also, make sure there are no duplicate device or scene names. Duplicates can appear when you replace your hub, reorganize scenes or rooms, or have multiple rooms with the same type of devices.

In case you need to know the MAC address of your Echo device, you can see it under Menu, **Settings** in the About section.

Duplicate Alexa Scenes

The Alexa app has an option to rescan scenes, or "forget" scenes. I think the easiest way to forget scenes is from a web browser.

1. Open the Alexa app in a web browser.

2. Click on Smart Home and then select **Scenes**.

3. You can forget individual scenes, or scroll down to forget all scenes.

To get at the root of the problem, look at the original smartphone app. For example, Philips HUE automatically creates scenes for each room you set up. Theoretically, then, you can have duplicate scene names. If you replace your Hunter Douglas hub, Alexa may show duplicate devices.

Learn more about Philips HUE scenes in Chapter 4, "Lighting, Electrical and HVAC" in the section "Scenes."

What did Alexa Hear?

Alexa keeps a history of what she heard. If you have concerns about Alexa eavesdropping, therefore, this is where you erase those conversations.

1. Go to the menu and select **Settings**.

2. Scroll down to History and select an item.

3. Play the recording, view the text, or select **Delete Voice Recordings**.

Alexa Doesn't Understand Commands

Alexa uses these phrases when she doesn't understand commands.

- *"Your phrase"* doesn't support that.

- "A few things share that name. Which one did you want?"

When this happens, go back to the original smartphone app and rename the device or scene, making sure you have no duplicates.

These additional steps may resolve the problem:

- Delete and rediscover the scenes.

- Disable the skill connection to Alexa and recreate it.

- Rename the scene or "trigger phrase" using words with hard consonants.

Alexa Doesn't Respond

The light ring flashes to indicate Alexa's mode. The color may offer a clue as to why Alexa is not responding.

The light ring flashes flash **purple** if "Do Not Disturb" is active. A pulsing green light flashes when Alexa is receiving a call or "Drop-in." Check all the Echos in your house to make sure they are not participating in a call together. At each Echo with a flashing green light, try the command, "Alexa, hang up."

When Alexa doesn't respond, and the light ring doesn't flash, try unplugging Alexa to see if that resolves the issue.

Alexa loses Wi-Fi Connection

Alexa does not work on all 5GHz channels. In your router setup, try configuring the 5GHz network to use channel 149 or higher.

Reset Amazon Echo

Resetting your Echo is the last resort. Keep in mind you'll lose some settings when you reset Echo.

To make a note of Alexa setup options before you reset your Echo see Chapter 9, "Basic Echo Setup."

Press and hold the "microphone off" and "volume down" buttons at the same time until the light ring turns orange. This should take about 20 seconds, and then the light ring will then turn blue. Wait for the light ring to turn off and on again. The light ring then turns orange, and your device enters setup mode.

Open the Alexa mobile app and follow the prompts to connect your device to a Wi-Fi network and register it to your Amazon account.

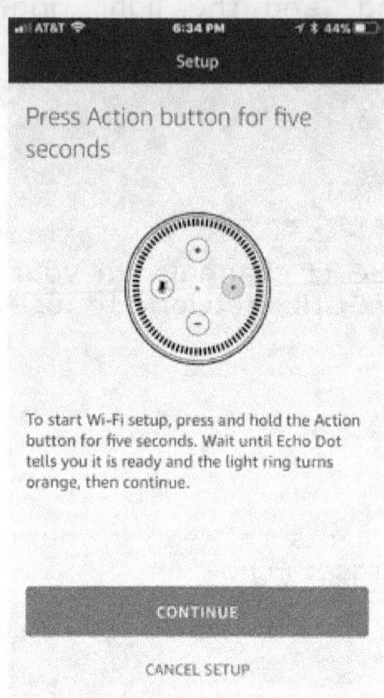

Figure 14.3   Echo 2nd Generation Action Button

Conclusion

Will the Internet of Things change the world? I honestly don't know, but I do wonder if we are at the cusp of a radical change in how we interact with the world around us. In fact, search the Internet for "cusp" and "Internet of Things," and you may be surprised by what you find.

Industries across the globe are implementing this new technology. Manufacturing, transportation, utilities, healthcare, consumer electronics, and automotive industries have embraced IoT. As I interact with my smart home devices and systems, they learn my habits and record my location. The flip side of this equation, is this data could be used to provide insights to manufacturers and retailers about my consumer lifestyle.

Citizens across the US are benefiting from government and municipality IoT integrations that improve their daily lives. Cities that implement beacons use Geofencing to monitor consumer location. Interactive mobile apps for cultural events, tourism, traffic information, and shopping use this information to customize the user experience in the app. Healthcare today has personal medical monitoring units, and the potential for mobile diagnostics in the future is a very real possibility.

We think IoT will have a real impact on energy conservation, and convenience in our lives. For those who have suffered a broken leg or other disability, a smart home drastically improves the quality of life. Whether it is listening to music, turning lights on or off, cleaning the floor, or sending a message, a smart home is an assistant worth having.

The book is specific to 2018, this moment in time, because the Internet of Things is rapidly changing. While this book won't be obsolete next year, there will be substantial changes in the technology. The smart home concept of virtual assistants, sensors, hubs and cloud services is not likely to change in the near future. With this knowledge you should be able to identify changes and understand how they fit into the smart home landscape.

The work of the Internet Engineering Task Force IoT Directorate, International Standards Organization, and others will continue, and accelerate growth and adoption of this technology. With exponential growth IoT will be mainstream before me know it. We're ready for change - bring it on!

The experience of talking to others and sharing ideas is very rewarding, and inspired me to write this book. For questions, advice, and to stay in touch, e-mail us at 2018SmartHome@att.net. Thank you for purchasing this book and taking the time to share this experience with us. We sincerely hope you enjoy your smart home for years to come!

Index

Smart Home

Trademarks

Warning and Disclaimer